Praise for
BURKE'S LAW

"Brian Burke is first and foremost a father and community activist. He's also a brilliant storyteller who's led an extraordinary life. You'll enjoy this book!"
—Rick Mercer, bestselling author and host of *The Mercer Report*

"'Truculent' doesn't begin to describe my friend Brian Burke. He brings that and hard-boiled honesty to every aspect of his life—including his friendships. But if you can't take his truculence as a friend, you definitely wouldn't want him as an enemy. The most belligerent and entertaining book you'll read this year."
—Mike Milbury, former NHL player, coach, GM, and broadcaster

"If you've only ever heard Brian Burke talking at a press conference, you probably think he's a gruff, old-school hockey hard-ass who could care less about other people. You would be only half right. I have known Brian since he was getting into the agenting business, and I can tell you he will never take a step backwards if he thinks he's right. But he's also a big teddy bear. If he gives you his word, you can take it to the bank, and you have to respect someone who believes in equality the way he does. Brian is an enigma wrapped in a riddle. This book may help some of us figure him out."
—Glen Sather, former NHL player, Stanley Cup-winning coach, and GM of the Edmonton Oilers

"Sometimes gruff, but brutally honest. . . . Poignantly penned."
—*Edmonton Sun*

"[Brian Burke] speaks directly and succinctly, with purpose and conviction. . . . To the point, as they say, is Burke's manner. But don't mistake bluntness for unkindness. . . . [*Burke's Law*] bubbles with barroom tales of boardroom conflict."
—*Sportsnet*

BURKE'S LAW

A LIFE IN HOCKEY

Brian Burke

with Stephen Brunt

PENGUIN

an imprint of Penguin Canada, a division of Penguin Random House Canada Limited

Published in this edition, 2021

First published in Viking Canada hardcover, 2020

1 2 3 4 5 6 7 8 9 10

LIBRARY AND ARCHIVES CANADA CATALOGUING IN PUBLICATION

Title: Burke's law : a life in hockey / Brian Burke with Stephen Brunt.
Names: Burke, Brian, 1955- author. | Brunt, Stephen, author.
Identifiers: Canadiana 20200177583 | ISBN 9780735239494 (softcover)
Subjects: LCSH: Burke, Brian, 1955- | LCSH: National Hockey League. |
    LCSH: Sports executives—Biography. | LCGFT: Autobiographies.
Classification: LCC GV848.5.B875 A3 2021 | DDC 796.962092—dc23

Cover photo: Alessandra Petlin / AUGUST

Printed in the United States of America

www.penguinrandomhouse.ca

Penguin
Random House
PENGUIN CANADA

To six amazing kids:
your dad couldn't be prouder.

"It is not the critic who counts; not the man who points out how the strong man stumbles, or where the doer of deeds could have done them better. The credit belongs to the man who is actually in the arena, whose face is marred by dust and sweat and blood; who strives valiantly; who errs, who comes short again and again, because there is no effort without error and shortcoming; but who does actually strive to do the deeds; who knows great enthusiasms, the great devotions; who spends himself in a worthy cause; who at the best knows in the end the triumph of high achievement, and who at the worst, if he fails, at least fails while daring greatly, so that his place shall never be with those cold and timid souls who neither know victory nor defeat."

—Theodore Roosevelt

CONTENTS

"YOU SHOULD NEVER START A FIGHT, BUT YOU SHOULD FINISH EVERY ONE"

I COULDN'T SLEEP.

Objectively, there wasn't a lot of reason to be nervous. We were coming home to Anaheim, up three games to one on the Ottawa Senators in the 2007 Stanley Cup final. We had lost only five games—total—during the playoffs, we had knocked off the mighty Detroit Red Wings in the conference final, and we had the series under control against an underdog team that should have been happy just to be there.

But I couldn't let myself think that way, and I kept tossing and turning all night long with worst-case scenarios running through my mind. What if Scotty Niedermayer gets the flu? What if somebody blows out their groin during the pre-game warm-up? If the Senators win, then we're back in their rink for Game 6. If they win that, then it's Game 7, and those are always a coin toss. I was worried about everything. It was a fucking nightmare.

The truth is, the Stanley Cup playoffs aren't fun for a general manager—they're exciting, but not fun. You're cursing your players, cursing the referees, worrying about everything that could go wrong, and it's all out of your control.

My wife, Jennifer, tried to reassure me.

"These guys aren't going to let you down," she said. "You're not going back to Ottawa."

She was right, of course, but that night, it didn't help a bit. We were so close to claiming the greatest prize in sports. There's no championship that's harder to win, and when they engrave your name on the old silver chalice, it's there forever. After the long, unlikely journey I'd been on since the first day I put on a pair of skates, there was no way I was taking it for granted.

The next morning, I pulled into the parking lot at the Honda Center at dawn, which was part of my daily routine.

If you run a hockey team in Canada, everyone knows who you are, and you can pretty much do whatever you want around the arena. But not in Southern California. Not down the block from Disneyland. The security guys at the rink never seemed to figure out who I was—or at least they never acknowledged it. They'd ask me for ID every time, and they would never let me enter through the door that was closest to where we parked, even though I had a master key that would let me in. I had to go through the official security entrance, which was a colossal pain in the ass.

Today, of all days, I wasn't in the mood to play that game again.

"I've got this key, so clearly I'm somebody here," I told the security guy. "I'm not showing my ID to anybody, and no matter what you say, I'm walking through this door. You can go ahead and call your supervisor if you like, but I'm going in—and by the way, I'm winning the Stanley Cup tonight."

At least they didn't throw me out.

Chris Pronger got hurt in that game—so all my crazy fears weren't completely unfounded. But they shot him up and he stayed on the ice, and by the third period we had a comfortable lead.

With five minutes left in the third period, John Muckler, who was running the Senators, came over to my box and congratulated me. Muck's a good guy, but in that moment, all I could think was that the fucker was trying to jinx us. I didn't start to relax until Corey Perry scored to make it 6–2 with three minutes to go.

This was the moment a hockey person dreams about their whole life, and I was going to enjoy it. I went down to the bench to watch the final seconds tick off the clock. The players were all excited and yelling, and our owner, Henry Samueli, was hollering as well, though mostly unintelligibly.

Our video guy came down, and when the clock hit zero, he shouted, "The Chiefs have won the championship of the Federal League!"—a line right out of *Slap Shot*. Everyone who loves hockey loves *Slap Shot*. We all laughed our asses off.

It got surreal after that. I went on the ice and did an interview with Ron MacLean, but I honestly didn't remember doing it until I saw it on an NHL Network replay years later. The crowd was so loud that I was yelling into the mike.

And then it was my turn to lift the Cup, but I have bad shoulders—I had surgery on one of them that spring. If you watch the tape, you can see that I have trouble getting my arms fully extended because my shoulders were fucked, even though the Cup weighs only about 35 pounds.

I was looking for my wife in the crowd, but I couldn't find her. Meanwhile, there was chaos all around me. What a moment. It was like climbing Mount Everest. But it wasn't like we didn't see it coming.

It's supposed to be bad luck to talk about winning a Cup before it actually happens, but with that Anaheim team, we started talking about it in training camp. We knew how good we were, and after we got Pronger, we were loaded. We had made it as far as the conference final the year before, which gave our young guys some valuable training experience. And then we started the season with at least a point in each of our first 16 games.

That was a team of destiny. I will believe until I die that those Ducks could have beaten any team that has won the Cup since. Maybe Washington would have given us a bit of trouble, but that's about it. Teemu Selanne. Ryan Getzlaf. Corey Perry. We had all kinds of skill. J.S. Giguere was the best money goaltender in the business. You want to hit? We'll beat the shit out of you. You want to fight? We do that better than anybody. We fought in the first round of the playoffs, we fought in the second round of the playoffs, we fought in the third round of the playoffs and we fought in the finals. You may never see that again. It was a tough team, but we could play—even our fourth-line heavyweights, George Parros and Shawn Thornton, could play. And Randy Carlyle was the perfect coach for them.

After the game, the dressing room was jammed. My parents were there, and I remember going into the coaches' office and sitting there with my mom and dad, just savouring the moment. My dad was so proud.

And then Pronger came in. When the game ended and our guys were celebrating on the ice, he skated off by himself and grabbed the game puck (some of the media guys actually criticized him for that, because he wasn't immediately with his teammates). He walked over to me and handed me the puck. "You put this team together," he said. "This is yours."

I still have it.

Now it was time for me to take a drink out of the Cup. My son Brendan and my daughter Molly had already had their chance. Then the players started chanting, "Burkie wants a drink! Burkie wants a drink!" Travis Moen and Parros were holding it, pouring in champagne and warm Bud Light. It was a disgusting mix, and 20 people had already slobbered on it—but it was the best, sweetest drink I've ever had in my life. At least it was until they tipped it up and poured it all over me.

The party was going to continue for most of the night, and I was exhausted. I told Jennifer that I was finished and had to go home. Let the players party on. I needed to get some sleep.

I'll never forget that night. I'll never forget the whole journey to win it. I'll never forget the satisfaction. When I went to bed that night, I slept well for the first time in weeks—because in the playoffs, you don't sleep. But that night, I slept like a baby as a Stanley Cup champion.

Looking back now, I savour those moments. They're what we strive for. The ultimate. As a general manager, you have to put the right players and the right coach in the room. You're not the guy who wins the Cup, but you're the architect.

We had the coaches over to the house the next day, and then later in the summer we had a big party back in Vancouver, where we closed down a restaurant for the night, and none other than Gordie Howe walked in off the street. It was a pure coincidence.

"Okay if I crash your party?" he asked.

Whatever you want, Mr. Howe.

We had the Cup in the room, and Gordie was showing people his name engraved on the rings.

Hockey has been a miracle in my life, and in my family's life. I've travelled the globe. I've educated four kids, and I'm educating two more now. The sport has given me so much, and it has given me a voice.

I'm hoping that when people look back on my career, they say five things: he had the right values and made a difference in the cities where he lived and worked; he was a family man, and he brought some good young people along with him. I've been a mentor, and I'm proud of that. Oh, and the fifth? He won a Cup.

It's been a great ride, and it continues. I'm still part of the hockey scene as part of the media, and I still love it. I can't wait to go to a morning skate tomorrow. I feel the same excitement I've always felt.

And I know, especially, that I have been extremely fortunate to have lived the life I've lived.

I know you're not going to believe this, but I was a shy kid. It will surprise you less to know that I was always up for a scrap.

I'm the fourth of 10 children in an Irish Catholic (I guess that part is self-evident) family. My oldest brother Bill, my late sister Ellen and my brother John came before me. We were born in consecutive years—May, June, May, June. My mother never got a rest. I was born in Providence, Rhode Island, in June 1955. Mom took a year off and then had my sister Joan Rachel, followed by Andrea, then Christa, then the twins—Matthew and Victoria—and finally the baby of the family, Meghan.

The great thing about having all those brothers and sisters was that there was always someone to talk to, always someone to read with, always someone to play a board game with.

I was a skinny kid with glasses and crooked teeth (I got braces in high school.). My older brothers could have been embarrassed having me hang around with them, but they never acted that way. They let me tag along, which is why I wasn't afraid of playing against older kids in sports, and why my musical tastes skewed a little bit older than those of other kids my own age.

My older brothers were my heroes then, and they still are today. Not that we always got along—and they were always willing to fight. Bill and John and I would fight at the drop of a hat.

Dad was bewildered by that. He'd been involved in only one fight in his entire life. When he was in the navy, he had a beef with a guy, and they settled it in the boxing ring.

"I've only had one fight in my life and you guys have 25 a year," he'd say to us. "What's wrong with me as a father?"

When you grow up with two older brothers who both looked after you and toughened you up, you wind up not being afraid of anything. I was never bullied, never picked on, even though I was a small kid.

Some of that attitude also came from my grandmother Burke. I remember a time when we were visiting her in Clifton, New Jersey. I was out playing by myself and these two neighbourhood kids jumped me and beat me up.

"You go right back out and fight them again," she told me.

So, I went out, full of fear and trepidation because those kids were bigger than me—but I had a mandate from Grandma, and I wasn't going back and facing her unless I carried it out. I beat 'em both up.

"That's all right, then," Grandma said—that was her favourite phrase. "You should never start a fight, but you should finish every one of them."

The Burke side of the family came from County Mayo on the west coast of Ireland. My great-grandfather Patrick Burke—my son is named after him—got off the boat at Ellis Island in 1861. The American Civil War had just begun, and like a lot of Irish émigrés, he joined the Union Army. He spent a year in the infantry before figuring out that riding a horse was easier than walking—that's when he re-enlisted in the cavalry, where he spent another three years.

After the war ended, they sent him to Colorado to fight Indians. He was mustered out there and moved back to Jersey City, where he got a job in construction as a hod carrier—one of the guys who carried the mortar up three and four storeys and delivered it to the bricklayers. It must have been back-breaking work.

Like a lot of Irishmen in those days, he didn't get married until his 40s—which is why it's possible for me to have a great-grandfather who fought in the Civil War, though some people find it hard to believe. He didn't have kids until the 1880s.

His son, my grandfather, became a clerk in Tammany Hall—the organization, dominated by Irishmen, that effectively controlled New York politics for about 150 years. Tammany Hall was known for patronage and corruption, but it obviously served my grandfather well. He would brag to us that during World War I, when food was being rationed, he had all the meat he wanted. He was proud to be part of the Tammany machine.

My father and his two brothers grew up in Jersey City. After serving stateside in the US Navy during World War II, my dad went to Fordham University on the GI Bill. My mother's brother, my uncle Roger, was a combat veteran who served on destroyers, and my father's younger brother, my uncle Bob, joined the US Army just as the war was ending and wound up with the occupation troops. He met and married a woman from Germany, then became a career army officer, serving in Korea and Vietnam before retiring as a full colonel.

I'm part of the first generation of my family that didn't serve, which maybe explains the strong allure the military has for me.

My father worked for Sunbeam, the appliance manufacturer, and climbed steadily up the corporate ranks. His job, and his promotions, kept us moving around. My parents started out in St. Louis, then went to Milwaukee, where the first two kids were born, then to Providence (two more), Philadelphia (three more) and Chicago (three more).

My first memories are of life in Chicago, where I went to kindergarten through Grade 5. We had a small house with a master bedroom and nursery on the main floor, and three bedrooms upstairs. Four of us boys shared one bedroom, the girls had another, and my mother insisted on keeping one empty for guests—we had 10 kids, and we still had a guest bedroom.

I wasn't an altar boy, but I was a devout Catholic kid. I'd get up at 5:30 in the morning and go to 6 a.m. Mass with the nuns who taught me, head back home for breakfast at seven, and then go to school. Like most Catholic boys, I briefly thought about becoming a priest, but then it was a firefighter, then a soldier—I went through all the classics.

Sports was certainly important in my family. My parents encouraged all of us to participate. My dad was a great baseball and tennis player— he played tennis on the day he died—and he especially loved Notre Dame football. He always carried a transistor radio so he could listen to the Notre Dame games, and he took the three older boys to see the Fighting Irish play in South Bend.

My parents would also take the older kids to one big sporting event a year. That's when I saw my first NHL game: the Black Hawks playing at the old Chicago Stadium. I hated it. They allowed smoking in arenas in those days, and by the second period there was a thick blue cloud hanging under the ceiling. We had cheap seats up high, and you could barely see the ice. All I can remember is coughing and gagging.

But I also had some great experiences. I saw Gale Sayers and Dick Butkus, my favourite player, in a Bears pre-season game at Soldier Field, and I saw the Cubs play at Wrigley Field. What I remember most about that afternoon baseball game was that we were sitting right behind the plate, and my mom noticed that I couldn't read the name on the back of the catcher's jersey. She dragged me off to the eye doctor as soon as she could get an appointment, and I wound up with my first pair of glasses.

My older brothers turned out to be terrific athletes in their own right. Both of them started on undefeated state high school champion football teams. But in our family, academics took precedence over everything else.

My father was valedictorian of his class at Fordham, a brilliant guy, and my mother earned a four-year RN degree from the College of Mount St. Vincent. They were both highly educated, and making sure that their children succeeded academically was their No. 1 goal. Every night at dinner, one kid had to bring a new vocabulary word to the table. We had to say it, spell it, define it and use it in a sentence. As a result, we all have great vocabularies.

And after dinner, we had a mandatory reading hour. At seven o'clock, the whole family assembled in the living room to read books. That was before we did our homework. No phone calls, no television. Just all of us gathered together, reading library books. That's where I got my life-long love of reading.

While we were living in Chicago, my dad was offered the presidency of Sunbeam. But when they told him he couldn't bring his management team along with him, he turned down the job. In 1966, he was offered the presidency of the rival Shetland Company, which made vacuum cleaners, and he accepted. That's when we moved to Boston from Chicago.

There was a pond out back of our house where I used to bird-watch. In winter it froze, and the local kids would play hockey out there. I had never put on skates before, but I found an old pair in the garage that didn't fit, found a stick somewhere, and went out and played—or at least tried to play—maybe a dozen times that winter. That's where I got my first hockey cut. I fell and smashed my head on the ice, and there was blood everywhere. It took six or eight stitches to close it.

I didn't play seriously until my family moved to Minnesota. My dad had figured out pretty quickly that he'd been sold a bill of goods about Shetland vacuums. The company was in way worse shape than he had been led to believe. He sued them—unsuccessfully—and took a job with Brown and Bigelow, which was a hot advertising company in those days. That's why we moved to the Minneapolis area. Dad didn't last long in advertising—those were the *Mad Men* days, and he was a very moral guy. After he left, he started his own consulting business, W.J. Burke and Associates (even though, at the beginning, there were no associates), and eventually became wildly successful.

We didn't have a lot of money in those days, but somehow my parents managed to buy a house in Edina, a high-end suburb of

Minneapolis. They chose Edina because it had the best public education system in the state of Minnesota. Ninety-four percent of my high school class went on to university.

It turned out we were also moving to one of the great hockey hotbeds in the United States—and that changed my life.

The moving vans hit a blizzard and took three days to bring our stuff from Boston, and we wound up stuck in a Howard Johnson's motel in Bloomington waiting for them—ten kids and two parents crammed into two rooms. The Minnesota state high school hockey championship happened to be going on then. It was a big enough deal that they showed all the games on television. It was a Thursday afternoon and there were 16,000 people packed into the old Met Center, where the North Stars played, to watch two games, and then they refilled the arena that night for another two games.

Sitting there, watching television, I fell in love with hockey.

I think I'm a team sports guy by nature. I could never have been a swimmer or a figure skater. Being part of a team appeals to me. I lack fine motor skills, so I'm not a golfer, and even though I played a bit of baseball, I didn't really have the kind of hand-eye coordination you need to succeed.

But watching that high school tournament, I was hooked. I remember how skilled the players seemed. I loved the grace of hockey. My brothers would become great high school football players—and I became a decent enough football player—but from that day, hockey was my love and my passion.

And seeing those crowds, seeing how excited people were, it dawned on me, even as a kid—we're in Minnesota now, and if you want to be somebody here, you'd better be a hockey player.

There was an outdoor rink in Creek Valley, not far from our first house in Minnesota, and that's where I really learned to skate. A guy named Bob O'Connor coached the local bantam house league team there.

I was standing by the boards one day, watching the kids practise, when he hollered over at me, "Why don't you join in?"

"I've never played before," I told him.

"Get some gear and give it a try," he said. (Bob O'Connor made it all possible. He was a great man.)

We had some stuff lying around from my older brothers, and my parents bought me a pair of skates. I went to my first hockey practice, and I didn't even know how to put on the garter belt that holds up your socks. I put my pants on first (they call hockey pants "breezers" in Minnesota), and then tried to put the garter belt on over them. It didn't work very well.

When I finally got that straightened out and got out on the ice, I could barely stand up. I was the worst guy on the team—by a long shot.

Before climate change, the ponds of Minnesota were a real gift. They'd usually freeze up by Thanksgiving weekend. The dads would go out and drill a hole to make sure there was four inches of ice, and once they were declared safe, we'd go out there and skate all day and into the night.

Not long after that, the outdoor rinks would open. They flooded them and plowed them every night, and you could skate as much as you wanted to—just like in rural Canada. I'd come home from school, grab my stuff and skate outside until suppertime. And then, after I finished dinner and finished my homework, I'd go out and skate until they turned the lights off at nine—even later on a moonlit night. If I didn't have chores to do on a Saturday, I would be down there before the warming house opened at nine, putting on my skates while sitting on a snowbank. We would take a break at lunch, take our skates off for maybe a half hour, eat in the warming house and then be right back out on the ice. Some days, I'd be out there for almost 12 hours. That helped me make up for my late start in the game.

My first two years, I played bantam house league—but by the second year, I was one of the better players. In my third year, I made the midget beltline team, which played in a B-level rep league. I was in Grade 10 by then. All the better players my age were playing in Midget A or playing for their high school team. It was quite a thing in my town to be playing Midget B in only my third year of organized hockey, but it certainly didn't suggest I had a future in the game.

It was during those teen years that I came up with my four rules. I knew that I had a pretty big hill to climb when it came to hockey. I started late and wasn't the most gifted athlete in the world. But I figured that if I was disciplined and committed and set my mind to it, there were ways I could overcome those disadvantages and succeed. That turned into my four rules. I followed them when I was a kid, and I followed them until the day I retired from hockey. They served me very well.

> **RULE 1:** Be the hardest worker on the ice, whether it's a practice or a game. (I don't like guys who only put in their best effort during games.) Never get outworked by anyone.
>
> **RULE 2:** Be a coach's dream. Be perfect positionally. Play mistake-free hockey. I would be invaluable to the coach. He'd never look at a game tape and be able to say, "Burke, you were out of position." I did everything by the book. Whatever the coach said, I did.
>
> **RULE 3:** Be a great teammate. Become indispensable. Be a leader when it's your turn. Be a follower until then. I was the guy who would go over to a teammate and say, "Hey, you seem down. Is everything all right?" When I was in college, I would take freshmen out to dinner, ask them about their studies and give them tips based on my experience.
>
> **RULE 4:** Play tough and fearless hockey. I'm going to play hard all the time. I'm going to be tough—which carries a premium no matter where you play.

By my fourth year in organized hockey, I was the alternate captain of the local Midget A team. That's also when I had my first exposure to hockey in Canada. Our team travelled north to Winnipeg and played four games against the locals. I thought we'd get murdered because . . . well, because they were Canadians and Canadians were supposed to be so much better at hockey than Americans. There was a mystique that we all bought into.

We stayed with billet families. I remember the dad of the family I stayed with welcoming me to their home. "We're glad to have you here," he said. "The hockey's not going to go well for you, but I hope you enjoy the visit anyway."

Well, fuck you.

We played the River Heights A team in the first game. They had Kevin McCarthy playing for them, who wound up being a first-round pick of the Philadelphia Flyers. We beat them, and then in our second game we beat River Heights B. There was a scheduling screw-up for our third game, against Fort Garry, which meant that we wound up playing them on an outdoor rink in 20-below temperatures.

By this point, I was one of our better players. The Fort Garry coach told one of their players to go after me. He swung his stick at my head—I think he was trying to break my nose. I turned and the stick hit me right by the corner of my eye, and naturally I was spooked. The blood didn't even make it down to my jaw before it froze. They took me into the warming house, where a doctor showed up and said, "Don't worry, I'll sew you right up." There were popcorn boxes all over the floor, and the room was lit by a single bare light bulb. I wasn't going to let anybody get that close to my eye with a needle in those conditions, so I told the doctor, "No thanks." I got stitched up at Misericordia Hospital instead.

We beat Fort Garry that day, and then tied St. Boniface the next day—so we finished the trip 3–0–1.

I thought, "I can play with these Canadian kids. There's no fucking mystique here."

We won the state midget championship that season, which meant that we got to play in the national midget tournament held in Dearborn, Michigan, just outside of Detroit. That's where I first met Lou Lamoriello, someone who would go on to have a profound influence on my life.

Lou was the head coach at Providence College in Rhode Island, and he was in Dearborn scouting the tournament. He and Bob O'Connor had played on the same Providence team.

Bob told Lou he had a kid on his team that Lou ought to see—a late bloomer who had been coming on fast and might be a good fit for college hockey.

Lou watched me play in the tournament and wasn't impressed.

"He's never going to play college hockey," he told Bob. "This kid will be lucky if he even plays high school hockey."

I did play high school hockey as a senior, but it actually required a bit of luck.

That year, Edina split its high school into two separate schools, Edina East and Edina West. If there had still been just one school, there's no way I would have made the team. But with the schools being split, I ended up starting for both the hockey and football teams at the new Edina West High—it was so new, we didn't have our own building ready that fall, so we had classes in my old junior high. Whatever the circumstances, playing at that level in just my fifth year of organized hockey was a real accomplishment.

Even with the split schools, Edina West and Edina East wound up playing each other for the district championship. We lost to them, which meant that I never got the chance to play in the state high school tournament. That's one of my few regrets from those years.

I also played high school football, at left guard and linebacker. But the only reason I got my letter as a senior was because of the school split.

That year of football did teach me an important lesson about team dynamics that I've carried with me throughout my career.

Our coach was a guy named Stav Canakes, who back in the day had played on an undefeated national championship team at the University of Minnesota. We were getting ready for a game against Bloomington Lincoln High School, and more specifically against their star running back John Gilliam. Beat them on Friday night, the coach said, and you'll all get Saturday off. Usually, there was a film session and a light workout the morning after a game. This was in the middle of hunting season in the fall—and in Minnesota, hunting is a big deal. The guys were all oiling their guns and running their dogs, getting ready for a rare Saturday off when they'd get to go out hunting with their dads.

The game was at Lincoln, and it was a hostile environment. Ron Olsonoski was our star middle linebacker, the nicest guy you would ever meet off the field, but just a belligerent, angry man on the football field, and our strong safety was a tough son of a bitch named Gary Heinzig. The two of them tracked poor Gilliam all over the field and hit him all night, and somehow we won the game.

We got back on the bus, and everyone was excited about having Saturday off. I wasn't a hunter in those days, but I was sore and looking forward to sleeping in. We got back to our locker room to change, and then Stav came in.

"See you tomorrow," he said. "Films at eight o'clock."

That wasn't right. I went to the offensive line coach and protested. He went in and talked to Stav, and then Stav came back and went nuts on us. Stav had huge forearms, and I remember him pounding them on the blackboard and screaming.

"When I call practice, you had better goddamn well be at practice," he yelled, and then he stormed out.

The next morning, four guys didn't show, with the full support of their parents. One of them was one of our captains.

On that team, when you got kicked off, they padlocked your gear in your locker. We assembled for practice on the field, Stav took roll call, and then he told the trainer to lock up the gear of the four guys who weren't there.

"What do you think of that?" he said to the rest of us.

I decided to push back.

"I think it's really unfair," I said.

The rest of the team started arguing with Stav as well.

"You promised us a day off. The guys are up north, hunting with their dads. It's not fair. And I think it's dishonest. If you want them to run some laps, that's one thing. But kicking them off the team when you didn't keep your word just isn't right."

The coach didn't say a word to me the rest of the season—other than ripping me during film sessions.

And the team was dysfunctional for the rest of the year. It split us right down the middle.

I filed that lesson away and have never forgotten it. You can't lie to players when you're coaching. Over the years, I had coaches I didn't like, but Stav was the first one that lied to his players. It was like your parents lying to you. Do that, and you can't succeed in a team sport.

My last year of high school hockey went better than my last year of football. At the end of the season, I was selected to play in the Minnesota North–South High School All-Star Game. There's a funny twist to that.

I was at home one night when I got a call from a guy with a heavy French accent.

"Hello, Brian," he said. "This is Coach Andre Beaulieu from Hill-Murray. I'm coaching the South team in the all-star game and I'd like you to play for me."

I assumed it was a prank—that it was one of my buddies trying to put one over on me.

"Fuck off!" I said, and hung up.

Luckily for me, Coach Beaulieu called right back.

"Is there a problem?" he asked. "Would you like me to call you back later?"

That's when it dawned on me that it was real. Honestly, I couldn't believe that I was being picked.

Playing in that game was big for me. I played with and against some of the top guys in the state, like Steve Jensen, who went on to play in the NHL. It was big time, and I did just fine. Coming out of that game, I was pretty confident that I could play college hockey.

By then, Dad's consulting business had started to take off. We moved into a bigger house and got a second car. My parents also bought part ownership of a pair of Minnesota North Stars season tickets. I went to four or five games at the Met Center that year, watching guys like Bill Goldsworthy, Lou Nanne, J.P. Parise and Cesare Maniago. I got hooked on the NHL in a way I never had been before. Not that I ever imagined I could play at that level. My whole focus was on college hockey and finding a way to pay for my education. My parents felt the same way. Junior hockey was just getting started in Minnesota, and I was pursued hard, but my dad laid down the law about going to college. There was really no debate.

I was recruited by four schools: Dartmouth, Yale, Providence College and, if you can believe it, the United States Air Force Academy, where they had a club team. I went on recruiting trips to Yale, Dartmouth and Providence. I didn't like Yale, and I didn't think the coach there would last four years; I liked Dartmouth, but I also had doubts about whether the coach would last, either because they'd leave for a better opportunity or because they didn't have the right attention to detail and would get fired. (I was right, by the way—they were both out of jobs after my second year.) Even at age 17, I was pretty mature and realistic about the fact that I wouldn't survive a coaching change. I wasn't good enough, and a new coach would bring in his own players. Guys like me get buried in those situations.

On my recruiting trip to Providence, they set me up in a dorm room. There were two twin beds, but I had the place to myself. Or at least that's what I thought when I went to sleep. When I woke up, there was a big, tall African American guy sleeping in the other bed. I tiptoed out of the room so I wouldn't wake him up, went down the hall and showered and shaved, then tiptoed back to the room.

I was struggling to tie my tie (I didn't know how to do it, so I had torn directions out of a magazine and brought them with me) when he woke up. He told me he was being recruited to play on the Providence basketball team. He asked me what I was doing.

"I'm a hockey recruit, and trying to put on a tie."

"Fuck that shit, man," he said. "They're recruiting *you*! Don't be sucking up to them!"

I loved his response, but I told him that he was probably a more significant player than I was.

I wore the tie.

LOU'S RULES

BY THE TIME LOU LAMORIELLO came to our house to meet with my parents, I was already pretty sold on him and on Providence.

My oldest brother, Bill, went to Stanford and played freshman football until he had to quit with a knee injury. My older sister, Ellen, went to Wellesley. My brother John went to Dartmouth, where he was a varsity wrestler. If I went to Providence, I would be the first kid in my family to go to a non–Ivy League school. But my parents were supportive. They told me not to worry about where my older brothers and sister went, and to find a school that fit me.

Lou's visit cinched the deal. He came to the house and didn't really talk to me at all. Everything was directed at my parents. He told them which courses I would take, and told them that all his players graduated. There was no promise of a scholarship right away. I'd be playing as a walk-on as a freshman. But even without that, Lou did a great job of selling his program.

When he left, my dad looked at me and said, "You're going to Providence."

That was fine by me. And those four years at PC turned out to be the most important of my life.

I have known Lou Lamoriello for 40 years. I played for him at Providence College, I worked for him at his hockey school, I competed against him as a rival NHL general manager and I dealt with him when I was handling player discipline at the league's head office. No one has been more influential in my professional life. I owe him a lot. He got me through four years of college and got me a scholarship to pay for my education. He's the only reason I went to law school. I have learned so much from him.

All in all, I ought to know Lou better than just about anyone outside of his immediate family. But the fact is, while I like him and respect him immensely, I don't really know him. If someone asked me if I was close to Lou the person, my answer would have to be no. He's as much of an enigma to me as he is to everyone else.

He's a very private guy, and that's never going to change. He's a dedicated father and grandfather. His kids are his whole life outside of hockey. But aside from family, he doesn't really have a personal life. He golfs a little bit now—at least so I hear—but otherwise he is either at the rink or at home. Nothing in between.

When you were around Lou, just when you started to think things were getting a little more personal and intimate—and even those moments were few and far between—the curtain would always come down.

When I was a freshman at Providence, Lou invited me, along with Ron Wilson and another freshman, over to his house for dinner, which was a really nice gesture. His wife made homemade pizza, and it was great. But the minute we finished eating, Lou said, "Okay, you guys get in the car and I'll drive you back to the dorm. You've got studying to do." No lingering, no socializing—get fed and get out.

Years later, when I was living in Boston, Lou asked me to be part of the radio broadcasts of Providence College games. It was really inconvenient to make the trip there and back, but I did it because Lou wanted me to do it. One night, he asked if I could give him a ride to Boston after the game. I actually lived south of the city, so taking him downtown meant driving 20 miles out of my way and back, but I said, "Sure, I'll give you a ride, but you have to promise to stay awake and talk."

As soon as we hit the highway, he was out like a light, snoring away in the passenger seat. He slept the whole way until we got to his hotel. I'm still not sure if that was because he was really tired, or because he just wanted to avoid conversation.

Lou's rules are Lou's rules, no matter who you are and no matter how long you've known him. I called him before the beginning of the season in 2018 and told him I was moving over to work for Rogers Sportsnet—this was soon after he took the job running the New York Islanders.

We chatted a bit, some small talk about our families, and then he said, "Okay, see you later."

"Don't you want to talk about your team?" I asked him.

"No," he said. "I don't talk to the media."

The flip side is that when I was working for the league, no one was easier to deal with than Lou, even when I was coming down on one of his players. I'd call him and tell him I was suspending one of his guys for a game or two or three, and he'd just say okay—no argument at all.

Most guys were professional, but some were really hard on me. A lot of GMs would plead for mercy, claiming they were going to lose their job if they missed the playoffs. Others would scream and curse at me. Pierre Lacroix was the worst for that, and Pat Quinn was a close second. I had known Pat for years by then and had worked for him with the Canucks. We were friends, and he was my mentor. Didn't matter. I remember calling him one night when I was driving from New York to Hartford to tell him we were suspending Gino Odjick for four games—that was the time Gino went off and tried to fight everybody on the ice.

There was a long silence. I said, "Pat, it could easily have been six games, and you know it."

"You know what your problem is?" he said. "You don't know enough about hockey to do this fucking job."

And then he hung up on me.

Remember, he'd hired that know-nothing to be his right-hand man in Vancouver. But that was Pat.

Lou, by contrast, was always very professional, very cognizant of being part of the league and doing what was best for the NHL. Whatever the league said goes—which has always been my philosophy as well. Try not to be a problem for the league. Don't complain about things that you don't like. Vote with a league hat on, not a team hat.

———

I made a couple of trades with Lou when we were both running teams. My first big deal with him happened when I was the general manager of the Hartford Whalers—I sent him Bobby Holik for Eric Weinrich and Sean Burke. It turned out to be a great trade for both teams. We got two pieces that we needed—Burke was our MVP that year—and Holik became a big part of New Jersey's first Stanley Cup team.

But Lou skinned me on the next deal I did with him. I was running the Canucks and traded him a second- and a third-round pick—those were non-playoff picks—for a guy named Vadim Sharifijanov. I didn't really want to make that deal. I knew Sharifijanov a bit and didn't like his skating, but our scouts liked him, and I figured Lou wouldn't screw me on something like this.

We got the kid, and he couldn't play. Not even a little bit.

When I called Lou to complain, he taught me a lesson.

"Hang on," he said. "This was your deal. *You* called *me* and asked about him. You can't complain about *your* deal. You can complain about my deal if I called you first."

I never forgot that.

But where I first got to know Lou Lamoriello was as a college coach. That's where he shaped me as a player and as a man.

Lou's drive and desire to win is contagious. If you play for Lou, you know the games are important, and you know that the practices are just as important. He's very intense—and that intensity transmits to his players. He has incredible attention to detail, and he has those rules—absolute, unbending rules. Playing for Lou is almost like being in the military. You had better never be late—you should be 15 minutes early for everything. I was late for a practice once, on Christmas Day, after I took the freshmen to midnight Mass. As a punishment, I had to skate at 4 a.m. for nine days. I was never late again, and I'm never late for anything now.

Lou's also a stickler for curfews, dress codes, hairstyles. No facial hair allowed, and nothing that resembled long hair. In an era when a lot of guys wore their hair like Jesus, Lou got us free haircuts from an

ROTC barber. It was cut so short that when we went and played a game at West Point, the army cadets came up to us and said, "What's with the hair?"

If you played for Lou, your manners had to be impeccable. He insisted that we be polite to everyone. If you didn't behave, you were gone. As a result, we were a pretty popular team around campus.

There were certain elements of Lou's rules that were more quirky. Team meals, for instance. The pre-game meal had to happen exactly five hours before puck drop. Every time, without fail, we got a steak, baked potato, green beans, a salad and two pieces of toast and two pats of butter—no more. You could butter your potato or your toast, but not both. One of the chefs was assigned to stand there and make sure no one cheated. He literally counted those pats of butter. You could have two pops to drink, or one milk and one pop, but not two milks—because Lou thought dairy was bad for you on game days.

I remember that on one of my first road trips with the team, we stopped at a steak house for our pre-game meal on the way to play Colgate. We walked in and Lou said to the manager, "I want to look at those steaks."

"What?"

"I want to look at those steaks."

Lou made the guy take him back into the cooler so he could personally inspect the meat before he let them serve it to us.

But for all the old-school stuff, what a lot of people don't understand about Lou is that he was also an innovator. Keep in mind that this was back in 1973—the year after the Soviets played Canada in the Summit Series, and everyone was baffled by their training techniques.

We did extensive stretching as part of our weightlifting program. No one else was stretching back then. We worked on shot blocking at a time when no one else made that a priority. We did circuit training, which was unheard of. Off-ice training in those days meant lifting the heaviest weights you could lift and maybe riding a stationary bike. Lou had us doing bench-press reps at low weights, then 30 seconds off, then curls, then push-ups. It's standard practice now, but it was cutting edge then.

He had the people from Bauer come in and provide our skates.

Most college players then would just wear whatever skates they could afford to buy. Lou had us properly fitted. He bought our sticks from Sher-Wood, and had their guys come in and look after us, the same way they would have treated an NHL team. We used video before most teams were using video. And Lou had a tight alignment with pro hockey—he would go to Boston Bruins practices and see what they were doing, and every once in a while he would arrange for injured players from the Providence Reds, the Rangers' American Hockey League farm team, to practise with us. That was a big thrill for us.

But if we had a bad game . . . well, then it was back to the old-school approach. Normally, you'd come to practice and he'd have the lines written out in chalk on the blackboard—first line wears red, second line wears green, and so on. After a bad loss, he would just say, "Any colour." That meant we weren't going to see any pucks in practice. Lou was just going to bag-skate us to death.

I arrived at Providence College with no financial guarantees, fighting for a place on the team. As a walk-on, I was going to have to beat out a scholarship player to win a spot. The freshmen came in on the Tuesday after Labour Day. Classes started that Thursday, and we had our first hockey meeting the following Sunday. After that, we had training camp—eight weeks of it before we played a game—two-a-days, and then one-a-days, on top of our classes. It was brutal.

Every day of camp included a two-mile run. There was a defence-man named Terry Nagel, a big guy from Minneapolis who could run like a deer. He won the two-mile run every time. But I wasn't going to give in. The first time, I tried to stay with him. He yelled back at me, "Rook, you're not going to win this race. I always win this race." I couldn't beat him. I finished a couple of steps behind him. The next time, same result: two yards back at the finish.

Lou noticed what was going on and pulled me aside. "It's clear you're serious about trying to make this team," he said. (He'd also seen me working hard in the weight room and during practice.) "If you want to make it, *there's* the guy you have to beat out."

He pointed to a player named Joey Rego. My heart sank.

Joey was an all-state high school player from Mount St. Charles High School in Rhode Island, a hockey factory. I think he scored 40 goals in his senior year, and he weighed about 195 pounds. In my senior year in Edina, I scored 7 goals. And in the fall of 1973, I stood 6-foot-2 and weighed 176 pounds. I was a bone rack. So, beating out Joey Rego was going to be a tall order.

Lou prized big forwards and he liked physical teams. We always had at least two or three guys who could change a game with a big hit. Fighting wasn't really the point, because you couldn't fight in college hockey games—if you did, you were ejected and automatically suspended for the next game. But if you were on the bench and Lou tapped you on the shoulder and said that things were getting a little rough out there, you understood the message: it was time to go out and get a piece of someone.

Part of my challenge as a freshman was to find a way to prove to Lou that I was that guy. The easiest way to do that was to take on one of my teammates. Fighting might not have been a factor once the season started, but in practice it was a different story. We weren't allowed to fight during drills, but once we started scrimmaging, all bets were off.

We had a defenceman named Kevin Gaffney (who ended up becoming a good friend of mine). He was two years older, weighed about 195 pounds and was getting on my nerves during the drills.

"As soon as we get to the scrimmage, I'm going to kick the shit out of you," I told him.

"I'm not hard to find," he said.

We were practising at the Providence Civic Center because our new rink was under construction. I was playing right wing, and Gaffney was playing right defence. As soon as Lou dropped the puck, I charged across the circle and dropped my gloves. We had a good, hard little fight. He landed a few and I landed a few before Lou broke it up. It didn't matter who won. I had sent a message to the upperclassmen that, one way or another, I was making this team.

I beat the odds and did make it, a marginal fourth-line player who did little more than kill penalties, but still part of the team. My four rules had worked. And Joey Rego, the guy Lou told me I had to beat out, never played a game at Providence College.

Which brings me to one of the most impressive things about Lou Lamoriello. A lot of kids who played in other programs and washed out as athletes never graduated. But all of Lou's players graduated, and he honoured every scholarship. Joey Rego had a four-year ride. Lou honoured it, and Joey graduated.

If you played for Lou and your academics started to slide, he would always come down on the side of school instead of the side of hockey. In my sophomore year, Terry Nagel, the guy who beat me in the two-mile runs, had a grade point average of 1.6, which is high enough to retain eligibility under NCAA rules, but short of the 2.0 that you need to graduate from Providence College. Lou made him ineligible for a semester, until he got his grades up. At any other school he would have played, but not for Lou.

He also had little ways of keeping you on your toes. For instance, we didn't know it at the time, but each of our professors would get a self-addressed postcard from Lou before the school year started. "So-and-so, your student, is a player on the varsity hockey team," it would read. "If he misses any classes, just drop this postcard in the mail."

I rarely missed a class, but once or twice when I did, Lou immediately called me in to ask what was going on. You started to think that he must have spies in every classroom.

As soon as I arrived at Providence as a freshman, I started hearing about a star high school player from Rhode Island named Ron Wilson who was going to be part of the team. I knew he was in one of my classes, but for the life of me I couldn't pick him out until he introduced himself afterwards. He was a small guy wearing little wire-framed glasses. He sure didn't look like a jock, but the truth was he was a great all-around athlete. Ron scored 100 points as a high school senior—and he was also an all-state shortstop, and pretty close to a scratch golfer.

People ask me to name the best player I played against in college—and I tell them I had the misfortune to practise against him every day.

It was Ron, by a mile. He had 37 points in his freshman year—and we only played 28 games. As a sophomore, he had 87 points. He's still among the top five scorers of all time in ECAC Hockey, even though we played a shorter schedule than colleges do today, and he was a defenceman, not a forward.

He would embarrass you with the moves he would make. He was a magician. And he worked hard at it.

I remember once in practice, watching Ron work on a move from the side of the net. It just didn't look like something that could work. "You'll never score that way," I said to him. But he kept at it. He stayed after practice for four days in a row, working on that one move for 15 or 20 minutes at a time. He worked his ass off.

Three games later, he scored from that exact spot. And after he did it, he went to the bench and sat down. He didn't gloat. He didn't say anything to me. Just went back to business.

Ron was a superstar who didn't act like one. He was a phenomenal player, a great teammate, and also just one of the guys. We wound up being captains together at Providence. And, of course, our paths would cross again down the road.

In March, at the end of the first season, two days before I was going to head home to Minnesota for spring break, Lou called me into his office and offered me a scholarship: a one-third ride the next year, two-thirds in my junior year, and a full ride as a senior. I was thrilled—and so were my parents. They were contributing to three other tuitions then, all at expensive Ivy League schools, so that scholarship helped out a lot.

I had struggled a bit academically as a freshman, in large part because I had enrolled in pre-med, which was an act of appalling arrogance on my part. Math and science were never my academic strong suits. Heading into the second semester, my eligibility was hanging by a thread. Lou made me promise to switch my major the next year.

Providence College had a wonderful program called the Development of Western Civilization, which is mandatory in the first two years. It combines history, literature, fine arts, philosophy and music. You go five days a week, and it counts for 40 percent of your GPA. It's tough enough that it has rendered more athletes ineligible at PC than all other courses combined.

I loved it, especially the history. When Lou leaned on me to change my major, it was an easy decision to switch to history.

In May, right before I drove home for the summer, Lou called me in and said he had moved some things around and could offer me a half scholarship in my second year and a full ride in years three and four. That was great news.

The Minnesota guys who played hockey for Providence drove home together. I never had a car in school, but some of the other guys did. Sometimes there were two of us, sometimes there were four, and we would make the 24-hour trip non-stop. We drove until the tank was empty, then we'd pull into a gas station, and while the driver refuelled the car, the other guys would run in, use the bathroom, grab a burger or some other form of grease, and then the driver would run in and pee and the next driver would take over. We'd leave Friday at noon after classes got out and we'd be home by 11 in the morning on Saturday.

I played summer hockey in Minnesota all through my Providence years, along with just about all the other college guys from the state. It was a great league with great players, and a really important development tool for me. I took it seriously, worked my ass off and had a lot of fun doing it. And I remember one really good fight that I had with Paul Holmgren.

It didn't teach me any great life lessons, but I should mention one of my summer jobs, because it was my first brush with celebrity. Bill Sims was a tight end at the University of Minnesota, and his father owned the biggest security company in the state. I had played high school football with him. Bill asked me if I would be interested in working security at a Rolling Stones concert. They had already hired half the Gopher football team. I was told to show up in jeans and a tight white T-shirt, to be as intimidating as possible. When they lined us up in front of the stage, I was easily the smallest guy there—the football guys on either side of me were all over 240 pounds. So I wasn't going to intimidate anyone. The manager told me I was too small and sent me off to perform a somewhat less intense task—guarding the stage door. It turned out great, though, because I got to talk to all the Stones—especially Charlie Watts, who was a really friendly guy. It was a very cool experience.

Bob O'Connor helped me get a summer job with a landscaping company. That's where I learned an important lesson that has stuck with me my whole adult life. I was part of a crew planting trees and shrubs and spreading wood chips at the Freshwater Biological Institute on Lake Minnetonka, just west of the Twin Cities.

There was a pile of wood chips, maybe seven feet high—it looked like a two-man, one-day job, spreading them around with a wheelbarrow and pitchfork. I told my boss that the guy I was working with and I would be finished by three in the afternoon. It turned out the job was a bit bigger than I thought. It was four o'clock and we still weren't finished. This was a Friday, and it was an hour's drive back to the farm.

The guy I was working with said, "Let's go, it's four o'clock."

"Fuck that," I said. "There's an hour's work here. Let's finish it. We can't spend an hour driving back, spend another hour driving out Monday morning, work for an hour, and then drive an hour back."

"Fuck you, man," the guy said. "I've got plans. You can't make me stay."

I thought for a minute, and then threw him the keys to the truck.

"You're right," I said. "I can't make you stay, so you drive back."

"What about you?" he asked.

"I will hitchhike back with my wheelbarrow and my pitchfork. And then, on Monday morning, I'm going to come to work and kick the living shit out of you in front of all the guys for fucking bailing on me here."

He thought about it for about 60 seconds, and then he threw me back the keys and started pitching chips.

When we were finished, I bought him a six-pack of beer and let him have a couple on the drive back. I didn't tell anyone that story—but he told everybody.

The next thing you know, they made me a foreman and gave me a four-dollar-a-week raise.

The lesson?

Don't waste time. Make yourself useful. And, especially, never cheat your employer.

3 ▼ "YOU'RE WRITING THE EXAM"

THE NEXT YEAR, 1974–75, I came into camp at 188 pounds. The way I played, that extra weight was crucial. Now I had some size, and the hits I was delivering were starting to sting people. I got a little bit of ice time with the third line and the second power-play unit, I killed every penalty (we called the penalty-killing unit "The Bomb Squad" and took real pride in it), and Lou put me on the ice at the end of games when we had a narrow lead. Off the ice, I was now a history major, and my grades shot up.

My junior year was even better. All the weightlifting and work during the summer had built me up to 194 pounds. Now I was really drilling guys. If I hit them right, somebody had to help them off the ice.

That season, I got to see yet another side of Lou Lamoriello.

We were scheduled to play an away game against Clarkson College, part of their Homecoming Weekend. Instead of the rink on campus, the game was moved to the much larger War Memorial Auditorium in Rochester, the home of the Rochester Americans of the American Hockey League.

We started the game badly and were down 4–0 by the end of the first period. The Clarkson students and alumni were going crazy in the stands. We went into the dressing room and Lou blew a gasket. He took off his watch and threw it across the room. I think he was trying to smash it against the wall for dramatic effect, but instead he hit one of our players, Dave Dornseif, in the chest.

Even though Lou's outburst didn't go exactly as planned, it got the desired result. We were on fire in the second period and tied the game up.

Then, for whatever reason, the referee started fucking us over. There were, I think, six straight penalty calls against us, and we lost the game. Lou was so mad that he sent me out late in the game with instructions to get a piece of someone. I did—and took another penalty.

I was always the last player off the ice at the end of a game—it's one of my few superstitions. As I was walking down the corridor in my skates on the way to the dressing room, I heard a commotion behind me. It was Lou and the referee, nose to nose. I have no idea who started it, but each of them had a hold of the other by the neck. The ref was wearing a helmet—it was actually the first game where I'd ever seen that—and one of those times when Lou jerked his neck, the helmet clipped Lou on the bridge of his nose and cut him. I'm not totally sure how it happened, but after that, the ref ended up on his ass.

Our assistant coach, Bob Bellemore, and I hustled Lou away. We were convinced that there was still a chance someone was going to arrest him. The other guys on the team couldn't believe it when I told them what had happened, but we all showered, dressed and got on the bus in record time. I was pretty relieved when we got out of town without anyone going to jail.

Two important things happened for me at the end of what was a pretty lousy season for Providence College.

Lou had the players vote on who would be the captains the following year. They chose me and Ron Wilson. It felt like a real accomplishment after starting as a walk-on. By the time I finished my senior year, I'd hold the school record for most games played.

And the Philadelphia Flyers claimed my professional rights. Under the old system, if you weren't drafted, a team could claim your rights later on. They would just add you to a negotiating list. I wasn't drafted, but Lou told me that there was another team who would have added me if the Flyers hadn't beaten them to it.

By the time I got to my senior year at Providence College, I had a plan for my life after graduation—I was going to go get a graduate degree in history, and then I'd get a job teaching and coaching college hockey. I had it all laid out. I won the award as the top history student in my class. Hockey players don't win those awards. Eggheads win those awards. But I had the highest GPA in history of anyone in my class. Notre Dame University was my dream school. A couple of the professors at Providence had studied at Notre Dame and raved about it. By my senior year, I had already signed up for the GREs—the graduate record exams—in history. When the time came, I would apply to different grad schools, see where I was accepted, and move on with my academic life.

Except there was a change in plans. Not a change in *my* plans. A change in Lou Lamoriello's plans for me.

In my last three years, I managed to schedule all my classes in the morning, between 8:30 and 12:30. Then I'd sprint through lunch, and try to get two hours of studying in before practice. I'd review my lecture notes, jotting down the important stuff in red in the margins so I'd have a study guide for exam time. My dorm room was close to the rink, and it was a short walk across a little parking lot and a soccer field. When the time came, I'd jog over in time to get dressed for practice at 3:30.

One day, I got to the rink and was intercepted by Lou's secretary, Alannah Mooney. She must have seen me running across the field. She stuck her head out the door and said, "Lou wants to see you."

Ah, fuck. That was never what you wanted to hear. Lou was not a fun guy, and if he wanted to see you, it almost certainly meant you'd done something wrong, at least in his eyes.

On the walk to Lou's office, I was trying to figure out what that something might be. The truth was, I didn't get in a lot of trouble. I was a very disciplined guy all through school. I had a girlfriend back home in Minnesota. I never broke curfew except to study—that was it. I thought that maybe one of the freshmen had gotten in trouble and he wanted to talk to me about that.

I got to Lou's office and sat down. He didn't say a word. Just pushed a piece of paper across the desk to me. I looked at it and saw the title: Law School Admissions Test.

"What's this?" I asked him.

"You're writing this exam," he said. "Your professors tell me that if you do well on it, you could get into law at Harvard or Yale."

I pushed the paper right back at him.

"I'm not writing it. I'm not going to law school."

Lou shoved the paper back in my direction.

"You don't understand," he said. "That was not a request. You're taking the fucking exam. You're writing it."

I tried to make my case. I told him I had no interest in going to law school, that I was going to do grad work in history and hoped to go to Notre Dame and then teach—maybe coach hockey somewhere.

Lou, not surprisingly, was unmoved.

"Trust me on this one," he said. "Write the exam."

So . . . I was writing the exam.

The LSATs were scheduled for a Saturday morning, from nine to noon. These days, most of the students who write them take a course to prepare for the exam. It can last months. I got a booklet with sample questions and instructions. The night before the exam, I read it from front to back. Then I read it a second time. Then I drank a cold beer and went to bed.

Here's how important it was to Lou: he let me arrive late for practice the day of the exam. And you were never late for practice when you played for Lou Lamoriello at Providence College. As soon as I finished, I ran over to the rink, got changed as quickly as I could and got out on the ice.

Lou skated over to me.

"How did it go?" he asked.

"Coach, I don't know. I might have aced it, I might have bombed it. But the one thing I can tell you is that I've got one of the worst headaches I've ever had in my life."

"Good," Lou said. "Get in line. I don't give a shit about your headache."

It was four or five weeks later before I got the results. In the meantime, I'd written to a bunch of law schools asking them to send me applications. You had to do it by mail then—you couldn't call, and of course there was no email. Some of the applications were simple, and some of them were 20 pages long, complete with essays.

I also prepared to write my GREs and sent out for applications to do graduate studies in history at Notre Dame and Georgetown—just in case.

At Providence, all the mail goes to one central mailbox in the Student Union building. I had the same mail slot all four years I was there. One morning, I went in to look and there was one piece of mail in there—a single envelope. I didn't get a lot of mail, so I had a suspicion about what it might be. The return address was ETS—the Educational Testing Service—in Princeton, New Jersey. It was a really thin envelope, so I knew it had to be the test results and nothing else.

Opening that envelope was going to determine which fork in the road I took. If I didn't do well, I was going back to Plan A—doing my master's in history.

Not that anyone was watching, but I felt self-conscious. If the news was shitty, I didn't want anyone around to see my reaction. So I went upstairs to the Student Union administrative offices, where there was no one around.

I opened the envelope, unfolded the single sheet of paper, and read the number: 704—a score that put me in the 98th percentile of those around the world who had written the LSAT that year.

For a second, I wondered if someone was pranking me—but admittedly, that would be a pretty elaborate prank. Still, I double-checked the postmark, just to make sure.

The first call I made was home. My mom answered—and one thing you should know about her is that she didn't like lawyers. I tried to explain what it meant.

"This is like Charlie Bucket getting the golden ticket in *Willy Wonka*."

She was supportive, but she wasn't all that excited.

Then I went to see Lou.

I made him take the paper out of the envelope.

"704?" he said.

"Keep reading," I told him. He saw "98th percentile."

"You're responsible for this," I said.

Harvard, Yale, Georgetown Law—all of them were possibilities for me, because Lou Lamoriello gave a shit about a young, red-headed kid from Minnesota.

Before the end of my senior year, I had been accepted by Harvard Law School. Another student—Angela Carcone—and I were the first Providence College students in 10 years to be accepted into Harvard Law.

But there would be a short detour on the way to Cambridge.

There was a chance that the Flyers might want to bring me to camp—which meant that there was at least an outside chance that I might be able to play professional hockey.

I asked Lou what he thought I should do if that happened.

"What do you want to do?" he asked.

If the Flyers ever signed me—and I didn't really think that was possible, let alone likely—that would be great, but I would also be willing to go to training camp with them the next fall without a contract. I really wanted to give it a shot.

"Could you defer your Harvard acceptance?" Lou asked.

I had already read through the acceptance letter, and they said that they took a maximum of 40 deferments a year. I applied for a deferment right away, and it was granted almost immediately. So now I had an option.

I figured that if the Flyers cut me in camp—which I absolutely thought they would—I would go and play the season in Europe. I wasn't good enough for the best leagues in Europe, but there are all kinds of places you can play over there. Even to this day, I still dream about living abroad for a year. And after that, I could head back to Harvard Law.

Providence College lost to Clarkson College in the playoffs—in fact, they smoked us, in part because they had a guy playing for them named Dave Taylor, who would go on to be one-third of the Los Angeles Kings' famous Triple Crown Line. He had five points against us.

That game was on a Tuesday night. We went out drinking after the game . . . and on Wednesday . . . and on Thursday. On Friday morning after class, the Minnesota guys began our familiar drive back home for spring break. And 24 hours later, after that great, non-stop dash across the country, we arrived.

Lou called me at home on Saturday morning and told me that the Flyers wanted me to play some games with their AHL farm club, the Springfield Indians. Right away.

I had gone three or four days with no workouts and drinking a whole lot of beer. "Coach," I told Lou, "I don't even have my gear with me. It's back in Providence. I haven't been on the ice in four days. And I've been drinking a bit . . ."

Lou, as always, cut to the chase.

"Get some gear, find some ice time and fly back here tomorrow."

I called the guy who ran the rink in our town, Larry Thayer, and he got me an hour of ice time. Then I found some guys I could throw the puck around with and borrowed some gear. We skated Saturday, and then I went out early Sunday morning and skated again before getting on the plane back to Providence.

The PC baseball team was on its spring tour in Florida, so I borrowed a car that the third baseman John Schiffner had left behind in Rhode Island. (Schiff went on to become the most famous manager in the history of the Cape Cod summer baseball league.)

It was about an hour and 40 minute drive to the rink in Springfield. Of course there was no GPS then—you had to rely on one of those Rand McNally road atlases to get around. And I got lost on the way to the rink. But luckily, I was so nervous about being late that I'd left three hours before practice was scheduled to start. I was the first guy in the dressing room, waiting by myself, and then the players started to trickle in.

They were really nice to me. They put me in a locker next to the captain, Andre Peloffy, who scored 99 points for Springfield that season. I went out for my first practice in professional hockey, and I thought it was the best thing ever. I was sitting there thinking, "This is really cool." The dressing room was pretty dingy, but it was a sunny day and the light was bouncing off the white walls and the locker stalls. I always put my skates on last, so I was sitting there in my bare feet, with my pants and shin pads on, reflecting on the journey—who would have believed it, 10 years earlier in Minnesota, when I played for the first time as a kid, if I'd said, "Guys, I'm going to be a professional hockey player." Everyone would have laughed at me, and yet here I am.

And then, after practice, I got my first dose of reality.

Springfield was a split team then—half the players belonged to the Flyers, and the other half to the Washington Capitals. The Flyers guys were pretty serious about what they were doing. The Washington guys . . . not so much.

Peloffy—his nickname was Peelo—elbowed me in the ribs and said, "Watch this." Mike McMahon, a veteran defenceman, yelled out for the trainer, whose nickname was Gooch.

"Hey Gooch!"

Obviously, Gooch had been through this routine before. He came over and handed Mac two plastic beer cups filled with ice. Great, big beer cups. Mac reached down under the seat, where the skates go, pulled out a jug of rye and filled up both cups right to the top. He handed one to Grant Cole, one of our goalies, and they clinked beer cups before having a sip. I remember looking up at the clock—it was 11:46 in the morning. Holy fuck. No mixer, no tonic, no nothing. Just straight rye.

After practice, I went back to the crappy Howard Johnson's where they had put me up and called my dad and told him the story.

"Don't you hang out with those two guys," he said. "If they ask you to go out, you say no."

After the first period of my first game, seven guys lit cigarettes and smoked in their stalls. There was a big tub of beer waiting when you came off the ice after the game. It was nuts.

I played weekend games and then returned to Providence in time for classes Monday morning. I remember that we played at home one Saturday night, and then bused part of the way to Hershey, where we were playing on Sunday. Gooch asked me if I wanted to buy beer for the bus. I asked what everyone was buying, and he said 12 beers. So I paid him for 12 beers. When I got on the bus, there were at least 14 cases of beer stacked in the aisle with bags of ice on them. You had to walk on the seat handles to get over them. Turns out the *team* put four cases of beer on the bus. The 12 beers each guy bought were on top of that.

The movie *Slap Shot* came out that spring. I remember telling one of my buddies that I'd lived it in Springfield.

Gary Dineen was the coach of that team, and he had no interest in me at all. I barely played—and the team that year was awful. But the experience gave me a much clearer picture of professional hockey and what I needed to do to prepare. And now I had friends going into training camp. All in all, it was a great two weeks. I got to meet the legendary Eddie Shore. The rink we played in was a great old barn that smelled like horse manure because of the agricultural shows they used to have there. They were paying me 200 bucks a game—I wound up playing seven games for Springfield that spring and making 1,400 bucks. A beer was 25 cents then, and our meal money was three bucks a game in college, and seven bucks a day in the pros—and you could eat just fine on that—so that was decent money.

I loved every minute of it.

And it turned out my timing wasn't bad. Keith Allen, the Flyers' general manager, came down one afternoon to watch the Indians play in New Haven. Tommy Rowe got into a fight on the very first shift of the game, pulled the guy's hair and got himself ejected. So I got a regular turn on the ice in his spot on right wing. I threw some big hits, made a couple of plays and caught a guy on the backcheck, breaking up a breakaway. There is no doubt in my mind that that's why the Flyers signed me a couple of weeks later—a one-plus-one contract (one year, plus an option) with a $10,000 signing bonus and $15,000 to play.

I went back to finish my final term at Providence with the acceptance to Harvard Law in my back pocket along with a contract with the Flyers. I started to think that if I had come so far, so fast as a hockey player, maybe I could take that next step. I knew I would need time in the minors, but I really thought then that I had a chance to play in the National Hockey League.

———

I loved my time at Providence College. I graduated with honours and won two academic awards—the Father Forster Award for excellence in European history, and the Alumni Award, which was given to the student who contributed the most to the school over four years. My name was called from the stage three times, and I know my parents were really proud. I was in tears when we drove away from campus after the convocation ceremony.

And in addition to my diploma, I had a copy of my standard NHL player's contract, and a cheque for $7,600—my signing bonus after taxes.

My parents weren't thrilled that I was going to be playing hockey instead of going to school in the fall, and they made no secret of it, but in the end, they supported my decision. I think they thought of it as my little Grand Tour year, my gap year. "Go and have your fun, but after that you're going to Harvard." My dad, in particular, was emphatic about that.

After graduation, I went home to Minnesota to spend some time with my family, and I bought a car—a forest-green Jeep CJ-7 hardtop. I loved that car. After my birthday, I packed up my belongings, put my dog in the Jeep and headed back to Providence, where I was going to spend a few weeks teaching at Lou Lamoriello's summer hockey school before going to my first—and, as it turned out, only—professional training camp as a player.

Lou didn't pay much, but it was an amazing hockey school. Not surprisingly, it was run along Lou's principles. There was no improvising. The drills for each workout were set up in advance for the entire week, so every kid had to work on every single skill. You were never on the ice for more than five hours. And the weight room was always open.

After the hockey school was finished, I had about four weeks left until the beginning of rookie camp. There was open ice time in the morning, and then I'd come back and lift around 5 p.m. By the end of the summer I was a lean, strong 206 pounds—precisely 30 pounds heavier than when I had arrived at Providence as a freshman, and in the best shape of my life.

I was ready.

The 1977–78 season was the first for the Maine Mariners, the Flyers' new AHL affiliate. Portland, Maine, wasn't the cleaned-up and restored tourist town then that it is now. It was more grimy and rundown. But I loved the place.

They made a big splash for the arrival of the new team. The day before rookie camp opened, all the players boarded a replica of one of Christopher Columbus's ships and sailed into the harbour, where we were greeted by a high school band and a pretty decent crowd, and then the town put on a dinner for us. I'll never forget one thing that happened that night. Gil Stein was the president of the Mariners—he would go on to work in the NHL head office, and was for about a year the league's president, the last one before Gary Bettman arrived and was given the new title of commissioner.

At the dinner, one of our players asked Gil how many of us would be invited to the Flyers' main training camp in Philadelphia after rookie camp was done.

"All of you," Stein said.

That wasn't even close to being true, though I don't think he really knew. The next day, at the first practice, the Flyers' assistant coach, Pat Quinn, called us all in and made that clear. "What you were told last night was bullshit," he said. "They can't take you all to main camp. Half of you are going home from here."

He could have gotten in trouble for saying that, but Pat had the guts to tell us the truth.

Rookie camp was held at the North Yarmouth Academy in Yarmouth, Maine, just north of Portland on the road to Freeport. They put us up at a place called the Eagle Motel, two to a room. My roommate was Tommy "TJ" Gorence, who wound up playing six seasons in the NHL. We were two of only a handful of Americans in camp, so maybe that's why they put us together. It was a lucky break for me—TJ was a great guy, and we'd go on to room together for that whole season in Maine.

On the second day of camp, I remember telling TJ that I hoped I would get a chance to fight. I hadn't fought much, but I knew that with the kind of game I played, I would have to fight to make it in the pros, and I wanted to make it clear to the coaches and management that I was willing to go when necessary.

It wasn't long before I got my chance. We were on a breakout and I passed the puck to my centre, and then tried to step around the defenceman, which would have set up a three-on-one. Instead, he tripped me. As he skated by me, while I was still on my knees, I pitchforked him down. If you know hockey, you know what comes next. We both came up swinging.

This would be a great story if I could claim here that I knew the player I was about to trade punches with was Frank Bathe, the toughest guy in camp, a minor-league veteran who had 250 penalty minutes the year before in the International Hockey League, who would go on to be a bit player over several seasons with the Broad Street Bullies. But the truth is, I had no idea who I was fighting.

I thought I hung in pretty well with him. I got a couple in. I ate a couple. No cuts. No problem.

When I got back to the bench, the guys asked me, "Do you know who that was?"

I said I didn't—but fuck him for tripping me.

The next morning in the local newspaper, there was actually a story about the fight—something about how the only two redheads in camp squared off and Frank Bathe won a clear decision over Brian Burke. Well, I'd dispute that. I told TJ that now everyone was going to get to see round two. I was going to fight him as soon as we were on the ice together.

I was in the dressing room in my underwear, getting ready for practice, when Frank Bathe gestured towards me to follow him into the showers. I thought maybe he wanted to fight me again right then and there.

We walked in, and I'll never forget what he said.

"I saw the paper. Don't worry about it. You fought the toughest guy in rookie camp. You did just fine in the fight. The other players will leave you alone now because they think you're a looney tune, and management noticed for sure. Just play hockey now. I'm not afraid of you, and we can go again right now if you like. But you did fine, and I think you should just concentrate on playing hockey."

What a great guy, and what great advice. He didn't have to do that. He was in Maine with me that year, and he became one of my first clients after I got into the agent business. We've been friends ever since.

This seems like as good a time as any to talk about fighting in hockey. It's become a bit of a debating point, but if you know anything about me at all, you know where I stand.

I have no problem with fighting, and I'm never going to apologize for being a fighting guy. I believe in it.

And I fought—and that's important. There are a lot of guys who are fighting guys who love to see other people fight but have never dropped their gloves once.

I wasn't a big fighter. I didn't do it a lot, because in college hockey, you couldn't really.

As a pro, over 60 games in the AHL, I fought maybe six times. Our coach Bob McCammon told me that if I had fought more, I would have played more, but I said it had to be the other way around. If you play me more, I will fight more because the fights will come to me. The way I hit, I will generate them. But I've got to play. I'm not coming off the bench to fight.

When I did fight, I fought for teammates. The fights I had in hockey—not to mention those I've had in my life outside of hockey—have generally happened when I was defending somebody else. When that's the case, there's a virtuous side to it—there's a legitimate reason for the fight. And I had no problem going against the other teams' tough guys to defend a teammate. I fought Billy Bennett—he was 6-foot-6, 230 pounds. I fought Nelson Burton, who had 300 minutes in penalties that year.

Once the fight starts, I don't mind being part of it. I don't mind getting hit. The only problem I had was that to be a good fighter, you've got to get mad fast, get the adrenaline pumping—and I tend to be slow to anger. That was the hardest part for me. Working up that hate right away.

I'm also not about to turn into one of those guys who get religion as they get older—guys who had really tough teams in the old days and now say, "Oh, we've got to get rid of fighting." Guys who write books saying, "Well, that was me at a younger age, and I've matured since then and now I know that fighting is bad."

Fuck that. I'm not changing anything.

Contrary to what some have suggested, I'm not a dinosaur who wants to go back to the '70s. We emptied the bench six or seven times the year I played in Maine. We routinely had three-hour games. I don't want to go back to that. No one wants to go back to that. There's a lot less fighting now than there used to be, and that's a good thing.

And, just to be clear, it's not about selling tickets—which is another argument the anti-fighting crowd likes to trot out. If that were the case, we'd just dress five idiots every night, and we'd allow fighting in the warm-up because that would get people drinking beer early. If the NHL is allowing fighting as a way to pump up the box office, they're doing a pretty poor job of it, because these days we're down to about a quarter of a fight per game. If you want to be guaranteed of seeing a fight, go to a UFC show.

But I don't always like the game the way it is now. There's too much flag football being played. I watch too many games that lack any emotion or passion. I think we need to have fewer games—I've been pushing for a shorter schedule for years. That would help. In the meantime, this notion that we're going to get rid of fighting completely and people are still going to enjoy our game is wrong. The amount of body contact and the fighting are distinctive features of North American hockey. Everywhere else in the world, the game looks pretty much the same, but in North America we hit more and we fight. I don't ever want to lose that.

Most importantly, I think there are too many cheap shots and not enough self-policing. Accountability on the ice has always been a part of our sport. That's the reason there's fighting in our game, and I hope that never changes.

Some people have argued that fighting is a necessary "safety valve" for players in a contact sport, but that's not true. I played plenty of rugby, another full-contact sport, and there's no fighting there. It's not about letting off steam. It's about accountability, something that has been part of hockey for over a hundred years. There are times as a player when you know it's your obligation to fight—when someone runs your goalie or runs your defence partner.

I don't want the referees and the Department of Player Safety to be the only regulatory forces in the game. I think it's a wonderful part of our game that, if a guy delivers a cheap shot, one of the victim's team-mates grabs him immediately and beats the snot out of him. I think that's fantastic. I don't ever want to lose that.

That being said, I don't think players should have to fight if they don't want to. Markus Naslund came to me in Vancouver, because he knew how my teams played, and asked, "Do you want me to fight once in a while?" I said, "No, no. You're not going to fight, and if you do fight, I'm going to kill you. But I do want my players to come to your assistance if you're victimized by a cheap shot."

One of the things I hear all the time is that people don't mind "real" fights, but they hate the staged fights. That's crap. People who talk about "staged fights" in hockey aren't really paying attention. Nine times out of 10, a "staged" fight starts after a cheap shot—maybe in the previous period, or the previous game between the teams, or three games ago. A visiting coach gets his guy on the ice, the coach of the home team has the right to make the last line change and sends out the guy he wants to fight him, and then they go. That's not a "staged" fight. That's an organic part of the game. If you talked to a hockey person about it, they'd say, "Look, we played them 16 days ago and this guy late-hit one of our guys, and now he has to pay his tab." I'm just fine with that. That's how we police ourselves.

I remember when Colin Campbell was running the league's player safety department, and he'd call me after one of our guys took a bad hit to let me know the league was looking at it. "Don't worry about us," I'd tell him. "You look after the other teams. The Anaheim Ducks will look after themselves. We don't need help from New York. We'll take care of this. Suspend him or don't suspend him, but we're going to look after it ourselves."

The league didn't like that very much.

One final thing. There is a lot of talk about brain injuries in hockey and in other sports, and a lot of research going on—and that's a good thing. But some people are using it as a reason to try and ban fighting.

The truth is, fighting causes a tiny fraction of the total number of concussions in hockey—well under 10 percent. Concussions occur far more often as a result of other aspects of the game. If you take away fighting completely, you're going to see more concussions resulting from hits from behind and other things that players are afraid to do now, because there is that accountability built into the sport.

So no, I don't buy that argument.

PORTLAND

BY THE TIME ROOKIE camp had wrapped up, half the guys had been sent home—just as Pat Quinn had said they would. But I wasn't one of them. I had a contract, and I'd scored five goals in our five scrimmages, so I was feeling pretty secure. I stopped off at Providence College for a night, then headed to Philadelphia for the start of the Flyers' training camp.

Rookie camp had gone very well for me, but this was a whole different thing. This was a Flyers team that still had most of the guys who won back-to-back Stanley Cups in 1974 and 1975. I admit that I was totally intimidated being on the ice with Bobby Clarke, Bernie Parent, Bill Barber, Moose Dupont and all the rest. And when I wasn't sitting back watching those guys, the difference between my skill level and theirs was all too apparent.

I felt lost—and out of my league.

After camp, I was sent back to Portland. It could have been worse: there were roster spots that had to be filled with the Flyers' IHL affiliate in Milwaukee, one level below Maine in the minors. But I managed to stick with the Mariners. And as a player, that was as far as I was going to get.

I practised hard. I pushed the other players. I was a good teammate. And I followed my four rules. But for the first time, I realized that they would only get me to a certain point. If everyone follows those four rules, you're fucked unless you're an elite athlete.

I'm not a natural athlete. I'm above average. But everything I got came because I worked hard, because I was big and because I was kind of hostile. But now I was playing pro hockey, and there were lots of big guys, lots of hostile guys, lots of guys who worked hard. But they were better at it than I was. They did everything I did, and they were better than me.

Flyers management did talk to me once about calling me up to play in the NHL. They were playing in Boston and somebody got hurt, and they asked if I was willing to fight Terry O'Reilly or Stan Jonathan. I said, "Absolutely." But instead, they called up Jimmy Cunningham, our tough guy in Portland—he was way tougher than me. And he fought O'Reilly. That was as close as I ever got to playing in the NHL.

By February, it was really starting to hit home that maybe I had gone as far as I was going to go as a player. Two of our right wingers got hurt, and I thought my ice time would go up. It didn't. (I know it surprises some people to find out that I was a right winger, because I'm a big guy who loves defencemen, and when they look at my stats and see that I only had three goals, they assume I was a defenceman. But I was a right winger who couldn't score.)

That's when I got discouraged. I had been going to the gym and lifting every day until then. But after that, I stopped going. It was tough playing out the last part of the year.

We had a great team in Maine that season. When we made it to the Calder Cup final, they dressed Steve Coates instead of me because they knew the series wasn't going to be physical. So that was another indicator to me that I wasn't really in their plans.

The only thing I had ever won as a player was a state midget championship back in Minnesota. When we won the Calder Cup, I didn't dress for the last game, and I was on the ice in street clothes for the celebration. I played in 73 games that season, including playoffs, so I was a part of it. But I felt a little left out.

I learned something that year about what makes a winning team—what kind of players and what kind of personalities you need in each position. Over the years, I kept thinking about it, watching those great Montreal Canadiens and New York Islanders dynasty teams, trying to figure out the formula for winning a championship.

POSITIONAL SKILLS AND PERFORMANCE

Every place on the roster, from the first-line forwards to the backup goalie

	LEFT WING	CENTRE	RIGHT WING
FIRST LINE ▼ ONE GUY WITH SIZE	TOP SKILL SIZE (EVEN IF NOT A BLACK-AND-BLUE PLAYER) ABILITY TO FINISH	TOP SKILL FOOT SPEED FIRST POWER-PLAY UNIT 65 POINTS OR BETTER LEADER	SNIPER FOOT SPEED GREEN LIGHT TO SCORE FIRST POWER-PLAY UNIT
SECOND LINE ▼ TWO GUYS WITH SIZE	SIZE (EVEN IF SKILLED) SECONDARY SCORING SECOND POWER-PLAY UNIT	SECOND SKILL LEVEL RESPONSIBLE DEFENSIVELY FACEOFF SKILL	SIZE (WITH SOME BITE) SCORING ABILITY SECOND POWER-PLAY UNIT
THIRD LINE ▼ SIZE, FIGHTER DISCIPLES	MUST BE SMART ABOVE-AVERAGE SKATING ABLE TO MOVE SHOOTOUT SKILL	PENALTY KILLER FACEOFF GUY HIGH HOCKEY IQ FOOT SPEED A MUST WORKAHOLIC RIGHT-HANDED SHOT	SIZE SECOND FIGHTER, MIDDLEWEIGHT SKILLED AND SMART ENOUGH TO SHUT PEOPLE DOWN PENALTY KILLER
FOURTH LINE ▼ GRIT, FIGHTER DISCIPLES	PENALTY KILLER RESPONSIBLE HARD TO PLAY AGAINST LAST MINUTE OF EACH PERIOD	SIZE FACEOFF SKILL SHOT BLOCKER SHUTDOWN ROLE AGITATOR	FIGHTER AND CAN PLAY PENALTY KILLER SPEED LAST MINUTE OF EACH PERIOD

13th FORWARD

TOUGHNESS
FIGHT IN ANY WEIGHT CLASS

POSITIONAL SKILLS AND PERFORMANCE (continued)

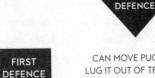
LEFT DEFENCE

RIGHT DEFENCE

FIRST DEFENCE PAIR ▼ SKILL

CAN MOVE PUCK OR
LUG IT OUT OF TROUBLE
TOP-END FOOT SPEED
HIGH HOCKEY IQ

SIZE
PLAY AGAINST TOP LINE
HARD SHOT
CAN SHUT PEOPLE DOWN,
BUT MOVE PUCK
RIGHT-HANDED SHOT

SECOND DEFENCE PAIR ▼ SIZE

SKILL
SECOND POWER-PLAY UNIT
GOOD DECISION-MAKER
ELIMINATE/PIN
(EVEN IF NO HARD FINISH)
SOME PENALTY KILLING

SMART
MOBILE
FINISH, PIN/ELIMINATE
SOME BITE
PENALTY KILLER
RIGHT-HANDED SHOT

THIRD DEFENCE PAIR ▼ BIG SIZE, ONE FIGHTER

PENALTY KILLER
HARD MINUTES AGAINST
BOTTOM-SIX FORWARDS
THIRD FIGHTER

SIZE
HARD TO PLAY AGAINST
FIGHT WHEN NEEDED
FINISH CHECKS HARD
PENALTY KILLER

GOALTENDERS

STARTER

BACKUP

PLAY 60–65 GAMES
BATTLES
ELITE ATHLETE
GREAT MECHANICS

GREAT WORK ETHIC IN PRACTICE
PUSH THE STARTER
MAKE SHOOTERS BETTER
SURVIVE WITH LOW WORKLOAD
POPULAR

Eventually, I put it all together in a chart that included every spot on the roster, from the first-line forwards to the backup goalie, each of which requires a specific skill set—and in some cases, specific personality traits. Some of it is based on common sense—the backup goalie, for instance, has to work hard in practice, push the starter, deal with the low workload and be a popular guy with his teammates. Other parts relate to my preference for a certain style of hockey. One of the fourth-line wingers, for instance, needs to be able to fight in any weight class. Not some little shit-kicking tough kid—I need a fucking heavyweight there.

I had only one season as the general manager in Hartford, so I didn't really have time to put all the pieces in place there, and by the time I got to Calgary I had to modify the chart to get rid of the fourth-line fighters because there was so much less fighting in the game by then.

But if you look at my teams in Vancouver and Toronto, you can see how I was trying to find players who could fit into each role. And if you look at my Cup-winning team in Anaheim, it's almost a perfect representation of the formula from top to bottom.

Despite all the frustrations during that one season in Maine, in my heart I wanted to keep playing. I had another year left on my contract with the Flyers' organization. Maybe one more summer of hard work could make a difference.

I had driven down to Cambridge on an off day to see if there was any way I could defer my acceptance to Harvard Law School for another year. I made an appointment with the dean of admissions and headed for the campus. I had actually never set foot there before. I walked around and soaked it all up before heading into the meeting.

I explained my situation to the dean, told her I had another year remaining on my hockey contract, and asked for a second deferral.

She said no. Simple as that. "Read the admissions material," she said. "It's very clear. It's one year."

I asked her if she'd give me a second deferral if I were running for Congress.

"Absolutely," she said.

"Well, I'm trying to be the best at what I do. What's the difference?"

That argument didn't sway her at all. And then she laid it out in black and white.

"You don't get admitted to Harvard Law in order to give up your spot," she said. "I've looked at your file. If I were you, I would come."

What she was saying, in so many words, was that I wasn't the first fucking person they'd admitted. I was at the tail end of the class, and I had better show up. She wasn't being a dick about it. She was just being honest—which I appreciated.

But that made my choice clear: I could play hockey or I could go to Harvard Law, but I couldn't do both. I had until the end of June either to confirm that I'd be going to school in the fall or to give up my place for another year in the American Hockey League.

I was torn, and so I stalled.

The Flyers flew the entire Maine team to Las Vegas as a reward for winning the Calder Cup. After that, I decided to take a trip into western Canada. Two of my teammates were getting married that summer—Drew Callander in Regina and Al Hill in Victoria. During the two weeks in between, I decided to drive the Alaska Highway.

I definitely wasn't acting like someone who was going back to school. I was going to buy a new weightlifting machine for the house and work on getting stronger, and then I'd take another shot. I also knew that when I was accepted into Harvard I'd also been accepted into some other excellent law schools, including Georgetown University. With my LSAT score and my academic record, I was pretty confident that I'd get in somewhere when the time came, even if it wasn't Harvard.

I was on the road, with the deadline fast approaching, when I started to have second thoughts. From somewhere in northern British Columbia, I called Lou from a pay phone. He had always given me great advice, and he always had my best interests at heart.

"You can keep playing if you want," he said, "but if you do, you're saying no to Harvard Law School. That's a pretty big boat to let pass by. I think you should get on the boat. But if you're still unsure, why don't you talk to Keith Allen."

Looking back, I'm pretty sure that Lou had already talked to Keith and set the whole thing up. But Keith was great.

"Brian, we love you," he said. "We'd love to have you back. We loved the role you played in the community."

(Bob McCammon once joked in the local newspaper that I was in the hospital so often, visiting patients, that the people working there thought I was an intern.)

"But if you were my son," he said, "I'd have to be honest with you. I don't think you're going to play in the NHL. I think you should take this opportunity and go back to school."

It was like getting kicked in the balls, but I will always be grateful to Mr. Allen for that. They were always looking for bodies to play in the minors, and they would have been happy to have me back. But he was looking out for me.

"I owe you five grand," I said to him. "You gave me 10 grand to sign to play for two years."

"Don't worry about the money," he said. "You earned it."

I made one more call—to my dad—and told him that the general manager of the Flyers was telling me to go back to school.

"Brian, it's time," my dad said. "It's unbelievable what you accomplished in hockey, but now it's time to get on with your life."

The next morning, I called Harvard and told them I was coming.

I missed playing hockey for years and years after that. I missed the guys. Harvard Law School is a very intense academic environment, but you don't get to blow off an afternoon drinking beer with your pals. I missed that camaraderie.

Before law school started, I hopped into my Jeep and drove down to Cape Cod. I was meeting friends at a bar, and when I pulled up, the attendant at the parking lot told me that I could only get a spot if I had four people in the car. So, I parked the Jeep illegally for a minute, ran into the bar where my friends were, and said, "I need three of you guys, now!" They jumped up without asking any questions, came outside, jumped in the car and we parked it.

There was a girl in the bar from Canton, Massachusetts, who had been talking to my buddies. After I came in and barked at them, she turned to her friends and said, "What an asshole!" When I returned, I apologized to everyone and explained what was going on. The girl and I ended up talking and staying up late and walking on the beach and talking some more. We fell in love.

Two years later, right before I started my third year in law school, I married Kerry Gilmore.

5 ▼ "THAT'S BRETT HULL'S MOM"

AT THIS POINT IN the story, you are no doubt expecting a hymn to Harvard, the oldest university in the United States, arguably the most famous institution of higher learning in the world, a place that so many have dreamed of attending, steeped in history and in myth, home to a law school that has produced Supreme Court justices, leaders of industry, presidents of the United States and some of the most powerful people on Wall Street.

Well, you aren't going to find that here.

Over the years, I've gone back to lecture at the law school. And I've spoken at the business school. I think I've been loyal and grateful to Harvard. But my three years there? This will be the shortest part of this book, because I didn't like them. I didn't enjoy Harvard at all.

Now, I don't want to be two-faced. Graduating from Harvard Law School has made a huge difference in my life. It's a jaw-dropper. When people ask me where I went to law school, I never say Harvard right away. I'll say Boston and then let them ask, "Oh, where? Boston College? Boston University?" It usually takes about five guesses before they get to Harvard, and then they step back. There's no question it's a game changer.

So, maybe it was worth it. But did I enjoy the experience? Not even close.

This was back in the *Paper Chase* days—if you're too young to remember, that was a novel that was turned into a film that was turned into a television series about students and professors at Harvard Law. They got it pretty much right. The professors tried to make it as unpleasant and intimidating as possible. I had Clark Byse for con-tracts—he was one of the professors that John Houseman's character in *The Paper Chase* was modelled on. These were difficult, acerbic people.

I admit that part of my problem was that I was out of my league aca-demically. You're going head to head with Princeton guys and Yale guys. That was hard. I had to work frantically just to keep up. And I was home-sick. Even though I had been away for school before, I really missed my family. I didn't have a great living situation in my first year. I was two miles from campus—I'd bike in when the weather was decent and walk when it was lousy. I was broke. I still resented having to give up hockey.

So, yeah, I hated it.

Second year was a little bit better. I had a decent living situation closer to campus with a couple of great roommates, and I had a part-time job doing research for a law firm where I was making good money. Maybe most importantly, I started playing rugby for the Harvard Business School RFC. I love that sport. I'd used up all of my NCAA eligibility playing hockey at Providence, but this was a club team that played some of the best sides in the area—Beacon Hill, Bunker Hill, Boston Gentlemen. I played against four or five American Eagles, members of the United States national team.

Now that Kerry and I were married, she moved into my apartment and my roommates, Gary Toman and Steve Eckley, moved out. Third year was my favourite at Harvard Law. You're taking nothing but elec-tives by that point, so I could choose courses that interested me. I made some friends, played a bit of hockey, worked part time, contin-ued with rugby and life was pretty good. But it's not like I'd suddenly fallen in love with the place.

Graduation was in the spring at the end of third year. Kerry was in the advanced stages of pregnancy with our first child, Katie. My par-ents came from Minnesota for the ceremony, and they were very proud. But I just wanted to get it over with.

I didn't even wear a cap and gown—I wore a suit. I was the only one in our class to do that. Senator Ted Kennedy was making the convocation address, but we didn't go. It was a fucking hot day. My wife was eight and a half months pregnant. And I remember that there was a gypsy moth infestation, and Harvard Yard was stripped of leaves. The trees were filled with the caterpillars, millions of them, and all you could hear was the sound of them chewing, with little bits of leaves falling to the ground. It was so loud, it sounded like the ocean. My wife was miserable. My parents were hot. We were sitting in the law school yard, trying to stay cool.

"Aren't we going to Harvard Yard to hear Mr. Kennedy speak?" my mother asked.

"Mom, we are staying here in the shade," I said. "My wife is eight and a half months pregnant, she's really hot and uncomfortable, and I hate this place. I'm so happy to be leaving."

I picked up my diploma and I got out.

Four weeks later, I was in downtown Boston, taking the bar review course in preparation for writing the bar exam. We were in a big auditorium, and the session lasted from seven to ten at night.

I called home at the break to check on Kerry.

"I'm in labour," she said. "You have to come home."

"How far apart are the contractions?" I asked her. "I want to stay for the rest of the lecture." I thought that if the contractions were still far enough apart, I'd have time.

"Get your fucking ass home," Kerry said.

So, I did. I picked her up, we went to the hospital and Katie was born. What a gift!

I passed the exam. "The first bar you ever passed!" my dad said.

By then, I had already begun working for Palmer & Dodge, a Boston firm where I had done my clerkship. Each of the new associates was required to spend their first year doing a series of three-month rotations in probate, litigation, corporate and public law, before committing to a department.

At the end of the process, I chose corporate law. It turned out to be an unwise choice.

The head of the department was an excellent lawyer and a partner. But right from the start, he took a dislike to me, and that opinion didn't change. The partner shunted me off to do "blue sky" work—which is what they do in a law firm when they have no real plans for you. For those of you who aren't lawyers, blue sky laws were enacted to regulate the sale of securities, for fear that without regulations, entrepreneurs would sell gullible investors shares in the blue sky. Blue sky work consists of clearing a security (for example, an issue of bonds by the Massachusetts Port Authority) for sale in every state, as well as verifying that it is a legal investment for pension funds and the like.

It's important in the grand scheme of things, but it is also mind-numbingly repetitive and boring. Even so, I was willing to stick with corporate law in the hopes of building my own client list.

In hindsight, given that I hated the work and my boss hated me, it was inevitable that the end of the line would come sooner rather than later. One day, I came across language in a New Hampshire statute that was slightly different from the language in virtually every other state. So, I went to the partner and showed it to him. We reviewed it, and he instructed me to clear the security in question.

I submitted my report and the partner went to the closing. That's when a lawyer from another firm told him, "I see your blue sky guy cleared this security for sale in New Hampshire. Well, the director of securities in New Hampshire is taking a different position."

The partner called me in a panic. "I showed it to you," I reminded him. "You cleared it. Don't give me this shit."

When the partner returned from the closing, he was in a foul mood. But he huddled with two other partners and they all agreed that we had the better position under the statute. That settled it—or so I thought.

The next week, we had our monthly department meeting. There were 15 people gathered in the boardroom at eight in the morning, before regular working hours. And the partner proceeded to rip me a new asshole in front of everyone. He didn't mention me by name, but everyone knew I was the blue sky guy, so everyone knew who he was talking about.

"I've never been more embarrassed in my life," he said. "We can't tolerate this sort of slipshod legal work."

At that point, I had heard enough, and I piped up.

"Hang on," I said. "Tell everyone what really happened. You originally cleared it for sale. After it blew up, you reviewed it with two other partners and again cleared it for sale. I don't mind taking shit when I've screwed up, but I do mind when I haven't screwed up."

That was the end of me at Palmer & Dodge. The very next day, I got a visit from George Mulhern, a senior partner. He told me I didn't figure in their plans. They don't fire you at a law firm; they say something like "You're not on a partnership track." I still had to stick around for another six months to finish work I already had in the pipeline. But within days, I had multiple job offers from which to choose.

I went with Hutchins & Wheeler. They had tried to hire me right out of law school, knew about my background in hockey and were interested in developing an athlete representation business. I had already helped a couple of my old Maine Mariners teammates, Mike Busniuk and Frank Bathe—the same guy I'd fought in training camp—with their contracts.

Hutchins & Wheeler also had me doing some industrial revenue financing work, which turned out to be pretty lucrative, but eventually, representing hockey players became my primary job.

These were still the early days for player agents. Bob Woolf was the first, and in hockey, Alan Eagleson had started with Bobby Orr and built a large stable of clients while also running the National Hockey League Players' Association. Beyond Eagleson, almost all of the other NHL players were represented by just a handful of guys—Gus Badali (who had Wayne Gretzky and Mario Lemieux), Art Kaminsky, Norm Kaplan, Bill Watters and Don Meehan.

And now Brian Burke.

To be clear, I was never technically an agent. I was a lawyer, billing players on an hourly basis rather than taking a percentage of their income. And I operated a little bit differently from the other guys. If a player wanted me to represent them, they had to be willing to follow my rules rather than the other way around.

The biggest part of that was that they had to agree to a budget. They could only spend so much money on a car. They had to put so much in the bank every month. My policies were very rigid. I had watched too many guys piss money away. If a player wanted help on the money management and investment side, I would set them up with advisors who were under contract to me so that I could sue them if they lost the players' money. I wanted to get them to understand that playing careers are short and uncertain, so they had to save their money. Every player thinks they're going to get another deal, that they're going to stay in the NHL for 10 years. I tried to persuade them to assume that the contract they had just signed might well be their last. And I had an education clause added to the contracts of guys who left school early when they turned pro, so that they could go back and finish their degrees after they were out of the game.

Let me give you a couple of examples of how it worked.

Peter Taglianetti, who played for the Winnipeg Jets, Minnesota North Stars and Pittsburgh Penguins, was a client of mine. He was a Providence College guy, and I got most of the players who came out of there and turned pro.

He had just signed a contract with Winnipeg, and he wanted to buy a new car. I set a spending limit of $14,000.

Peter called me from a Saab dealership in Rhode Island. "Burkie," he said, "I've got the car I want, but the guy will only go down to $14,400. Can I buy it?"

"No," I said. "Put the salesman on the phone."

I said to the guy, "Look, in five minutes he's going to walk out of there with that car for $14,000 or he's going to walk out with no car. That's not negotiable."

He got the car for $14,000.

Another time, I was negotiating Ray Staszak's first contract with the Detroit Red Wings. Ray and I had agreed that if I could get him at least $250,000, he'd leave school.

The Wings sent a limo to meet me at the Detroit airport. To that point in my life, the only time I had ever been in a limousine was on my wedding night. So, I climbed into the front seat with the driver.

"Sir," he said, "I think you're supposed to be in the back."

"Just drive the fucking car," I said. The truth was, I didn't know better.

I was negotiating directly with Mike Ilitch, the Wings owner. One of the things I remember most vividly about that day was that I had a terrible case of the flu—I had to leave for the bathroom about four times while we hammered out the details of the contract. I was sick as a dog.

It turned out to be a ridiculous deal—something like $750,000 to sign.

When I got to the airport, I called Ray from a pay phone.

"Well, am I leaving school?" Ray asked.

"Yeah, you are."

"So, you got the 250?"

"A little north of that . . ."

"Two sixty?"

Then I told him the number. Of course he was pretty happy.

"So, how much can I spend on a car now?" Ray asked.

"Twelve thousand dollars," I told him. "The same as everyone else." That number didn't change, no matter how large the contract. (This was a couple of years before Peter Taglianetti, by which time the amount had increased.)

If guys weren't willing to follow my system, I was happy to encourage them to sign with somebody else. I remember there was an All-American goalie from the University of Minnesota Duluth (Rick Kosti), a really good player, who wanted to hire me. I told him about the budget and he said, "But I like to spend a lot of money on clothes."

"You know what?" I told him. "This won't work, you and me. You should find a different agent."

I didn't recruit players. They were all referred to me by their coaches or by players I already represented, and most of them came out of American colleges. That was my natural base for contacts because I was from Minnesota, played at Providence College and played in the Minnesota summer league with guys from all the top schools in the country (including 13 members of the 1980 Miracle on Ice US Olympic team).

Junior hockey was more foreign to me. At one point, in order to try and understand that world better, I did a tour through the Ontario Hockey League, stopping in Windsor, London, Toronto and Kingston. I got a better sense of the product so that I could at least speak knowledgeably about it. But I never did wind up with many players out of the junior game.

A bunch of my guys were college free agents—like Joel Otto and Dave Poulin.

Joel was a great story. He had been selected out of Bemidji State—a Division III school—to play in the US Olympic Committee's sports festival. I had told him that if someone was going to sign him, it was probably going to happen very late, so he'd need to be patient.

I was working at the Maine Mariners' hockey school in Portland when they called me off the ice to tell me Craig Patrick was on the phone—Craig was the general manager of the New York Rangers then. It was about Joel—he wanted to sign him and was offering a two-plus-one deal (two years, plus an option for a third), with a $35,000 signing bonus.

"Okay, Craig," I said, "that sounds great. I'm going to talk to Joel tonight after I get off the ice and I'll call you back tomorrow and let you know what he says."

Before I could even relay the offer, Craig called me back to say he was withdrawing it.

"Why?" I asked.

"One of our guys says he can't skate."

"Craig," I said, "you made me an offer in good faith. I haven't even relayed it to the kid. You owe it to me to keep it open for 24 hours." Craig agreed—which shows you what a class guy he is.

That night, Calgary GM Cliff Fletcher called and said that the Flames were interested in Joel. They were offering a one-plus-one, with a $10,000 signing bonus, with a side agreement that he wouldn't sign the option—so it was really just a one-year deal. The Flames only wanted to commit to one year.

"That's fine, Cliff," I said. "But if he signs a second contract, the bonus is $55,000."

"Fifty-five?!" Cliff shouted.

"That's right: 55. If I'm taking 10 on the first year, the second one is going to cost you 55."

Cliff reluctantly agreed to it.

I called Joel that night and went through the two offers with him.

"Well, I guess I'm a Ranger then," he said.

"No, you're taking the Calgary deal," I told him. "You'll get that second contract and you'll get that 55." (That was good money in those days.)

He wound up having a tremendous 12-year career with the Flames and is widely regarded as one of the best college free agent signings, ever.

I wasn't just hands-on with my clients when it came to budgeting. I was also hands-on when it came to their hockey careers. I spent countless non-billable hours travelling to rinks to watch games and practices my players were involved in. I went to every one of their training camps. I thought it was part of my job to make them the best hockey players they could be—and indirectly, of course, I would benefit from that. But even if they dumped me after I got them to the NHL, at least I had helped turn them into a hockey player.

And a few guys did dump me. Bob Froese got pissed with me because I couldn't go to the awards ceremony after he won the Jennings Trophy. He went back to Bill Watters. But I didn't lose too many guys, and that's because I was always transparent—this is what I do; if you want to do it my way, great, and if you don't, no problem. I never sold anyone. They had to buy in.

I was especially hard on my minor-league players. It was all about getting a kid to the Show by employing tough love. If one of my players had a bad game, when he came out I'd just give it to him. I would tell him, "You're going to die here if you don't change some things."

I remember going to an AHL game in Rochester to watch Gates Orlando. He had a terrible game. When he came off the ice, he saw me waiting for him and knew what was coming.

"I know, I know," he said.

I still went off on him. "You're stealing money playing like that. You should buy a McDonald's in Rochester because you're going to retire here. You've got to get your shit together."

That's how I talked to my players. Not all of them liked it, but if they signed with me, it was part of the deal. That applied to marginal players, and it also applied to future superstars like Brett Hull.

I was working out of Boston and teaching business law on Tuesday nights at Providence College. (I love teaching. When I was with the Canucks, I taught sports law as an adjunct professor at the University of British Columbia Law School during all five years I was an assistant GM and for the first five years when I was GM. There are a lot of things that I'm not really good at, but I think I'm a pretty good teacher.)

At two o'clock in the afternoon, I picked up a message from a Joanne Robinson, with a telephone number in the 604 area code. I didn't recognize the name or the number, and I didn't call her back. I left the office, took the train home and was grabbing my stuff before heading to Providence when my assistant called.

"Joanne Robinson called," she said.

"I know," I said. "I got the message. I'll call her back tomorrow."

"No, you're calling her back now," my assistant said. "That's Brett Hull's mom."

Of course I did. I knew all about Brett—Bobby's kid (Joanne was Bobby's ex), playing at the University of Minnesota Duluth, a big-time prospect who had been drafted by the Calgary Flames.

I got Joanne on the phone and the first thing I said was, "You're going to think I'm crazy, but I can't talk to you now because I have to go and teach a class." I called her that night after I got home, and talked to her and her husband, Harry, for the better part of an hour.

"How did you get my name?" I asked her.

"Well, we asked Cliff Fletcher for some names of agents, and he gave us four or five. You weren't on it, so we figured we'd go with you."

They invited me to come out to Vancouver and continue the conversation in person. I was on a plane first thing the next morning.

Joanne, Harry and I ended up having a great conversation, and we really hit it off. When we were finished, Joanne told me that they wanted to hire me to represent Brett.

"I can't agree to that until I meet him," I said. "I don't represent just anyone. I might not like him—and he might not like me."

The next day, I jumped on a flight to Minneapolis and then drove to Duluth. We met at a bar called the Garage, where the players used to hang out. I explained to him how I operated—the budget thing and all the rest. Ten minutes in, he said, "I want you to represent me."

"I'm not done, Brett," I said. "I've got to know if you're my kind of guy."

I didn't know if Brett was the kind of kid who could handle the kind of criticism I'd give him. He had grown up as the son of one of the most famous hockey players in the world. The name on the back of his sweater could have made him a bit of prima donna.

But as it turned out, he wasn't like that at all. Brett was great—a great client and a great kid.

I got him $100,000 from the Flames to leave school, plus a $10,000 donation to the university.

I remember Cliff saying, "I can't believe I'm doing this."

"Well, you are," I said, "or he's going back to Duluth."

In Brett's rookie year as a professional, he played for Terry Crisp, who was coaching the Flames' AHL farm team in Moncton. From the start, it wasn't a great fit. To call Terry Crisp old school would be an understatement. In the middle of the season, Brett called me and said, "You've got to get me out of here. All Crispy does is swear at me and tell me I'm a fucked-up, fat, spoiled college kid."

I flew to Moncton and quietly snuck into the rink to watch the team practice. Brett wasn't lying. Crispy was all over him during practice: "You fucking fat college puke bonus baby" and more stuff like that.

Brett and I drove back to his apartment. I remember they had a crazy amount of snow in Moncton that winter—the most in 20 years. The snowbanks were so high that you couldn't see houses from the street.

I sat down with Brett and he said it again. "You've got to get me out of here." It was pretty obvious that he expected me to be sympathetic to his plight. But I turned it around on him.

"How much do you weigh?" I asked him.

"I don't know," he said.

"You are fucking fat, Brett."

When I had guys who were overweight, I used to make them take a five-pound bag of sugar and hold it out at arm's length. They wouldn't think that being five pounds overweight was a big deal. But after 30 seconds, their arm was sagging. "That's what you're carrying around with you on the ice," I'd tell them.

I didn't have a bag of sugar to do the demonstration with Brett, but I told him right off the top that I wasn't getting him out of there. His hair was real long at the time. I told him, "Tomorrow, practice is at 10. You're going to be there at eight and you're going to ask Crispy if you can work on some extra stuff. And after practice, you're getting a fucking haircut. You get your shit together, you drop 10, and I'll think about getting you out of here. But until you get your shit together, I'm not doing anything. You start acting like you care, and they'll start treating you like you care."

At Christmas that year, he had only 14 goals. He lost 10 pounds, got a haircut, started working with Crispy and went on a tear. He finished the season with 50 goals, was named the AHL rookie of the year and never played in the minors again.

Brett did that all by himself. But he needed somebody to tell him the truth. He needed somebody to punch him right in the face. (I have *so* much respect for Brett Hull.)

After I was established in the player representation business, I got a call from Billy Cleary, who was the hockey coach at Harvard University. He told me that one of his former players wanted to become an agent, and wondered if I'd be willing to give him a half hour of my time.

I told Billy that I worked alone, that I wasn't looking for a partner. But Billy is a good guy, so I went ahead and agreed to the meeting. The former player was Bob Goodenow.

I'd actually played against him, and I know a lot of people run him down, but he was a good college player. He played hard and he played tough.

He was also a great guy back then—a guy you could drink beer with, tell jokes with. He had a good sense of humour. He understood hockey players. He got it, like me—I had a bond with my players that the other agents didn't have because they never played the game.

We ended up talking for a couple of hours and discussed working together. I want to make one thing clear: despite what some people have said, I was never a partner with Bob Goodenow. We just cooperated. I would talk to his guys when they were in the East, and he would talk to my guys when they were in the West. He was helpful to me and I was helpful to him. And when I got out of the business, he ended up with about half of my clients.

And I helped him get the job as head of the NHL Players' Association after Al Eagleson was taken down. Helping to put him in that position is one of my bigger regrets.

The idea of going after Eagleson had come up once before. Mike Milbury was the player rep for the Boston Bruins, and he was really unhappy with the way things were going with the union. He invited my wife and me to have dinner with him and his wife, one night after the Bruins had played a matinee at the Garden, to talk about the union.

Mike is a great guy. Very direct. In a lot of ways, we're very similar. I actually played against him in college when he was at Colgate. He didn't remember it, but I sure did. It was the bloodiest hockey game I've ever seen. It was like Vietnam.

One of our guys hit their goalie in the face with a slapshot, and his mask broke and cut him so badly that there was blood all over the ice. Later, one of our captains, John Martin, got rubbed out on the boards, and he got caught up on a bolt that was sticking out and it ripped a nine-inch gash in his forearm. He came back to the bench and was getting ready for his next shift when the trainer said, "I've got to look at your arm."

"Fuck off," Marty said.

"Look at the floor," the trainer said.

There was a pool of blood on the floor of the bench. He was leaking bad. It took 30 or 40 stitches to close that cut.

Then our other captain, Mike Marvell, got a stick in the eye. Lou Lamoriello didn't trust the doctors at Colgate, so we bused all the way back to Providence with Mike moaning in pain in the back. We kept trying to persuade Lou to pull over at a hospital, but he wouldn't do it—he said he had the doctors lined up at home.

Mike wound up losing half the sight in that eye. (Not because of the delay—just because of the injury.)

But back to dinner. Milbury didn't waste any time getting to the point.

"What are we going to do to take out Alan Eagleson?"

I gave him a few suggestions—things that they might go after him on, the questions players could ask in meetings. But I knew it was easier said than done. Pete Peeters was one of my clients. When he was playing for the Bruins, he went to an NHLPA meeting, and Eagleson asked if anyone had any questions. Pete stood up and tried to ask a couple of things.

Eagleson said, "If you weren't so fucking stupid, Pete, you wouldn't have to ask that. Next question."

Pete was embarrassed and sat down. That's the way Eagleson bullied the players.

Milbury wasn't so easily intimidated, but that first revolt never went anywhere. This was back in 1982, and the player reps were afraid of Eagleson. Mike couldn't get any support.

Four years later, Goodenow got wind of a big agents' meeting in Toronto where they were going to talk about taking on Eagleson. Of course he wasn't invited and I wasn't invited—the other agents were nervous about me, and Bob was having too much success. We weren't really part of the club that, in those days, was dominated by Meehan, Kaminsky, Badali, Herb Pinder and Pierre Lacroix.

Bob said we ought to crash the meeting and put something on the table. I met with him at his office, and we stayed up all night putting together an eight-page memorandum detailing what we thought had to change at the players association. We wanted disclosure of salaries. We wanted Eagleson to get out of the representation business, because it was a conflict of interest. We wanted to address the players' insurance coverage. It was pretty heady stuff, and really detailed.

The next morning, we caught the first flight to Toronto and then walked into the meeting—where we were about as popular as a porcupine at a balloon party. But then we presented the document, and the other agents were blown away. They said it was exactly what we needed. They decided that they'd send three guys to meet Eagleson and present him with the document—Badali, because he represented the two most important players in the game, Gretzky and Lemieux; Lacroix, because he represented the French side of the sport; and me.

The three of us went to Eagleson's office and handed him the memorandum. He couldn't have been more polite about it. He went through it and said, "Yeah, we can do that, and this makes sense, and this is tricky, but we'll work on it." We got the impression when we left that things had changed.

And then we found out that as soon as we left the room, he ripped the document in half and threw it in the trash in front of all his staff.

"That's the end of that," he said—and for the time being, he was right. Until the players were galvanized to act, we had no avenue, and so it died. It took Russ Conway and Paul Kelly to finally bring Eagleson down.

I have to say that I always got along well with Al personally. He's a charming guy. After he got out of prison, he had paid his debt as far as I was concerned. When I was running the Canucks, he'd call me from his place in Whistler and ask for a couple of tickets, and I always looked after him. My personal relationship with him was always good—but professionally, there were things going on that had to change.

After Eagleson was deposed, I got a call from a headhunter in Toronto who had been hired by the players association to find his replacement. This would have been 1992. "Your name keeps coming up," the guy told me. "I can't offer you the job, but I'm telling you that if you want it, you can get it."

I've never been in a union in my life and had no interest in being a union leader. I told him to call someone else. "We can probably triple what you're making," he told me. I still wasn't interested.

Finally, he asked: "If you were looking for someone to do this job, who would you talk to?"

I said Bob Goodenow.

That's one thing I look back on and wish I'd handled differently. I wish I'd suggested someone else, or even taken the job myself.

The job changed Bob. It made him really intransigent and bitter. By the end, he was this cynical, distrustful guy. You could hardly talk to him, and he wasn't any fun to be around. He was bullying the players, just like Eagleson did. (Though it should be said that Bob is absolutely honest. He wouldn't take a paper clip off the desk that didn't belong to him.)

Maybe that's what happens when you're constantly being attacked and criticized. In any case, he was no longer the same guy I'd worked with—which would become all the more apparent when we faced off in labour negotiations after I went to work for the league.

Player representation was a good business. The firm was happy. I was working with about 30 players, including 15 in the NHL. Not bad for only having been at it full time for two years. And I was at the point where I thought maybe I should do this on my own and have an office five minutes from my house instead of commuting every day to downtown Boston. I actually looked at some office space.

But one day I was in Rochester, New York, hanging around after an AHL game to see Gates Orlando again, and I saw Donnie Meehan down the hall, waiting to see some guy on his way up or down the hockey ladder. Donnie is a great guy, and a great agent, but he is also 10 years older than me. I thought, "That's going to be me. I'm still going to be the guy standing outside a dressing room, waiting to talk to a player." I had started to find the work repetitive—the same grind on contracts, the same guys complaining about ice time. And I thought, "I'm good at this, but I'm bored with this. I don't want to be doing this 10 years from now."

"GENTLEMEN WEAR
FRENCH CUFFS"

THEN PAT QUINN STEPPED in and changed my life.

In 1987 they held a reunion for the Maine Mariners teams that won the Calder Cup—the 1978 team that I was on, and the group that repeated the win the following season. It was a great chance to see the guys. A lot of them were still playing, but just about all of the guys who had retired came back as well.

They put on a nice dinner for us. Afterwards the wives went to bed and it was just the guys, sitting around and drinking beer, including me and Pat Quinn.

I admit that I had worked very hard to manufacture a friendship with Pat. I worked really hard on that relationship, because I respected Pat and liked him. During the years when I was representing players, any time I went down to Philly, I would call him and ask him if he wanted to go out for lunch after practice. And I worked on Sandra, his wife, too—who is lovely. I kind of forced that friendship to develop. We had a lot in common, and we got along great, so I don't think it was a hardship for Pat, but make no mistake—I worked to make it happen.

Now we were at the reunion and our wives were in bed and it was about three o'clock in the morning. This was during the time that Pat was suspended by the National Hockey League. He had accepted a signing bonus on a contract to become the president and general manager of the Vancouver Canucks while he was still coaching the Los Angeles Kings. His lawyer told him it was kosher because the Kings had missed a deadline to pick up his contract option, and in any other business or any other walk of life, it would have been—but not in professional sports. So, he was expelled from the league for the rest of the season, and barred from coaching for the next two years. (It's worth noting that those penalties were later reversed, substantially, in Pat's favour.)

Pat was looking for advice. He said, "I've never been a GM before. You deal with all 21 teams. Tell me which teams do it right and how their front offices are set up." I went through the whole thing—the assistant GM, the farm teams, amateur scouting, pro scouting. I spent 45 minutes explaining what I thought was the best way to put together a first-rate NHL organization.

At the end of it, Pat said, "Why don't you come and work for me in Vancouver?"

I was really embarrassed. The last thing I wanted was for Pat Quinn to think I'd been talking him up in an effort to get a job. I apologized to him and went to bed.

I woke up the next morning and the first thing I thought was, "Jesus Christ, Pat Quinn offered you a job last night." It would be a dream to work for him. He had just provided me with a great opportunity, not to mention the perfect escape from player representation.

I left the room and found him and said, "If you're serious about that job offer, I'm your man."

"I *was* serious," Pat said. "I don't joke about stuff like that."

After I accepted the job, I told the law firm I was leaving, and then met with each of my clients face to face. Bob Goodenow wound up with about half of them.

My dad thought I was nuts to take the Vancouver job. "Let me get this straight," he said. "You were about to go on your own with a successful sports agency. Now you're going to move out of the country and work for a team that hasn't made the playoffs in years. And as part of the package, you get to pay Canadian taxes?"

"That's right," I said.

"I can't approve of this. I can't tell you this makes sense to me."

My dad was his own boss, and he figured it was everybody's dream to be their own boss. He wanted me to have my own company.

"Dad," I said, "I never dreamed that one day I could work for an NHL team, just like I never dreamed that I could play professional hockey. Other kids did, but I didn't. And now I'm getting that chance."

I'm still not sure he really understood, but he gave me his blessing.

"Good luck," he said. "I love you, and I'm sure you'll do well."

I will never forget my first day on the job as assistant general manager of the Vancouver Canucks. Pat called me and offered me a ride to work—and then he got lost on his way to the rink. I said, "Pat, you fucking played here. You must know how to get to the Coliseum." But he didn't remember. We wound up pulling over and stopping a guy on the street—who happened to be one of the game night officials, Terrino Barbiero.

"Welcome back to Vancouver, Pat!" he hollered. "And welcome, Brian."

"Thanks, Terrino," Pat said. "How do we get to the rink?"

The first thing Pat said to me when we finally found our way to the building was, "What do you think we should do?"

The way I saw it, my job was to take all the detail work off Pat's plate so that he could spend his time putting together the best 20-player roster possible. I'd take on the grunt work, the time-consuming stuff—staff contracts, player contracts, building issues. I told him that I should probably spend the first week reading the arena lease and going over every staff and player contract.

"While I'm doing that," I said, "you should start making some calls. You're the GM."

The truth is, we were both green. Neither of us had ever worked in a front office before. That summer was a blur of long, long hours in the office. And there wasn't much of anyone left in the organization to show us the way. The two senior management guys, John Whitman and John Chesman, both quit when the Griffiths family hired Pat. Glen Ringdal, the sales and marketing guy, stayed on, and so did Darcy Rota, who handled PR. But that was about it.

How small an operation were the Vancouver Canucks in the 1980s? Well, consider this. I remember a summer when we were worried about resigning Robert Nordmark—his contract was up and it looked like he might head back to the Swedish Elite League. Pat was famous for saying "one of us" had better go over there and talk to him—by "one of us," he always meant me. It was clearly my job to fly to Sweden and try to talk the kid into coming back.

I had just left home, telling my wife I'd be back for supper. Now I was calling and telling her I probably wouldn't make it—because I'd be in Sweden. But I needed some cash and I didn't have time to go to the bank before heading to the airport (back then, the most you could get out of an ATM was $200).

So, I went to the team gift shop in the arena and asked Irene, who ran the place, if she had any extra cash on hand.

"Oh, I've got lots," she said. "I can give you 400 bucks."

I went to the airport and got on a plane to Sweden with just those 400 bucks from the gift shop as my operating funds. Mind you, $400 was a lot more money back then.

We were blessed with great owners in Vancouver: Frank Griffiths Sr. and his wife, Emily. Frank made his fortune in the media business, owning and operating television and radio stations, before he got into hockey. He was an old-school gentleman. And Mrs. Griffiths was a nice, nice lady, but beneath that surface, she was tough as nails and wanted things done in a certain way. But she was also fair.

One of my first decisions as assistant general manager was to let the team physician go. We had a dispute over money right before training camp. He also happened to be the Griffiths family's personal physician, so that was a difficult conversation. I thought I was going to get fired, but Pat backed me up and told Mr. Griffiths he approved of the decision, and that was that.

Frank Griffiths took me aside early and told me that he had never lost money on a business deal, and that he was tired of losing money on the Canucks.

"Really?" I said. "You've *never* lost money on another business deal?"

"Never," Frank said, unequivocally.

So that was a pretty strong indication of how he expected us to run his hockey team. Remember, we were taking over a team that had missed the playoffs, that had no prospects of making the playoffs, that was not drawing well and wasn't making money.

So the outlook was kind of bleak.

I remember that at the end of our first year, we were debating whether to raise the price of tickets in the lower bowl from $26 to $27. I came in prepared with all my arguments against doing it—foremost among them that we couldn't raise ticket prices after missing the playoffs once again.

Mr. Griffiths held up his hand and said, "Son, we are raising ticket prices. The only question is how much." He was going to protect his bottom line.

We wound up raising the price by a dollar. And we lost a couple dozen season-ticket holders because of it, all of them people who objected to a non–playoff team raising prices.

So, maybe I was right about that one. I learned a lot about running a team during those first years in Vancouver, starting with the fact that the foundation of the business is selling tickets, and the only way to sell tickets is to win.

But I firmly believe, and I still believe, that you can make a community fall in love with your team before they're successful on the ice. I came to believe that there were three pillars you could apply to any team in any city— and that if you followed them, things would eventually work out.

The first is that you run the team like a business. You might say, "Of course you run it like a business—it *is* a business." But the fact is, a lot of guys in professional sports don't operate the way they would if they were selling any other kind of product.

It's not just that you're being responsible to the owners. The fans actually appreciate it when you're careful about how you spend money. My view is that if I pay a guy a million bucks and he winds up in the minors, it's not just the owners' money that I've wasted—it's the season-ticket holders' money. So, wherever I've been, I've always counted every dollar. Players know they have to fight for the money on a Brian Burke team. I don't give it away, because it ain't mine. And people appreciate that. Canadians, especially, hate overpaid athletes.

The second pillar is community service. My teams performed more community service than the next three teams combined. People start to see the players at Canuck Place, at the B.C. Children's Hospital, see them out in the city doing charity work, and they start to like the players more, whether we're winning or not.

The third pillar is that my teams are going to play an entertaining style of hockey. We'll never trap. We'll try to score goals. We'll trade scoring chances. When I see a coach being interviewed on television after a game and he says, "I'm really proud of our guys because we only allowed two scoring chances after the first period," I'm thinking, "Yeah, and I bet that sold a lot of tickets."

I have told all my coaches that I don't mind giving up scoring chances just as long as we get as many as they do. I don't mind if the hockey is a little riskier but more entertaining. And I don't mind if we hit—even though, when you look for a hit, you take yourself out of position a little bit.

Of course, I also don't mind when my players fight. I want to give the fans a reason to put up their hard-earned money for a ticket, even when we're not in first place. I want them walking out of the arena feeling that even if we didn't win, the team is fun to watch.

By sticking to those three pillars, we started selling out games in Vancouver long before we became a contender.

It certainly helped that the local view on the team changed the day they hired Pat. Those first five years were kind of magical. The team got better and better. Pat made some really good trades and had some really good drafts. Plus, he is one of the most honest and believable guys you would ever meet. We would have meetings with season-ticket holders and he would get up and talk, and these people would leave planning to reserve hotels for the Stanley Cup final. Attendance went up, and we were treated like gods.

Before I got to Vancouver, I didn't realize all the little perks that come with working for an NHL team in Canada. We'd go into any restaurant in town and as long as Pat was along, they'd always give us the best table. If the owners of the place didn't pick up the tab for dinner, they would at the very least give you a nice bottle of wine on the house.

There was one place Pat loved, called Pietro's, that was normally closed in the afternoon between lunch and dinner. But if Pat got hungry at 2:30, he'd call them and they would open the place up, just for him.

There were little bonuses, too. I remember stopping at McDonald's with my kids one day before going to the rink and the guy at the window wouldn't let me pay. And my kids thought that was the greatest thing ever—free McDonald's! I would go to the car wash or the movies and the guy wouldn't let me pay. Need an oil change? Someone comes and picks up your car and brings it right back. People who work for teams expect that kind of thing now, but in those days, when it came to hockey, it only happened in Canada.

Those weren't the only differences in my new adopted homeland. A lot of people think that Minnesota, where I grew up, is the part of the United States that is most like Canada—including the shared passion for hockey. But there are also some significant differences.

As soon as I got to Vancouver, I was struck by the very leftist politics and the very heavy union orientation in British Columbia. I'm not from a union background, so that took some getting used to. I also believe there is a very strong undercurrent of anti-Americanism in Canada. I heard a lot of comments about how stupid Americans are, how greedy they are, how loud they are. I had to bite my tongue. (But the truth is, after you fly on Air Canada enough times, you can pick out the Americans on the plane—because they really are louder.)

But those anti-American sentiments didn't seem to be directed towards me—maybe because I believed that when you immigrate to another country, it's your job to fit in, not their job to accept you. I did everything I could to understand my new home, and I spent the first six months in Vancouver trying to blend in like a chameleon. I read both local papers cover to cover every day. I could tell you how all the local high school girls' basketball teams were doing. I knew who my MLA was. I knew what mattered locally.

When you make that kind of effort, people notice it and appreciate it. They understand that the new guy is proud and grateful to be here.

The average person might not make that effort, and so they don't get the benefit of the doubt. My goal was to fit in and pass for a Canadian, and I did that long before I got my Canadian citizenship.

And I loved the city. I loved going to work. Vancouver was so beautiful and the people were so nice to us. My biggest issue in my entire professional career has been to avoid getting a speeding ticket on the way to the office—that's how much I enjoyed almost all of my jobs. My advice to any young person is that if you want to be happy, find a job you really love.

That's exactly what I had with the Canucks. I would get to work between 5:30 and 6 in the morning—because when the Boston Bruins were open for business three time zones ahead on the East Coast, we had to be in business.

Those early mornings were the origin of the untied-tie thing that has kind of become my trademark. I came in wearing a T-shirt and jeans, worked out and then changed into my suit and tie at work—and sometimes I didn't quite get around to tying it.

Pat would roll in around seven, and he was always immaculately dressed. His wife, Sandra, had something to do with that, but for a working-class guy who grew up in the rough east end of Hamilton, he was very fashion conscious. He always looked great behind the bench or at the general managers' meetings. He tried to bring me along a little bit in that department, but I never managed to be quite as flamboyant as he was.

I remember coming into his office one morning with my tie hanging around my neck.

"What's with the shirts?" Pat said.

"What do you mean?"

"You don't wear French cuffs. Gentlemen wear French cuffs."

Pat wore French cuffs every day of his working life, complete with beautiful cuff links. And I have never worn anything else since.

The truth is, I wanted to *be* Pat Quinn. Over the years, a lot of people have come up to me and said, "You're just like Pat." That's the highest compliment I could ever receive—to be compared to him. I learned so much from him during those first years with the Canucks.

We would begin the day talking for maybe 20 minutes, maybe an hour, while I updated him on everything I was working on, from issues with the building to contract negotiations with players and their agents. He had his fingertips on everything, but he didn't like the grinding-it-out part of the job, so he left that to me. I'd brief him on building issues, front office issues, tell him that there were a couple of kids in the draft that he probably needed to see. He would do the odd scouting trip before he took over the coaching job, but normally he would give me a list of things to do and I would keep him up to date.

I trusted Pat with everything in my life, and he'd always give me great advice. He had the legal training—he wasn't technically a lawyer, because he never took the bar exam, but he had a law school degree—and so he knew how to ask the right questions.

As I was sitting in his office, other people started filing in to work. Pat was brutal with names—he could never remember them. But he'd wave to everyone and give them a great big smile and they were happy just because Pat had acknowledged them.

We set aside two hours a day when players and other people could wander into Pat's office and shoot the shit—two hours a day of people coming in to worship at the Pat Quinn shrine. It was amazing. He'd sit there smoking a cigar and just listen. Pat was the best listener I ever saw, and he had a great gift for making people feel important. He could sit there for hours, never saying more than "Go on . . . ," encouraging you to tell him what you had to tell him.

Guys would show up who had played with him years before, who had grown up in the same neighbourhood in Hamilton. They'd ask Pat if he had a minute, and an hour later, I'd have to go in and break it up, just so he could get back to work.

Pat had very strong morals. I remember a time when our vice-president of business operations was celebrating a birthday, and the other guys hired a stripper to come in and surprise him. She pulled up in a fancy sports car, came in with her boom box, turned the music on and started stripping right in the middle of the office. I didn't know any of that was happening until it was too late—by that time, she was already down to her whatevers.

Luckily, Pat wasn't there to see it.

I broke it up as soon as I could, and then lit into the guys.

"Are you out of your minds? This can never happen again. If Mrs. Griffiths had walked in, we'd all be out of a job."

Pat came in later, and someone told him what had happened. He called me into his office.

"What the hell is the matter with you?" he said.

I tried to explain that I didn't know it was happening, that as soon as I found out, I stopped it, but he wasn't having any of that.

"You really let me down," he said.

I felt terrible because I had disappointed him. He was pissed at me for about a week because of that. He was such a family guy. He just didn't understand that type of thing.

And when Pat got mad . . .

It only really happened a few times a year. His fuse was miles long, but when he went off, that was it. He had a terrible temper—a true Irishman. He'd start to shake—physically shake. And you would think, "Shit, he's going to kill somebody."

Usually, though, that really intense, blind anger was saved for stuff that happened on the ice, especially for referees, and for one referee in particular: Don Koharski.

Pat hated Koharski. Hated everything about him. They had a history going back to the AHL, where Pat claimed Koharski had stared him down one night during a game and grabbed his own crotch—in other words, saying, "Fuck you."

There was a night when he was coaching that Pat yelled obscenities at Koharski all the way through the national anthem. The game hadn't even started yet. That's how much bad blood there was between them.

I remember we were playing at home one night when Koharski was working the game. I was walking with Pat on the way to our dressing room. We had to pass the officials' room. In those days, there weren't any security guards hanging around.

Pat stopped in front of the officials' room door.

"What are you doing?" I asked him.

"I'm going in there to take a piece out of Koharski."

He was shaking already—so that was a bad sign.

"You are not going in there, Pat," I said.

"Get out of my way, or in 30 seconds, you're going to wind up as a fucking corpse."

I didn't know if I could take a punch from Pat Quinn. I might have wound up knocked out cold. But I knew what the consequences would be if an NHL GM attacked an NHL referee. So I got between him and the door and I wasn't moving.

Pat stood there for about 30 seconds, shaking, trying to decide whether or not to drop me.

"Fuck you!" he said, and stormed away.

I didn't persuade Pat to do a lot of things that he didn't want to do, but I did sell him on hiring a young, untested assistant coach.

As an agent, I had represented my old Providence teammate Ron Wilson after he came back from Europe and played for the Minnesota North Stars. When Ron decided to retire as a player, I pushed Pat to hire him as an assistant with our IHL farm team in Milwaukee—and Pat pushed back.

"We're not hiring all your fucking cronies," Pat said.

I tried to convince him just how valuable Ron could be to the organization. In addition to his sky-high hockey IQ, he was something of a computer genius. Remember, this was back in 1988, before everybody had their own personal computer. Ron was already doing his own programming.

Pat still resisted. "We don't have a budget for an assistant coach in the minor leagues," he said.

I told Pat it would only take 25 grand, and that I'd find the money somewhere in my budget. Finally, he relented—and I hired Ronnie for $25,000 a year. He was married, with two daughters, and it wasn't even enough to pay his expenses, but he really wanted to stay in the game.

Ron was brilliant. Pat watched him work and said, "All right, he has to be here," so we moved him up to become an assistant coach with the Canucks after one season in the IHL. He was invaluable to us.

When the Mighty Ducks of Anaheim came into the league as an expansion franchise, their president, Tony Tavares, called me and said he wanted to talk to me about hiring Ron as their first head coach.

"You shouldn't talk to anyone else," I told him. "This is the guy you want. He's going to be a great head coach."

He was. Ron was a miracle worker in Anaheim, and then he moved on and took the Washington Capitals to the finals.

And of course, our paths would cross again.

The other guy I hired in Vancouver, and who would play a big role in my career, was Dave Nonis. I got a call from Shawn Walsh, the legendary coach at the University of Maine, asking if I had a job for one of his former players, the captain of his team. I had met Dave when I spoke at a banquet at the university—it was almost like a roast. I crapped all over Dave in a funny way when I spoke, and then he got up and gave it right back to me—I remember he had a line about how the next time I was buying a suit, maybe I ought to find a tailor who could see. I liked that. I liked that a college kid wasn't afraid to go toe to toe with an NHL assistant general manager. So when Shawn called and asked if I had a job for Dave, I was immediately interested.

Dave was a great college player—a small defenceman, but really skilled offensively. And for a little guy, he hit like a ton of bricks. I admired him as a player.

"What's he been doing since graduation?" I asked Shawn.

Dave had gone to Denmark and played pro there for a year, then came back to Maine as a graduate assistant. He was working towards his MBA while acting as assistant coach with the hockey team.

I was interested, and so I went to Pat and told him about Shawn's call and the kid he was recommending. Pat's first response was that we didn't have the budget to hire another body—and, really, he was right. Things were tight then. But I found a way to justify hiring Dave, with half of his salary coming out of hockey ops and the other half out of the ticket sales department—he was going to have to do both jobs.

Dave made a great impression right away. He's very bright, a very smart guy. And he's mentally tough. He's not afraid of tough decisions. He's also a fun guy, and that was really important. It's a hard job, and you want to work with people who you like to be around. And he's very devoted to his wife and son, a good family guy, which is very important to me. I don't like guys who aren't good family guys.

So Burke, Wilson and Nonis all started their careers under the late, great Pat Quinn.

One of the problems I tried to solve in the organization was our two-step approach to filing scouting reports. Our scouts would file handwritten reports, and then someone in our office had to manually punch them into the computer. There had to be a better way to do it.

"How do we get rid of that extra step?" I asked Dave. "Why can't the scouts file by computer?"

"They can," he said, and he started to tell me about these new things called laptops.

In those days, "laptop" was a bit of a misnomer. The portable computers of the time weighed about 30 pounds. But if we could get one for each of our scouts, they would be able to punch in their reports and send them directly to our office in Vancouver using a modem (you may remember what those were like, where you connected the laptop to the phone line, and the two computers talked to each other in a series of squeaks and squawks).

I brought the idea to Pat—because, among other things, he was going to have to approve the money to buy the computers.

For a big, tough Irishman, Pat Quinn was one of the most progressive thinkers in the sport. He wasn't wedded to the past at all. We were the first team in the NHL to hire a strength coach, and Pat hired sleep experts to make sure our guys were getting enough rest. He loved new ideas. So, when I told him about the computer idea, he was all for it—even though computers were going to cost in the neighbourhood of $8,000 each.

"Figure out a way to do it," he said.

I didn't know exactly how we were going to do it, so I asked Dave Nonis. Dave is one of those guys who can solve any problem. If I called Dave and said, "I want to hire a master Chinese architect," he'd say, "Well, I don't know anything about master Chinese architects, but give me an hour." If you told him you needed a new carburetor, give him an hour and he'd show up with one. He's very smart, but also very practical.

I asked him how we could make this computer scouting system work. It's not like you could just go out and buy the necessary software. You had to start from scratch. Dave called a buddy of his who understood computer programming, and he found a way to modify an existing program to fit our needs, and before you know it, we'd bought eight laptops, programmed them all and sent them out to our scouts. We taught them how to punch in their reports and how to file them— I made sure that they did it after 11 o'clock at night, after the long-distance rates went down.

In the beginning, our scouts were the laughingstock of the league, lugging around laptops and filing late at night. All the other scouts would be down at the bar while they were up in their rooms, getting the modems to connect.

But within a year or two, every team in the league was doing it that way. They started to figure out that we had an edge with our system, and eventually, everyone copied it.

That was Pat's vision, and that was Dave Nonis's execution. You can understand why I wanted Dave next to me at different points in my career.

One of the tasks Pat assigned me in Vancouver was to deal with the local media. Over the years, I've earned a reputation for being . . . well, let's call it combative with certain reporters, broadcasters and columnists. That really started during those first seasons in Vancouver, which was also the first time I was asked to be the public face of a hockey team.

Pat had previous experience dealing with the media in his past coaching jobs—and in his mind, it wasn't good. So he already had his back up, and he was walking into an environment that was pretty volatile.

Vancouver is kind of a strange, split-personality hockey market. There was a lot of negativity in the media directed towards the Canucks. But there was also a great fan base that loved Pat and wanted the team to do well.

We wanted to have an arm's-length, professional relationship with the media covering the team. But that was impossible. The media guys in Vancouver were vicious, led by two guys—a radio talk show host named Tiger Al Davidson, and the *Vancouver Province*'s hockey columnist, Tony Gallagher. They took horrible shots at the team all the time.

Gallagher didn't like me, and I had no interest in him liking me. We had some legendary feuds over the years.

Tiger Al worked for CKNW, the same station that carried our games—and which was owned by the Griffiths family. I remember one time where he took a shot at me on air—we were having a dispute with our goalie, Richard Brodeur, who was one of the heroes when the Canucks went to the finals in 1984—and Davidson said something about me being disrespectful to him. (The truth is, I didn't hear it myself—someone called me and told me about it.) This was at 5:30 in the morning, and of course I was already at work. When I heard what he said, I was infuriated. I thought it was completely unprofessional. I left the office, jumped in my car and headed for the CKNW studios.

It was still dark and it was raining, and there I was outside, pounding on the locked door at CKNW. Finally, Davidson came to the door and said through the glass, "If I open this door, are you going to beat me up?" He really thought I was going to hit him.

I said, "No, I'm not going to beat you up, but we're going to set this straight right now." Finally, Davidson opened the door and let me in. By 6:30 I was on the air, telling our side of the Brodeur story.

Pat and I both knew that, ultimately, the way to change that coverage was by doing better on the ice. But at the same time, we didn't think we had to take that kind of shit from the media. You don't have to let someone knife you in the back and then buy them dinner.

So we decided to change the rules of engagement. We would be professional at all times. We wouldn't lie to them. We would make ourselves available. But we were not going to bend one inch for them, give them free shit or bow to their influence. We weren't going to bother trying to win them over to our side.

All of that came straight from Pat.

With that in mind, I was reading through the arena lease during my first days on the job, and got to the part where it talked about media parking. A bunch of spots were reserved right next to the door where they entered the building—and the team paid for them.

I showed that to Pat.

"Do you realize," I said, "that we're buying a parking spot for Tony Gallagher and the other mortal enemies of the team?"

Pat didn't have to think twice about that.

"Get rid of them," he said.

I called a guy from the Pacific National Exhibition, which was our landlord at the Coliseum. "If we're paying for those spots," I said, "that means we can put anyone we want there—right?" For instance, we could put team management there.

"You can do whatever you want with them," he said.

So, we moved the media parking to the farthest reaches of the lot. That doesn't sound like a big deal, but if you know anything about the weather in Vancouver in the winter, you would understand that it is. It rains. A lot. Cold, nasty rain. Under the old arrangement, the media guys could scramble for about 30 feet to get from their cars to the door. Now it was going to be a whole lot longer, wetter walk.

Needless to say, they weren't happy about it. They'd walk in from the far reaches of the parking lot in the pouring rain, and then walk by my office and grumble, "Burkie, what the fuck's the matter with you, you fucking asshole?"

Funny. I had a really short walk in from my car and didn't get wet at all.

Next, we got rid of the free meals in the press box. We were one of the first teams in any sport to make the reporters pay for their pre-game food. That didn't go over too big.

And we started having closed practices. It's not allowed now, but it was allowed back then. We would station cops everywhere. The building was big and there were a lot of ways to sneak in—especially if you knew a friendly security guard or somebody. We made sure that didn't happen.

But the biggest change we made was having our own radio show in Vancouver. Guys like Tony and Tiger Al used to brag that the guys who ran the Canucks were terrified of them, that they'd read and listen to every word, afraid of what was coming the next morning.

We wanted to send notice that we weren't afraid of anyone with a microphone or a pen. And so we went on the offensive. We wanted to prove that we didn't need these assholes. You want an arms race? Well, then, buckle up, because we are about to go nuclear.

During my early days on the job, I got a call asking me to appear on Dan Russell's late-night sports talk show on CKNW. Dan was one of the pioneers of sports talk in Canada. His show was the go-to destination for Canucks fans. I remember they sent a limo for me, and again, like an idiot, I got in the front seat instead of the back (it took me a while to figure out that limo thing). I went down to the station, did the show and it felt like things went well. Afterwards, Dan asked me if I'd be interested in coming on with him once a week.

Before saying yes, I needed to run the idea by Pat. He didn't hesitate a second before approving it. Among other things, Pat Quinn was a genius-level innovator. He understood where things were headed in hockey—and in sports in general. He knew instinctively what it would mean for us to be the first team in any North American professional sport to have one of its senior executives speaking directly to the fans once a week. For a start, it would be a great marketing tool. We weren't good then, and we weren't going to be good for a few seasons yet. Having someone out there explaining the decisions we made and our plans for the future would help us sell tickets.

It would also give us a platform to fight back against the negative elements in the Vancouver media.

Pat didn't tell me I had to do it. He warned me there were going to be nights when I would hate having to go on the air, when the team wasn't playing well and the people weren't happy and I'd have to take a lot of bullets, sometimes unfairly. But if I was willing, Pat loved the idea of speaking directly to Canucks fans without having our message filtered through other broadcasters or writers.

What became known as the *Canucks Weekly Update* almost immediately became a bit of a sensation in Vancouver. It was true appointment radio. Every Wednesday night, Dan's listeners knew I'd be on the show for an hour, talking about the team and taking calls. They had eight phone lines, and the switchboard would already be lit up an hour or an hour and a half before I went on. People would wait on hold forever just to get their call in.

Before each appearance, I'd talk to Pat. This wasn't going to be Brian Burke's take on life. Pat was the puppeteer; I was the puppet. I'd run everything by him: What did he want me to say about a trade we'd made? How hard did he want me to go after Tony? He'd tell me I could go as hard as I wanted if Tony had done something like question our integrity, but sometimes he'd tell me to just ignore what he'd written or pretend that a story didn't happen.

But if something was written that Pat really didn't like, I would go right back at the writers. Taking them on directly gave us great credibility with the fans. It got to the point where Tony would take his worst shots at us only on Thursdays or Fridays, because he knew he could escape the radio wrath of Brian Burke. If he wrote something bad about us on Monday or Tuesday, I'd carve him to pieces on air. It was hilarious.

The show was a huge hit. I couldn't go anywhere in Vancouver without people coming up to me and telling me that they listened to every show, every week, and they loved it. I had a guy tell me he got divorced because of the show—he had some kind of pillow speaker in his bedroom, and he'd lie there listening while his wife was trying to get to sleep. Finally, she had had enough of me—and of him.

Even when I was away scouting in Europe, we'd find a way to keep the show going. Dan would have coffee sent up to my hotel room in Sweden or Finland, where it was early in the morning, and then we'd do the hour over the phone.

It was all part of Pat's vision. That's how brilliant he was. He knew exactly how it was going to play out.

———

To be fair, my relationship with the media wasn't all bad. I developed working relationships with a bunch of guys. And I handed one of them the scoop of his life.

In the summer of 1988, Arthur Griffiths, who had recently begun helping us and his father as an informal advisor to the team, walked into the Canucks offices and told Pat and me that we had a chance to trade for Wayne Gretzky. That was a mind blower. The Edmonton Oilers had just won the Stanley Cup, and Gretzky was the greatest player in the world, arguably the greatest player of all time. There had been rumblings that Peter Pocklington, the owner of the Oilers, was having money trouble and might be looking to sell Gretzky. But those were just rumours. This was real, as was the possibility that Gretzky could skate out on opening night of the 1988–89 season wearing a Canucks uniform. There were only two teams in the running: us and the Los Angeles Kings.

But it was going to cost us a crazy price: $25 million in cash, Greg Adams, Kirk McLean and three first-round draft picks.

Pat sent me home to tear the deal apart and come back the next day with a cost-benefit analysis.

Try as I might, I couldn't come up with a way that the deal made sense for the Canucks. We would never recover the $25 million in our market. Even if we raised ticket prices 10 bucks across the board (which in 1988 in Vancouver would have been a significant bump, considering that our top ticket price then was about $30), we couldn't have made the money back in 10 years. I maxed out everything. I went through all the models, taking into account private-box revenue and advertising revenue and everything else. There just wasn't enough money in the market. Besides handcuffing us at the bank, losing three first-rounders would handicap us on the hockey side. And the fact was, at that point, Gretzky was no spring chicken.

I told Arthur and Pat the deal just didn't make sense for us. And, God bless him, Pat agreed with me. Arthur was great, too—he acknowledged that I was probably right, and that we shouldn't do it.

One problem, though. The fact that Gretzky was being moved—and specifically to Vancouver—had started to leak into the media. (I always figured Arthur might have had something to do with that.) Our fans, understandably, were in an uproar. Expectations had been created that we knew weren't going to be fulfilled—by then, the deal to send Gretzky to the Kings was all but done—and there was a pretty good chance we were going to get blamed.

"Pat," I said, "we've got to do something about this. They actually think he's coming to Vancouver. We have to nip it in the bud."

The only way to do that was to plant the real story with someone.

The next day, at around 6:30 in the morning, my phone rang. It was a guy named Gord Miller, who was working for some bumfuck station in Alberta. I didn't really know who he was, but I had heard from others that he was a good, young, ambitious guy. Obviously, he had at least figured out that I had a habit of coming into the office early. But otherwise, it was just random. If it had been anybody else, calling me later in the day, they would have got the story.

He introduced himself and stammered a bit. He was obviously nervous.

"Is there a question in there somewhere?" I asked him.

"I hear Gretzky is coming to Vancouver," he said. "Is that true?"

"Grab a pen," I said. "He's not coming here. He's going to Los Angeles."

"You're serious?"

"I'm serious. He's not coming here, and Pat Quinn doesn't want people thinking he's coming here. He told me to give it to someone, and I've heard good things about you. So get it out there."

I laid out the whole deal for him. I had one small component wrong, but otherwise I had the whole transaction, including the money and the inclusion of the Kings' Jimmy Carson in the deal.

Of course there was no social media in those days. Miller phoned Oilers GM Glen Sather and told him he heard Gretzky was going to Los Angeles. Sather denied it, and added that if Miller reported that, he would sue Miller and the guy would never work in the Canadian media again.

But Gord told him he had a pretty good source and he was going with the story. And then he went with it. Of course, he has had a long and distinguished career with TSN since then, but breaking that story was the thing that really put him on the map.

They sent Gord to LA to cover Wayne's arrival. He didn't have enough room on his credit card to cover the two nights in a hotel, so Gretzky had to lend him some money to pay for the room.

Eventually, a story came out that I was the one who killed the trade. I will never forget the headline: "Burke Says No to Gretzky."

I had no regrets, and to this day I have no regrets. You've got to live within your means. Would I have liked to have Wayne Gretzky on our team? Goddamn right! But at a price we couldn't afford? No thanks.

THE RUSSIAN ROCKET

IT WAS NOT LONG after the Gretzky trade that I had my first dealings with the Russians.

The Griffiths family had a long-standing interest in trying to acquire players from the old Soviet bloc. They got Ivan Hlinka and Jiri Bubla out of Czechoslovakia in 1981, but they were both over 30 by then. The big prize would be Russians, though that was going to be a whole lot tougher. There had been defections of players in their prime from behind the Iron Curtain—most notably the Stastny brothers—but the Russians had managed to keep their guys under control.

Still, just in case they ever got permission to leave, Vancouver drafted two-thirds of the Russians' famous KLM Line: Igor Larionov in 1985, and Vladimir Krutov in 1986.

And most famously, we drafted Pavel Bure in 1989. But back to him in a minute.

The Canucks organization made a point of trying to build relationships with the Soviet hockey authorities. They invited the famous coach Anatoli Tarasov to training camp in 1987. He was out of favour back home by then, old and in ill health. One of the reasons he was happy to make the trip was that the Griffiths family arranged for him to have a hip replacement that Russian doctors had refused to perform.

They also brought in the great goalie Vladislav Tretiak. He did a tutorial for our goalies, but what I remember most about him is that he showed up and said he didn't have any equipment with him. We gave him a full set of goalie gear. And then the next day, he showed up and, once again, no equipment, so we gave him another set. It turned out the stuff wasn't for him; he was taking it for goalies back in the USSR. That's how tight money was getting over there.

It wasn't quite a quid pro quo, but the Griffiths Family seemed to have an understanding that in return for those gestures, the Canucks would have the inside track on signing the first Russian players who were allowed to leave. The Soviet system was in its death throes, and they were getting ready to sell off some of their best talent. We met with the Russians at the 1988 Olympic Games in Calgary and were assured that we were first in line.

Except it turns out that we weren't. In the spring of 1989, they made a deal to sell Sergei Priakin to the Calgary Flames, and he became the first Russian to play in the NHL. Our reaction, naturally, was "What the fuck?"

Later that year, Pat got a call saying the Russians were ready to make a deal for Larionov and Krutov.

The Flames owned the rights to the third member of the KLM Line, Sergei Makarov. Cliff Fletcher, who ran the team in Calgary, called Pat and suggested that they fly over together and negotiate in tandem.

That sounded like a bad idea to me.

"Don't do it," I told him. "You're not going to fuck this up, but Cliff is going to fuck it up. They're going to separate you as soon as you get to Russia and they're going to get Cliff to agree to a whole bunch of shit that doesn't make any sense and that the league won't allow, and we're going to be fucked. I won't let that happen. Just bring me along."

But Mr. Griffiths wanted this to be a Pat Quinn production. "He thinks you're involved too much sometimes, and the public can't separate us," Pat explained. This was an issue—a real one.

I offered to fly over on a different flight and stay in the background—I didn't have any interest in being the public face of the deal. But Pat wouldn't budge, and so he and Cliff went over together, leaving me in Vancouver.

So, guess what? The first thing the Russians did was separate them. On his own, Cliff agreed to a 50/50 split—that is, the Russian federation would get half of everything. The deal was $1.5 million a year, and $750,000 of that was going right back to the Russians. There was also a no-trade clause—which was illegal in the NHL back then—along with seven or eight other dubious clauses. Then they came back to Pat and said, "If you want your two players, this is the deal Mr. Fletcher has agreed to."

And Pat wasn't coming back without them.

When he got back, I asked him what the fuck had happened. "They separated us," he said. "I knew you were going to be mad at me."

Cliff told me later that he expected the league to step in and say no to the contracts—and I believe him to this day. Cliff is a very smart guy, and that was a reasonable assumption on his part. But it wasn't happening. I went to Gil Stein and tried to persuade him to fight for us. "These deals have language you can't approve," I told him. "Just void them, and then we'll negotiate new deals." But there was no way he was doing that. "You fucking made this mess, you get out of it" was the attitude—and I have to admit that when I went to work for the league a few years later, I had the same feeling when a team got itself into a jam.

They let the three Russians start playing on deals that clearly violated NHL rules. I think the league was anxious to get the guys in, and in any event it didn't have any interest in helping us get out of a situation that we had created.

The story doesn't end there. Not by a long shot.

Krutov was a disaster. He was a peasant, a hockey-playing peasant who was way past his prime and drank way too much. He soaked us for a lot of money. He hadn't seen a dentist in 10 years and his teeth were falling apart. We paid to fix them—and his wife's teeth. I remember Doug Lidster was driving him to the airport one day. Krutov was sitting in the back, and all of a sudden, Liddy heard him cracking a beer. Liddy had to explain to him that we don't do that here.

"*Da, da,*" he said.

When Pat was in Russia, they told him we could send the guys back any time we wanted, because they were "national treasures." With Krutov, they were more specific: "If he does too much of this," they said, giving the universal gesture of a guy tipping a bottle into his mouth, "you ship him back, no questions asked."

But none of that was actually in the contract. We sent Krutov home after a year—he had 34 points in 61 games—but the Russians still wanted their $750,000, and they took us to the Arbitration Institute in Stockholm to try and get it. We had agreed to that arbitration process in the contract, but of course the NHL could have voided that as well, given that it had sovereign rights over the players in the league. But it refused.

This time, I flew over, along with Joe Weiler, a professional arbitration lawyer. The hearing went great. Krutov's lawyer offered to settle, and I was so confident that we were going to win that I refused. Then the arbitrators came back and said they had found in favour of the Russians in every instance.

I was never so devastated or dumbfounded in my life.

"Did you even try over there?" Pat said. "Did you even put up a fight?"

Just to rub it in, they tried to charge us another $150,000 for legal fees. I had to go back to Sweden for that hearing, and I got it reduced to $50,000.

Stockholm had always been one of my favourite cities, but I couldn't make myself go back for about 10 years after that.

Igor Larionov was a different story. He was a delight. What a hockey player. Our whole team changed the first day he came to practice. He started making passes that guys weren't expecting. We got sharper immediately. If you weren't paying attention, he would hit your stick with the puck and it would bounce into the corner.

Off the ice, Igor was way more sophisticated and savvy to Western ways than Krutov, but he was still a product of the old Soviet Union. The first night Igor and his wife, Ylena, came to Canada, Stan Smyl and his wife, Jennifer, took them out to dinner. On the way, they stopped at a convenience store to pick something up. Ylena began grabbing all the packaged sliced meats from the rack.

"What are you doing?" asked Jennifer.

"We need to take it all as long as it's here," Ylena said.

There were such severe food shortages in Moscow that people just grabbed everything whenever it was available. Jennifer gently took the meat away from Ylena and replaced it. The next day, she took Ylena to a supermarket. Ylena burst into tears.

But Igor wasn't without his own complications. Not long after he arrived, I was sent a bill by three different agents, all of whom said they represented him, and all of whom were claiming their percentage of his contract.

I called Igor in after practice and tried to get to the bottom of it.

"Did you sign with three agents, or just with Mark Malkovich [the one we had been dealing with]?"

"*Nyet*," Igor said. "Just Mark."

"Okay, are these your signatures?"

"*Da*."

"So, you signed with three agents?"

"*Da*."

"You just told me you didn't," I said. "You lied to me."

"I didn't lie to you," he said. "You're not Russian."

That's what they had told him back home: you could lie to anyone with impunity, as long as they weren't Russian.

"Igor, I'm the best fucking friend you have. You're not paying these other two assholes. I will make them go away. But you had better start trusting me. You can't lie to me."

Igor told me later that he would have signed with 20 different agents if he had to, in the hope that one of them would have got him out of Russia.

Igor also surprised us by publishing a book during his first season in Vancouver. It caused a bit of a sensation because he revealed that while he was playing with Red Army, they tried to get him to take mystery injections of a "milky white substance" and he refused. The clear implication was that they wanted him to use steroids. This wasn't long after the Ben Johnson scandal, when the whole world was waking up to the reality of performance-enhancing drugs.

Excerpts from the book started leaking out during one of our games, and understandably they caused a stir—starting with Pat Quinn.

"What the fuck?" Pat said. "The Russians are going to sue him for libel."

I went downstairs after the game and pulled Igor into the coaches' office before the reporters could get to him.

"You're going to get asked by the fucking media about this. Is it true?"

"Why would I say it's true if it isn't true?"

"But is it true? Will other teammates say it's true? What if you get sued for libel?"

"Yes, yes, it's true," he acknowledged.

"Okay," I said. "We've established that. Now, what else is in there?"

Igor smiled.

"Buy the book," he said.

I fucking loved it. A communist had turned into a capitalist.

Igor played only three seasons for us. Pat agreed that he should leave after his third year in order to get out from under the 50/50 contract with the Soviets. He went to Switzerland first, and then came back to the NHL and played in San Jose and Detroit. What a great player, a great father, a great person, and a deserving member of the Hockey Hall of Fame. If he had been able to play his whole career in the NHL, he'd be remembered as one of the all-time best.

In the first two years Pat Quinn ran the Canucks, there were some encouraging signs. He hired Bob McCammon as our head coach, with Jack McIlhargey and Mike Murphy as assistants. In 1987–88, Pat's first season on the job, the team finished dead last in the Smythe Division and second-last in the league. With the No. 2 pick, we selected Trevor Linden, and things looked like they were turning around.

The 1988–89 season was magical. In September, Pat traded a third-round pick to Calgary for Paul Reinhart and Steve Bozek, and then traded Dave Richter for Robert Nordmark. He also re-signed Harold Snepsts, and the team started to take on a personality. Harold Snepsts, Stan Smyl, Garth Butcher—we had an old-time edge. Kirk McLean and Greg Adams came over and added skill along with Tony Tanti and Petri Skriko. We were moving north.

We finished fourth in the Smythe Division, snuck into the playoffs, and then took the Calgary Flames—who won the Cup that year—to overtime in Game 7 before bowing out in the first round. After a bunch of lost years, Canucks fans were beginning to see the light.

Which brings us to draft day, 1989. One of the most important moments in Vancouver hockey history.

Everyone in hockey knew about Pavel Bure, and knew that he was going to be a special player. No, let me change that. *Almost* everyone knew about Pavel Bure—except for Pat Quinn. He just wasn't on Pat's radar. Pat was mad about Krutov, and he hadn't seen much of Bure.

Bure made his debut with the senior Red Army team—CSKA—as a 16-year-old and was obviously the best young talent Russia had produced in a long time. He was the breakout star of the Soviet team that won the World Juniors in 1989 in Anchorage, Alaska. His skill set was being compared to that of Valeri Kharlamov, arguably the greatest player of the Soviet era.

In 1989, Bure was 18, and under the NHL's rules at the time he could be picked at any point in the first three rounds of the draft, but not after that. Given that there was no certainty when—or if—he'd ever get out of the USSR, no NHL team was going to risk a draft pick in the top three rounds to get him. It would be a different story in 1990, when teams could draft him in any round.

There was one exception to that draft eligibility rule: if a player had spent at least two seasons with an elite-level club, and played at least 11 games in each of those seasons, he was eligible to be taken in any round.

Bure had just finished his first full year with CSKA and had been named the top rookie in Russia. When you looked through the records, he had played only nine games for Red Army the year before. So, as far as anyone knew, he was ineligible to be selected in 1989.

But then our chief scout, Mike Penny, got a phone call.

Mike had good contacts in Russia. One of them called and told him we could draft Bure. He said he had two additional game sheets from St. Petersburg—the writing was in the Cyrillic alphabet, so Bure didn't look like "Bure" on the page. If the game sheets were real, what they proved was that Bure had played 11 games, not nine, during his debut season in the Soviet elite league, and that meant he was eligible to be drafted in any round.

Mike's contact faxed us the sheets. They looked legit. And as far as we knew, we were the only team in the NHL with that information in the days leading up to the draft.

But that qualifier is important—"as far as we knew." We also knew that in those days, everything was for sale in the Soviet Union. If someone had found a way to get the information to us, it was entirely possible that they had also sold it to another team in the league. The draft would be a game of chicken. We obviously weren't going to use one of our early picks on a guy who might never get out of Russia. But if we waited too long, somebody might beat us to the punch—if his eligibility wasn't challenged—and we'd lose out on one of the most talented young players in the world.

It was up to me to make the case to Pat. I told him we had to take Bure in the sixth round.

"Wait," he said.

I pushed Pat. "Are you sure no one else has those game sheets? In Russia, you could eat for a month on 10 dollars. Do you think maybe someone else would be willing to pay 10 bucks for that information?"

We argued about it.

"You'd better not cost me a sixth-round pick for some communist," Pat said. But then he approved the pick—and he was the boss.

I remember joking with Dave Nonis about it later: can you imagine passing on Bure because Pat didn't really know how good he was, and didn't know how cutthroat the Russians could be?

Finally, I won the argument.

When our pick was announced, all hell broke loose on the draft floor. Everyone charged the stage. Jack Button, who was working for the Capitals then, was cursing and swearing. "He's not eligible," they argued. "He's not on the list of draft-eligible players from the league's Central Registry."

That last part was true. But Central Registry doesn't list every player, and you're free to pick anyone you want—at your own risk. Jim Gregory, who was one of the finest people ever to walk on this planet, made that clear to us. The league would register the pick, but wouldn't approve it. There would be an investigation, and if it turned out Bure wasn't eligible, we would lose our claim to him and forfeit the draft pick.

I told Jim we understood, and we were fine with that.

The investigation took a full year. I learned later that we weren't, in fact, the only ones who knew that Bure was eligible. I think there were four or five teams that had the same information we did, including the Edmonton Oilers, who were going to pick him in the seventh or eighth round. Imagine how NHL history might have been different if that had happened.

To his everlasting credit, Glen Sather sent a letter to the league saying that he had the same information we had about Bure playing those two games in St. Petersburg, and that the pick should stand. Glen never told me that he did that—I heard it from the league. Think about it. That's a division rival doing the right thing. That's why I love our game. There is still some honour in hockey.

The 1990 draft was held in Vancouver. The night before, there was a knock on the door of our suite. It was Brian O'Neill, the NHL's vice-president, who told Pat that league president John Ziegler wanted to see him.

I knew it had to be about Bure. As Pat grabbed his jacket, I whispered to him, "Don't accept anything less than the player is ours." Pat left with Brian, the door closed, and then about five seconds later, there was another knock. It was Brian again. "You'd better come, too," he told me.

We walked into the league's suite, and Gil Stein handed us a press release that announced the NHL was upholding the pick and awarding us the rights to Pavel Bure.

It was a great day for the Vancouver Canucks.

Now all we had to do was find a way to get Bure out of Russia.

He had a year left on his contract with Red Army, and there was no way the Russians were going to let him go early, or let him play internationally and take the chance that he'd defect, as Alexander Mogilny had done.

In July, a month or so after the draft, I got a call out of the blue from Ron Salcer, the player agent who was going to represent Bure when and if he got to North America.

"Burkie, how's it going?" he said. "You want to say hi to Pavel?"

He passed the phone to someone.

"Hey Burkie," he said. "It's Pavel." You could have knocked me over with a feather.

He was in Southern California, with his father and his younger brother. Somehow, they got him out. Now the challenge was to try and clear up his contract in Russia and cut a deal to play for the Canucks.

"One of us ought to go down and see him," Pat said.

As always, "one of us" meant me.

I flew to California and met Pavel for the first time. I liked him, and I still like him. He fucked me later on when he wouldn't play for me, but I like him and his brother Valeri. His father, Vladimir, the former Olympic swimmer, not so much—he was pretty intense. He was suspicious of everybody, and everything we told him. He could be a problem.

I asked Salcer for a copy of Bure's contract with Red Army. He had signed it as a 17-year-old—so, a minor—but his father had counter-signed, which would make it legal and binding in most Canadian and US jurisdictions.

"What do we do now?" Salcer asked me.

"Let me research the law a little bit and find the state where we have the best chance of getting out from under the contract."

All my research led me to Michigan, where there had been multiple cases of contracts that had been signed by a minor and counter-signed by a parent or guardian being voided by the courts. I talked to Pat and said we ought to launch a suit in Michigan to break the contract. It was our best chance, but the truth was that the Russians could have—and should have—simply ignored it. All they had to do was maintain that the Michigan court didn't have jurisdiction, and we wouldn't have had any recourse.

Instead, they responded the day after we filed. I couldn't believe it. I remember saying to Pat, "There is a God. I can prove it now." Once they engaged with us in the courts, it would come down to money;

there was no longer any question that Bure would be playing for us. The only question was how much it was going to cost.

The Russians hired Howard Gourwitz, a top-notch attorney from Detroit and a good guy (who was Mike Modano's agent). We also hired a local law firm. We had two lawyers sitting on one side of the courtroom who would argue that Bure's Russian contract should be invalidated, and two other lawyers on the other side of the courtroom set to argue that if the court ruled the contract was legitimate, he should be sent back to Russia.

That last part might surprise you. But Pat had only authorized me to spend $200,000 for Pavel's release, even though I told him it probably wouldn't be enough, and we needed some leverage with Salcer negotiating Pavel's NHL contract. If he didn't sign with us, we needed him to think that he was heading back to Russia, which was the last thing Pavel wanted.

I hired a private detective to look into what Bure had been up to during his short time in the United States. We were thinking there might be something we could use—maybe he got busted with a hooker or something like that. Just some dirt.

We found out that Pavel had entered into a quickie marriage in Las Vegas to try and prevent being sent home. He paid the woman $10,000 to marry him so he could get his green card, and then walked away. I had that information in my back pocket, just in case we needed it. We didn't let on to anyone that we knew about the sham marriage. It was perfectly legal—but a judge might not like it.

On Monday morning, we went to court and presented our case and Gourwitz presented the Russians' case before Judge Kathleen MacDonald. The judge heard us out and said it seemed pretty obvious that there were grounds for a settlement. It was just a matter of figuring out the financial terms.

The Russians asked for 400 grand.

"Mr. Burke," the judge asked, "how much are you prepared to offer?"

"I don't think we should pay anything," I said. "I think you should simply release him. We don't pay anything to release European players from their contracts."

(Today, NHL teams do pay, but in those days they didn't.)

She said that in this case, we were at least going to have to pay a transfer fee.

I offered $100,000.

Judge MacDonald made a face when she heard that number, because she knew there was zero chance the Russians would take it. With that, we adjourned for the day.

I got back to my room and called Salcer. At this point, I'd been in the law office since six in the morning, in court most of the day, and now I was going to be negotiating with Ron until 11 or 12 at night. I'd never been so tired in all my life.

Salcer was asking for crazy money—millions of dollars to get Bure to sign with the Canucks. This was before all entry-level players were capped. I told him we weren't doing that, and I rolled out a few comparables, but he wasn't buying my arguments, and we left it at that.

On day two in court, our lawyers presented the case law and did a hell of a job. They laid out all the precedents in Michigan where contracts signed by a minor and countersigned by a parent or guardian had been thrown out. The lawyers for the Russians went next, offering up their own case law, but none of it was from Michigan, so it felt like we had made some major points.

I didn't make a serious offer on the first day, but after the second day, Howard pulled me aside and tried to make a deal. "We both know the kid's special," he said. "Give us 400 grand and he's yours."

I put on a show, slamming the table and yelling at Howard, calling him a fucking greedy fuck. And Howard's a nice guy who doesn't swear. He was taken aback, and he physically shrank away from me.

"We'll fucking give you a hundred grand and not a nickel more," I said. "You're lucky we're giving you anything."

That was the end of negotiations on day two. No progress with Salcer that night.

The next day, the judge tried to force a conclusion to the case. She called me into her chambers and told me she didn't think I was being reasonable. I told her I could go as high as 200 grand—the limit Pat had set—but no further than that.

"I don't think $200,000 is reasonable," she said. "I'm going to let this guy out of his contract and he's either going to be wandering around free or I'm going to send him back to Russia. Either way, he's not going to be a Vancouver Canuck."

"Your Honour," I said, "I don't know how to say this without being disloyal to my boss, but I don't think $200,000 is enough, either. But that's all I'm authorized to spend at this moment. I cannot move on it. I don't want you to think I'm being intransigent here."

"You'd better talk to your boss," Judge MacDonald said. "As it stands, I'm going to rule for the Russians unless you up your offer." (She then called the Russians and told them $400,000 was too high. It was good old-fashioned arm-twisting.)

That meant I had to go back to Pat—and of course, he wasn't happy about it.

"Are you deaf?" he said. "We're not moving a dime. The Griffithses authorized $200,000. That's it."

I pleaded with him. "Pat, it's not getting done at that number," I said. "Why don't you trust me? I'm here, I know what the deal is, and I know we're going to lose Bure if we don't sweeten the pot."

He wasn't interested in hearing that argument—and the truth is, the strength of Pat's position wound up saving us a lot of money in the end.

With my back against that wall, I managed to make a deal with Salcer for Bure's services. Our intelligence gathering came in handy.

"I know all about 'Mrs. Bure' in Las Vegas," I told him. "I was hoping not to have to play this card, but you're being a fucking douchebag. So either you agree to terms right now and we finalize this deal to play for the Vancouver Canucks, or Pavel is going back to Russia. At this point, I don't care which way it goes, but those are your only two options."

There was a long pause while he digested that information. And then we got a deal done.

(I should point out that I really like Ron Salcer. Some guys in the business don't, but despite how hard we went at each other, I do like him, and I think he did a good job for Pavel.)

Thursday morning, we were back in court. The judge had announced that she was going to make a ruling today, one way or another. She asked each side where they stood. The Russians had moved down to $300,000. And we, of course, were stuck at two hundred.

It was pretty clear to me that Judge MacDonald thought it was the Russians who were being more reasonable.

And then Pavel piped up.

"I'll pay 50," he said, in his then-broken English.

"Pavel," I whispered to him. "Shut the fuck up. I'll get you out of here for less than that."

"I'll pay 50," he said again. "I need to play, Your Honour. I can't go back. I sign a contract last night. I've got money. I'll pay 50."

The judge turned to the Russians.

"Will two-fifty do it?"

"Yes," they said.

She looked at me.

"Will two-fifty do it?"

"Yes," I said. "We have a deal."

We all shook hands. I hugged Pavel.

And then I called Pat.

"You dumb fucking Irishman," he said. "I told you—"

I stopped him in his tracks.

"Pavel has agreed to pay the last 50," I said.

There was a long silence on the other end of the line.

"There's no way we will let him pay that," Pat said.

So we had him.

I was exhausted. It had been a gruelling few days, and it was also the best work I ever did for Pat.

Now it was time to bring Pavel to Vancouver and introduce him to the local media. He had been training in Spokane, Washington, with his brother Valeri. I flew to Seattle, met him there, and we went to the Canadian consulate to get his immigration papers sorted out.

Brian Coxford from BCTV met me at the consulate with a heads-up—there was a mob of media people waiting at the airport, and it was already a zoo, he told me. So we decided to drive up instead of flying. We could cross the border at the Peace Arch, slip into the back of the arena, meet the trainers and get him settled in before facing the reporters.

On the drive north from Seattle, Pavel spent the whole time pointing out the car window and asking questions.

"What's English for that?"

"River," I'd say to him.

Then he'd repeat it. "River . . . bridge . . . lake . . . mountain."

I thought, "This kid is going to be fine."

"YOU'RE GOING TO KILL RICHARD"

THE FIRST TIME SOMEONE tried to hire me as a general manager was in 1989. The New York Rangers job had come open after they fired Phil Esposito, and John Diller, the executive vice-president of Madison Square Garden, reached out to Pat to ask for permission to interview me.

I didn't have an out clause in my contract, and Pat told me he was going to turn down the request. But he wanted me to sit in his office and listen on speakerphone while he talked to Diller—who had no idea I was there.

"Nobody knew about this guy until I hired him," he told Diller. "He's doing great work here and I need him."

"What kind of an asshole are you to hold back a young guy like this?" Diller said. "He's our top candidate."

"You're not talking to him," Pat said, and that was that.

After he hung up the phone, Pat looked at me and asked, "Are you okay with this?"

I told him I was, that I understood, that I wanted to be a general manager someday but I didn't have an out in my deal, so it was perfectly fair for him to say no to Diller. Plus, I liked working for him and for the Canucks—which was true.

But when I did my second contract with Pat, there was an out clause. And a year later, the Philadelphia Flyers called and asked me to interview for the general manager's job there.

I was free to go now. But I didn't want to go to Philadelphia. I didn't like the direction the franchise was heading. They had just fired Bobby

Clarke, who had become a dear friend of mine and who is an icon for Flyers fans. I first met "Whitey" (his player nickname) in training camp. Jay Snider, the son of owner Ed Snider, had taken over running the team, and I liked Jay, but I didn't have confidence in the organization. So I was going to turn down the interview.

Pat talked me out of that.

"You're going to that interview," he said.

"But I don't want the job."

"Interviewing is a skill," he told me. "You have to learn to interview. You don't represent yourself well. You're reluctant to talk about what you bring to the table. You're a modest guy. You've got to learn to shed that in an interview. You've got to say, 'Here's what I can do for you' . . . toot your own horn."

I called Jay back and said I would interview for the job on one condition—that no one knew I was being considered. I wanted it to be completely on the down-low.

The Washington Capitals were playing a home playoff game the next night. We missed the playoffs that season, and it would be perfectly natural for me to be there watching. The next morning, I could quietly drive up to Philadelphia and have the meeting.

I arrived at the arena in Washington, and a camera crew and reporter from Comcast—the Flyers' broadcast network, which was also owned by the Sniders—were waiting for me. Obviously, someone in the organization had tipped them off that I'd be there, which pissed me off.

"Brian, we understand you're interviewing for the Flyers job tomorrow," the reporter said to me.

They asked me if Bobby Clarke deserved to be fired and I said what I honestly felt—no, he didn't. The next morning, that was the headline in one of the Philadelphia newspaper sports sections.

I arrived at the Flyers offices at eight o'clock the next morning. Jay Snider threw the newspaper down in front of me.

"What the fuck is the matter with you?"

So, this wasn't starting well.

I told Jay that he'd just fired the most popular guy in town. Bobby Clarke and Mike Schmidt were the two biggest sports stars in

Philadelphia over the past 30 years, and I wasn't going to be blamed for one of them being axed.

"You take the hit for this," I said to Jay. "I don't want any blood on my hands."

To his everlasting credit, Jay said, "You're right."

So the interview went on . . . and on. All day long. Eight hours. The longest job interview of my life. And all just with him.

He was painstaking. "Tell me about Grade 1. Who were your friends?"

Finally, by the time we got to about fourth grade, I asked him, "Is this a date or a job interview?"

"I have my reasons," Jay said.

I liked him. I liked him enough that I started to change my tune about the Flyers organization.

My flight out was at eight o'clock at night. I remember that it had rained all day, massive thunderstorms that finally broke right about the time we finished the interview. He suggested that we head out and get a sandwich before I left for the airport.

We were walking down the sidewalk, and I noticed that there was a huge puddle of dirty, shitty rainwater in the middle of the road. A bus came along. The driver saw us, saw the puddle and saw an opportunity.

"Jay, look out!" I hollered, then jumped out of the way.

He got soaked from head to foot. I'll never forget him standing there, stamping his feet and shaking his fist and screaming at the driver as the bus drove off.

The time came to catch my flight.

"So, what's next?" I asked him.

He told me he was going to narrow his search down to two finalists, and that they would be interviewed by his father and the family lawyer. He told me I was one of those finalists, and that he hadn't decided on the other one yet.

"Head back to Vancouver," he said, "and I'll be in touch."

I got to the airport and Les Bowen, who was the most important sports columnist in Philadelphia in those days, was waiting at the gate (back in the days before 9/11, you could do that sort of thing). He knew I had been interviewing and asked me if I was interested in the job.

"Yeah," I admitted. "After talking to Jay, I am."

The whole experience had kind of got my juices flowing. You start thinking, "It's the Philadelphia Flyers, it's a general manager's job, I like the guy I'd be working for, maybe I want this after all."

I got back to Vancouver, and the only thing Pat wanted to talk about was the team getting reimbursed for my flight. They had paid for it on the understanding that I would pay them back. Every day, he'd ask me, "Have we been reimbursed yet? I want my money back."

I told him to quit bugging me, to take it out of my next paycheque if it meant so much.

What bothered him wasn't just the money—it was that it was the Flyers, the team that had fired him.

That was Pat.

And then I waited, and waited, and a week passed, and I didn't receive so much as a phone call.

Finally, nine days after the interview, Jay Snider called me and said, "We're going in a different direction."

No shit.

"Who are you hiring?"

"Russ Farwell." The general manager of the Seattle Thunderbirds of the Western Hockey League.

"Good man," I said. "I respect him. I wish you luck. Thanks for considering me."

Even though the ending was disappointing, it was a valuable experience. In addition to learning how to interview, just going through the process had changed my status—which is another reason Pat encouraged me to do it. Once you're a finalist, you're always a finalist. Once you've been one of four or five guys in the running for a job, you're going to be on the list for every general manager's job that comes up.

There would be more opportunities now, and the next time one came along, I'd be ready.

There were some bumps in the road during the early 1990s, but Pat's vision for the team was sound. It took time, but in 1994, the team he

had built from the ground up went on a thrilling playoff run that cul-
minated in just the second finals appearance in franchise history—a
series in which they lost to the New York Rangers at Madison Square
Garden in Game 7.

But I wouldn't be around for that.

I had my first encounter with the Hartford Whalers a few years
before they hired me as general manager. In 1986, before Pat brought
me to Vancouver, I was contacted by a couple of businessmen from the
Hartford area who had attended Providence College. They were interested in putting together an ownership group to buy the Whalers, and
they wanted me to be the president and general manager.

The franchise had begun life as the New England Whalers in the
World Hockey Association. But they'd had a checkered history once
they entered the NHL, playing in a market that had traditionally been
part of the Boston Bruins' territory. The team was up for sale, but the
Providence College guys didn't have the money to do it themselves, so
they approached Richard Gordon, who had made his fortune in commercial real estate. Gordon had been a great collegiate tennis player
and was on the board of the Tennis Hall of Fame. He wasn't originally
from the area, but he spent his summers living in a huge mansion in
Newport, Rhode Island, called High Tide.

Gordon told them he had no interest in owning the Whalers. Then
he went out and bought the team with a different set of partners.

Not long afterwards, the Whalers approached Pat, asking for permission to interview me for their general manager's job. Pat told them
he wanted a first-round pick in return—and I told the Whalers' lawyer,
Bob Caporale, that I didn't want the job without that first-round pick.
So they hired Eddie Johnston instead.

In 1992, they fired Johnston, in large part because he had engineered what is remembered as one of the worst trades in NHL history:
sending Ron Francis, who was an icon in Hartford, and Ulf Samuelsson
to the Pittsburgh Penguins in return for John Cullen and Zarley
Zalapski. (As you may recall, Pittsburgh went on to win consecutive
Stanley Cups in 1991 and 1992, with both of those guys making a sub-
stantial contribution.)

The Whalers asked me to come in for an interview. I was more than willing, but asked them to make sure to keep the process confidential. As I said about my Philadelphia experience, it's important to be viewed as a finalist for one job, because then you'll be viewed as a finalist for every job that comes along. But at the same time, it's in your interest to keep things quiet, just in case you don't get the job. If people know you've been rejected a few times, teams will tend to view you as damaged goods. So, getting shot down once was good for me. But I didn't want to publicly fail to get the Hartford job.

The interview process was bizarre. I showed up at Richard Gordon's office, only to find out that a guy named Jerry would also be in the room.

"Who's Jerry?" I asked Richard.

"He's one of our season-ticket holders," he said. "I want him to be comfortable with this hiring, too."

Richard—and Jerry—went through my education and experience and asked me which contracts I had negotiated and which trades I had been a part of. When you've only been an assistant GM, you don't really have a track record or a resumé you can shove in front of somebody and say, "I'm the guy," because you were working under somebody else.

When the interview was over, I wasn't really sure how it had gone. The process was just so strange. As for confidentiality, it turned out that everyone and their dog knew I was in town. There was a TV crew waiting for me when I came out. It was goddamnedest thing I've ever been through.

That same day, the local newspaper, the *Hartford Courant*, ran a poll asking fans who the Whalers should hire as their new GM: me or Mike Liut. Liut was an extremely popular former Whalers goalie, and I figured I'd get smoked. But it wound up about 50/50. I was surprised that people even knew who I was.

A few days later, Richard called and offered me the job. We negotiated a contract that would pay me $275,000 a year, which was serious money back then, especially for a rookie GM (it was three times what I was making working for Pat). But we didn't sign the contract right away. In fact, we didn't sign it until the end of October, with the season already underway. I had to confront Richard to make it happen—I think he was hedging his bets, figuring he could fire me in November or December if things weren't going well and then not have to pay me out. I knew by then that Eddie Johnston had been forced to go through hell to get the money Richard owed him after he was fired.

"This is clearly deliberate," I said to Richard. "I know you want to be able to fire me and not pay me. That's fine. I'll work without a contract from now until the end of the deal if that's what you want. But the first job that opens up that I think is interesting, I'm going to grab it and walk out."

They had the contract ready for me to sign that week.

But the first clue that some things were seriously wrong in Hartford came well before that. On my first day on the job, they held a press conference to officially introduce me to the local fans and media. My parents came to town, which was a big thrill.

Afterwards, we all went to Richard's beautiful house in Avon, Connecticut. He asked me what the first thing was that I wanted to do as GM.

"I'd like to go and take a look at our practice rink," I said.

Richard offered to lend me one of his cars, and asked Tommy Rowe, our assistant GM, to do the driving.

That's the same Tommy Rowe I played with in Springfield, the guy who got himself thrown out of a game for pulling someone's hair, opening the door for me to play a regular shift and make an impression on Keith Allen. If that hadn't happened, I would have never been offered a professional contract by the Flyers, and who knows what different direction my life might have taken.

We were walking out to the car, and Tommy said to me, "Have you signed your contract yet?"

"No."

"Don't sign it," he said. "Don't come here."

We got into the car, and I started thinking, "Either things are really bad here, or Tommy just wants me out of the way so he can take the job for himself."

It was the former.

"You're going to kill Richard before this is over," he said. "He inter-feres. He changes his mind constantly. You're going to physically kill him before you get out of here."

He wasn't the only person who warned me against working for Richard. Bobby Orr and Rick Ley had told me the same thing. Maybe I should have listened to them. Though in hindsight, I still wouldn't trade that experience for the world.

We sold our house in Vancouver and bought a beautiful place in Simsbury, Connecticut. The Hartford area is a great place to live. Every morning on my commute to the rink, I'd hit the road at 5:30 and be dodging deer and wild turkeys as I drove through a couple of state parks on my way into the city.

Your first job running a team is always magical. You never forget it. But we weren't very good that year. The way I saw it, my job was to go in and establish a style of play, and also establish the way I wanted to do business. One way or another, we were going to have a tough team and play Brian Burke hockey. I inherited Jimmy Roberts as head coach, who is a great guy, but I wanted somebody harder. I interviewed Brian Sutter for the job, but the Bruins heard about that and snapped him up for themselves (a lesson learned there about protecting information). But the guy I really wanted from the beginning was Paul Holmgren, whom I had admired ever since I fought him in Minnesota summer hockey. I lost the fight but won his respect, and we had remained friends ever since. We kept Darcy Regier as one of our assistants, and Paul hired Kevin McCarthy as the other. Before the end of the summer, the Islanders hired Darcy away, making him their assistant general manager. Paul convinced me to bring in Pierre McGuire as his replacement. I fought him hard on that, because I had never heard anything good about Pierre.

Beyond that, I kept everyone in the front office and gave them a chance to show me what they could do.

Pat Verbeek was my captain, and he was excellent. What a solid player and a solid person. Geoff Sanderson scored 46 goals for us. And that might have been the toughest team I ever had. Jimmy McKenzie was our heavyweight, and we also had Jimmy Agnew and Nick Kypreos—Nick scored 17 goals that season and had 325 penalty minutes. But we didn't really have the talent to compete.

I remember calling Bruins GM Harry Sinden early in that season and complaining about my team.

"What did you think you were getting?" he asked. "Why do you think they brought you in here? You always inherit a leaky ship."

Harry gave me some great advice about mistakes that I ought to avoid. He told me to go slowly before making my first big deal. Make a smaller deal first. Dip your toe in the water. Don't rush into anything. He was absolutely right.

(Harry and I went on to become very good friends. I remember, years later, we were out hunting together and he admitted that it had taken him a long time to warm up to me. "I used to hate your guts when you were in the agent business," he said. "It took a while, but now I think you're a decent guy.")

I realized that once you become a general manager, you've got to let your players (and their agents) know you're willing to fight over money. It's very important that you let the players know that every contract is going to be a battle. And in Hartford especially, it was going to be hard to get money out of Brian Burke. We were deep in the red. There was a hard core of about 8,000 fans when I was there, and you wouldn't attract any more unless you were winning. So we had to run a tight ship.

As I've already mentioned, my first big trade was with Lou—sending Bobby Holik to New Jersey for Eric Weinrich and Sean Burke. It worked out great for both teams. But I also decided it would be a good idea to make a splash at the end of my first season. It's a pattern I followed in Vancouver, drafting the Sedin twins, and in Toronto, making the Phil Kessel trade. End the year with a bang.

With the Whalers, I would make my big move at the draft.

———

I think Richard Gordon is a good person, a smart man, a committed family guy. To this day, I'm not mad at him. Owners have a right to run a team any way they want to run it. But I'm not necessarily going to go along for the ride. I said the same thing all four times I was interviewed for a general manager's job: if you hire me, there's two hands on the fucking steering wheel, and they're both mine. If you don't want to give me that much autonomy, I'll help you hire the right guy. But if you hire me, you listen to me.

Looking back, Richard was just the wrong man to be running a professional sports franchise in that city at that time. People in Hartford didn't like him. The locals viewed him as an outsider, and he was resented in some circles because he got the better of some people on real estate deals. I wouldn't say he was hated, but the community never really warmed to him.

And just as Tommy Rowe had warned me on the day they announced my hiring, Richard couldn't avoid meddling in the day-to-day operations of the team. He had a tendency to believe whatever he heard from the last guy who talked to him—and I mean that literally. Someone would tell him what a great player Ray Bourque was, and he'd be in my office demanding that we make a trade for Ray Bourque—as if that could actually happen.

One day, he came up to me and laid out a trade he wanted me to make.

"Who did you talk to now?" I asked him.

"The shoeshine guy downstairs," Richard said. "He's a huge hockey fan. You shouldn't be out of touch with the fans. You should know what the fans think."

I don't disagree with that. I think you should stay in touch with your fans and you should know what they're thinking. But you don't want them running your team.

Richard's daughter Ashley worked in our office. Every night, she'd go home and tell him over dinner what she thought was wrong with the organization. He'd come right back to me and tell me this guy should be fired and that guy should be fired—especially the sales and marketing guys. I know how hard it is to sell, because it was part of my job in Vancouver. And it was especially hard in a place like Hartford, where the economy was shot. So I'd stand up for our people as best as I could, but we were constantly fighting.

I remember there was a game in February against the Rangers in Hartford. We took them to overtime, and then Holmgren sent out five rookies for the first shift. Herb Brooks, who was coaching the Rangers, countered with five veterans, they scored right away and we lost the game.

Paul found me right after the game, before he talked to the media, and apologized.

"It's fine," I told him. "Those kids will never forget what happened tonight. Just don't do that when we play at home."

Richard, though, had other ideas. He got right in my face.

"Well?" he said.

"Well what?"

"Did you fire him?"

"Fire who?"

"Fire the fucking coach!"

Richard wasn't normally a guy to swear, or even raise his voice, but he was yelling and swearing now.

"He started five fucking rookies!"

I pointed out that the kids had learned a valuable lesson, that we'd essentially been out of playoff contention since November, that it was *my* call, and that if we were going to fire anyone, he ought to fire both of us.

Richard stormed out.

Paul called me on the way home to ask if he still had a job. I told him to come to the office the next morning, and if our keys still worked, we were probably okay.

Around that time, I got a call from Gary Bettman, asking if I would be willing to meet him to talk about an opportunity with the league.

Gary was still relatively new on the job—he had been hired as NHL commissioner in February 1993. I'd met him once before, just after he took the job, when I attended a board meeting as Hartford's alternate governor.

Gary likes to tell the story of what I said to him that day—something along the lines of "You're a basketball guy, you're short, you're American. Good luck."

We didn't really know each other then, but before the NHL hired him, I was asked to connect with some of my contacts in the National Basketball Association, where Gary had been a vice-president under commissioner David Stern, and find out what I could about him.

I called Bob Stein, the president of the Minnesota Timberwolves, whom I knew from the Sports Lawyers Association. "If there's any chance you can get Gary Bettman, you should break your arms dragging him out of the NBA office," Bob said. "He's tough, he's brilliant, he's a good guy." He couldn't say enough about him.

I asked Bob if other NBA executives would say the same thing. "They would," he said. "Gary is universally respected." So I was comfortable when the NHL hired him. I thought it was a great move for the league—and as history shows, it was.

I met Gary at a diner off the New York State Thruway, halfway between where we each lived. He wanted to talk to me about a new vice-president's position, which would include looking after player discipline. (He also talked to Harry Sinden and Glen Sather about it.)

"This will be a fascinating job because you'll be involved on a variety of different fronts," he told me. "You'd have a large role in collective bargaining. We need your legal skills and your hockey skills at the table when we negotiate with the officials and the players. And I'm going to expand the shit out of international hockey. I want tighter relationships with USA Hockey and Hockey Canada—you'll be involved in that."

Everything he told me that day came true. But at that moment, I only had a half season under my belt as an NHL general manager. Whatever my reservations were about Richard, I didn't think I could walk on the first owner who had been willing to hire me.

"You have to find somebody else," I told Gary. "But I don't think you'll have any trouble filling this job."

At the end of the season, with the Whalers long out of the playoffs, I was asked to be the general manager of the US team at the World

Championship. I decided to bring Holmgren along, and Richard decided that he wanted to go with us. We flew economy—that was Richard's style—and I remember the transatlantic flight as being one long lecture.

Richard came home before we did. When I got back to Hartford, it was as though the wind had shifted.

Our trainer, Skip Cunningham, told me that he'd come into the practice rink one morning and found pizza boxes in the trash. The next day, it was Chinese food containers. He couldn't figure out where they'd come from. As far as he knew, no one was supposed to be there. So he came back that same night to find out who had been doing the eating.

He found Richard, his wife, his three children and Pierre McGuire watching playoff games on our satellite dish. Pierre was telling Richard which players he liked and which he didn't and critiquing the coaches. He was trying to work his way into Richard's good graces, while at the same time undermining me.

I've made my peace with Pierre since then. We sat down at Gord Miller's wedding and talked it out. He was a really aggressive young guy who wanted to climb as fast and high as he could, and he made some mistakes. "I bear no resemblance to the guy I was back then," he said, and he asked me to give him a second chance.

I'm a second-chance guy. It's always been one of my pillars. So I forgave him. We remain friends to this day.

But Pierre had poisoned the well. The damage was done.

There was still the draft.

Tommy Rowe and I had scouted one of Chris Pronger's junior games with the Peterborough Petes. I don't think I have ever seen a better defenceman at that level. It's a big deal these days for a defence-man to play 30 minutes in a game. We put a stopwatch on Pronger in the second and third periods—he played 30 of the final 40 minutes.

There was one sequence I will never forget. He was on the ice for a shift, then the Petes took a penalty. He killed the first minute of the penalty. Then the other team took a penalty, so they were four on four for a minute, and then Peterborough went on the power play for a minute.

Pronger never left the ice. I couldn't believe it. I think he played at least 50 minutes in that game.

And what a player. He was the best first passer who ever played for me—better even than Scott Niedermayer. Even in junior, his first pass was a thing of beauty. He could put it right on someone's tape at full speed.

And he was mean.

I just fell in love with the guy, and I thought, "We have to draft him." There was no doubt in my mind that he was going to be a star.

We had the sixth pick that year. Ottawa had the first, which they used for Alexandre Daigle (that didn't work out so well). San Jose was picking second. They would be our target. I talked to the Sharks' general manager, Dean Lombardi, about swapping picks, and at first he told me to fuck off. But we had managed to glean some intelligence about what the Sharks were thinking, which gave us a bit of an edge. They wanted to draft Viktor Kozlov. And they really coveted Sergei Makarov, who was playing for the Flames.

I made a deal with Calgary for Makarov. Then I talked to the teams that were drafting three, four and five—Tampa, Anaheim and Florida. They promised me they were taking Chris Gratton, Paul Kariya and Rob Niedermayer, in that order.

The night before the draft, I went back to Dean and promised him that if he did the deal to flip picks, he'd be able to get Kozlov at No. 6—and if he couldn't, I'd give him our first-round pick the following year.

The draft was held in Quebec City. We were all staying at the Château Frontenac—I was in a garret suite that had a long corridor leading to a bedroom on the right and a meeting room at the end.

Two of our scouts, Bruce Haralson and Ken Schinkel, hung in with me, waiting to see if we could close the deal. Passing on Kariya was a tough call for all of us. We knew how good he was going to be. But they both really wanted Pronger.

I called Dean and asked, "Are we doing this or not?"

"Not tonight," he said. "Maybe tomorrow."

He admits now that he was convinced I was going to put more assets on the table. He was wrong.

"Dean, this is the deal," I told him. "I'm not sweetening the pot. If you're working on something with another team, that's fine. But this will still be our best offer tomorrow. I don't want you thinking I'm going to throw anything else in, because I'm already overpaying."

It was getting late, and I was frustrated and angry. I sent Bruce and Ken home. Then out of the blue, Mike Milbury called. He was working for the Bruins then.

"What are you doing?" he asked.

"Sitting here with my thumb up my ass."

"I'll come over and have a drink with you."

Mike turned up and we killed a bottle of red wine. I really like him. He's so intense, but he's also so funny. People who don't really know Mike might get a different impression, but he's a great human being.

We polished off the last of the wine, and then Mike said good night and walked down the corridor towards the door. I didn't notice at the time, but he made a little detour before leaving. The scouts had ordered some room service—soup with some crackers on the side. Mike saw the dishes left behind, grabbed a couple of packs of saltines, slipped into my bedroom, soaked the bed with water, crumbled up the crackers and sprinkled them over the sheet, and then pulled the bedspread back up so that everything looked normal.

And he also swiped two bottles of wine, just to annoy me.

It was 12:30 in the morning, I was exhausted and sour because I couldn't close the deal. I finally slip into bed . . . and into the wet sheets and crackers. I could have killed Milbury.

I curled up against the wall on the only dry spot left and eventually fell asleep.

On draft day, I'm always the first guy in the room. I arrive at least three hours before things get started. It began as a habit, and then it became a bit of a superstition.

I had to wait quite a while for Dean Lombardi to arrive. When he did, I went straight to him.

"Are we doing this deal or not?" I asked him.

"Yeah, let's do it."

It was stinking hot in the old Colisée that day. The president of the Nordiques, Marcel Aubut, was trying to shame the city into building a new arena, so he didn't turn the air conditioning on. I told our guys they could take their jackets off, but when it was our turn to pick and then go up on stage, they had to put their jackets back on.

We had to move fast now. In those days, you had to write out the terms of a deal, sign it and physically hand it to someone from the league. Ottawa was already on stage, making their pick, while we were scrambling to get the details down on paper.

When it was done, I hustled over to our table. The guys were sitting there in their shirtsleeves because, as far as they knew, we weren't picking until sixth.

"Put on your fucking jackets, boys," I said. "We're up."

I have never felt better about a trade in my life. That's the best deal for one guy I ever made. I got the Sedins, but that was two guys. If you're talking about one guy, it has to be Chris Pronger.

He's very bright. He's done real well with investing and he's interested in lots of things other than hockey. Chris is also very opinionated and stubborn, but those are traits that lots of successful people have. I think stubbornness is a flaw at some point, but all successful people are stubborn deep down because they believe in themselves. You can pick any successful person in the history of the world and you'll find they'll have a stubborn streak. But Pronger's is a mile wide—you could drive a truck on his stubborn streak.

Chris is a natural leader and a vicious competitor—as competitive a guy as I ever had on any of my teams. He'd break your arm to get a loose puck and not think twice about it. You'd be lying on the ice, screaming, and he'd just skate right by you and say, "Get up!" He's just a mean guy. It's no coincidence he was suspended a bunch of times. He put the fear of God into people and then used that fear as a tool.

But he also had an amazing skill set. His first pass out of the zone was always tape to tape. With his reach, Pronger could stand behind the net, take one step, and fire a perfect pass to the red line, right on a guy's stick. It was unbelievable to watch. He's a Hall of Famer and deservedly so.

It's just a joy having guys like that on your team, even though Chris is also one of the grumpiest people I know. Just miserable. He would come in every day and complain that the coffee wasn't hot enough or the weather was bad. He complained about everything. But the players put up with him because he was so good at what he did.

It didn't work out in Hartford, but I won a Cup with Chris in Anaheim. (I also suspended him a couple of times when I was with the league.)

There's a Pronger effect—you can look it up. He took three teams to the Stanley Cup finals. The year after he left, none of them made the playoffs.

If there was any justice, Chris Pronger would have more than one ring.

BETTMAN'S LEAGUE

9

AFTER THE DRAFT, I hired Joel Quenneville to coach our AHL team in Springfield. So chalk up Paul Holmgren and Joel Quenneville on this stop, with Randy Carlyle, Dallas Eakins and Kevin Dineen still to come. Then it was time to clear the air with Richard—or, more likely, bring things to a head.

I wrote a five- or six-page memo, outlining everything I thought was wrong and discussing the changes I thought had to be made. It was brutally honest, and I knew he wasn't going to like it. Among the things I told him was that he needed to move the hockey people out of his office, and that he needed to stop interfering in our business. I also told him I'd like to move his daughter Ashley to a different team. I had written her a recommendation to go to Harvard Business School. But in the meantime, it wasn't helpful having her in a position where people knew she was reporting everything to her father. I thought that the Boston Bruins might take her.

That last part really set him off.

I couriered the memo to his house in Newport on a Friday. He didn't work on Fridays, so he wouldn't get it until Saturday. That would give him the weekend to think it over.

My phone rang early on Saturday morning. Richard is normally a very quiet guy, but he was screaming and cursing like a longshoreman. I could tell he was holding the receiver two feet away from his face.

"You fucking asshole. Who do you think you are? Do you think you come ahead of my family?"

He signed off with a not-so-veiled threat: "You're going to find out in about an hour just where you fit in my universe."

Clearly, I was about to be fired.

I called Gary Bettman.

"Is that job still open?"

At first, Gary tried to talk me out of it. He argued that I had started to turn things around in Hartford, that the team was going to get better. "You're too important to the league where you are," he said. "I like the moves you're making."

"Gary," I said. "I'm going to be fired in the next hour."

He told me to stay off the phone. Then he called Richard. He told him that he was willing to take me off his hands, but not if I was fired—he wasn't going to hire general managers who had been fired to work for the league. Richard was okay with that solution.

Gary called me back. "You're working for me now," he said.

But we still had to agree to a deal. He told me that the job wasn't going to be a parking lot for out-of-work general managers. "If you come," he said, "you've got to promise me you'll give me five years."

We had just moved back east from Vancouver, close to my wife's home, and she was happy with that. Now I was going to have to relocate to New York City, a place I never really grew to like. Being from Minnesota, it always seemed too big to me. And Gary wanted me to commit to five years there.

"Does that mean you're offering me a five-year contract?" I asked him.

"Hell, no," he said. "I don't know if you can do this job or not. But I can offer you three."

He asked me how much I was making in Hartford. I told him—and told him I didn't want a penny more, because I didn't want anyone thinking that I left the Whalers after one season just for money.

We made a handshake deal over the phone, and then the next day they announced that I was joining the National Hockey League as the new senior vice-president and director of hockey operations.

———

I know that a lot of hockey fans—especially in Canada—are going to roll their eyes when they read what comes next.

It breaks my heart that Gary Bettman is not more popular in Canada, because he has done a staggering amount for the game of hockey and the NHL. When I speak in Canada, I'm invariably asked, "What's Gary Bettman really like?" and my answer is "You're already convinced that you don't like him, and there's nothing I can do to change that, so why bother?"

Hockey fans think he's not one of us, that he's American, that he came from basketball. He still gets booed at every rink in the NHL, and I guess that's never going to change.

But the truth is, he *is* one of us. He watches hockey and he loves hockey. If you go into his office late at night, he's got games on two or three TVs while he's doing other work. He knows the game.

You really want to know what Gary Bettman is like? He's a great human being and a brilliant human being. His family comes first for him, above everything else. As a boss, he's an amazing leader and he's tough as nails. If you're ever in a foxhole and you look over and Gary Bettman is in there with you, that's a good thing. He's fearless.

He treats everyone respectfully. When I was working for the league, I only saw him tee off on an employee once, and that was someone who had it coming. If Gary hadn't done it, I would have done it myself. Gary expected the best from you every day, and expected you to act like a league official 24/7. His philosophy is: "Don't tell stories about the league behind my back. Don't gossip about other people in the league. We are a family, so we stick together."

And he's so smart. We had a saying when I worked for the league—there's smart, and then there's Bettman smart. He's on a whole other level. Sometimes, when we were in meetings with the union, he would get so far ahead of us all that Bob Goodenow would be shaking his head and so would I. I'd say to Gary, "You're going too fast. Slow down. I went to Harvard Law School. I'm no slouch. And you're losing me." He was always three steps ahead. Visionaries look and see the next mountain and ask, "How do we get there?" Gary looks ahead and sees six mountains. Working for him was like getting an MBA.

I especially hope people here understand by now what a friend Gary has been to the Canadian NHL teams. The year I arrived for my second stint in Vancouver, the Canucks lost $36 million. We were dealing with a 61-cent Canadian dollar. It was Gary who put in the Canadian Assistance Plan. The American teams were sending us a cheque for $3 million a year. If we didn't have that plan, you wouldn't have all the Canadian teams now. Some of them would have folded.

Never mind all the money the league has put back into the Canadian Hockey League, the US National Development Team and hockey in Europe. Even when we were losing money as a league, he kept the talent pipeline going. He improved our international hockey relationships. He got us to the Olympics.

That's all Gary Bettman.

When you talk about Bettman, you really also have to talk about Bill Daly, Gary's second-in-command, who has become such an important figure in the NHL in his own right. My office used to be right next to his in the New York headquarters.

In a lot of ways, Bill has become a Bettman clone, but he didn't start out that way. When he was first hired by the league, he realized he would have to earn the trust and friendship of the group first. In that sense, he's like me—when I got to a new team, I knew it was my responsibility to try to fit in. Bill did that masterfully with the NHL general managers and owners. He could be a bit of a chameleon when required. He asked a lot of questions and didn't offer brash opinions.

Like Gary, he's a lawyer by trade, and like Gary, he's got an incredible memory for detail. Bill can answer questions about the fine points of the pension plan, the CBA and franchise agreements off the top of his head.

Now that he's established, he's got a much harder persona when he's around the professionals. He's a legitimate tough guy who played college football. Like Gary, he doesn't mind a fight. If there's a choice, they'll avoid it, but if we're going to have a fight, let's fight. He knows how to act in an owners' meeting and he knows how to act in a general managers' meeting. It's very different. With general managers, every once in a while you've got to tell them to fuck off and let them know in no uncertain terms that this is what we're doing. With the owners, you have to be a lot more solicitous—say that this is what we *should* do. Bill understands the difference and he works well with both groups. He's very popular with the GMs, which is saying something because they're all hockey guys, and Bill didn't start out as a hockey guy.

But like Gary, he's a hockey guy now.

When I went to work for the league, the NHL was still in its Wild West phase. Bruce McNall, who engineered the Gretzky trade to Los Angeles and eventually wound up in prison, was the chairman of the board of governors. The owners were used to running the league any way they wanted, and board meetings were chaotic. Bill Wirtz of Chicago would interrupt Gary and interrupt other owners as though he owned the place. It was a circus. Never mind some of the shady characters who came and went: John Spano, who briefly owned the Islanders and wound up in prison; Boots Del Biaggio, a minority owner of the Nashville Predators, went to prison; John Rigas, who owned the Sabres, went to prison. There were teams threatening to move, teams threatening to fold. Gary spent his first 15 years as commissioner putting out fires and establishing order. He put up with the personal slights, put up with being disrespected and pushed ahead.

By the time I left the league in 1998, Gary had complete control of the room. There was still some dissent, still some second-guessing, and the meetings were still interesting, but there was no question who was boss.

And today, those meetings go like clockwork.

Gary surrounded himself with top-notch people. Jeff Pash was a genius, Bill Daly is a genius, Steve Solomon is a brilliant business guy. But it was Gary who had the vision. He was determined to grow revenues, stabilize the weak franchises and improve our broadcast deals. He took what was still a mom-and-pop operation, at least compared to the other major sports leagues, and turned it into a modern, sophisticated, growing sports entertainment business. That's what the NHL is today, and it's entirely because of him.

———

My first year with the league, I lived in a furnished apartment at 62nd Street and Lexington Avenue. My family stayed in Hartford, and I drove back and forth on weekends. The old NHL offices were at 56th Street and Fifth Avenue, and I'd walk over first thing in the morning. I remember one day I walked in and ran into Gary, picking up a newspaper off the floor of the washroom. I said, "Boss, we have someone to do that, you know"—sounding like a wiseass. Gary wheeled on me and said, "Yeah, and when do they come in? After work. Meanwhile, all day, we have players, sponsors, broadcasters, advertisers and owners walking in here. Keep it clean." And out he goes. He was right, of course. I have never left a washroom messy since.

My job responsibilities included liaising with the NCAA, USA Hockey, Hockey Canada and the CHL, which wasn't just empty diplomacy. The league was about to embark on an aggressive expansion. Gary wanted to make sure that there was enough player talent available to stock the new teams without watering down the overall product. I did the research with Dave Nonis, who had moved over to join me with the league.

We concluded that with 20 more junior teams in existence than the last time the league had expanded, and 18 more college teams, there were enough players to make it work, and so expansion went ahead.

Gary expected me to attend all major NHL events—the All-Star Game, the entry draft, overseas exhibition games, board of governors meetings, general managers' meetings. He asked me to take over running the GM meetings, a job that in the past had been handled by Gerry Meehan, a lawyer by trade and the general manager of the Buffalo Sabres. "I need you to be at your best," Gary told me. I was nervous the first time, and I prepared for it as if it was an exam. I was going to be standing up in front of a bunch of guys who would look at me and think, "You never played in the league, you were a GM for a year, and now you think you're in charge?"

I went into it forcefully. No one interrupted me. I showed video to explain rule changes and enforcement. I said, "Here's what we're doing. If you don't understand it or like it, I will walk you through it. We will go through the tape."

Afterwards, Gary complimented me. "That's how you run a meeting," he said. "When you're at the microphone, you're in charge."

And of course I was also put in charge of supplementary player discipline, which turned out to be the most public part of the job.

It was a demanding job and a crowded schedule.

During my second year with the league, my first marriage ended. I'm the first to admit that I have never done a good job of balancing work and personal stuff, so I will take the blame for that. I always put parenting ahead of being a spouse. And my ex-wife had married an attorney, and she expected he would spend his entire career in Boston, near her family. She had no interest in living anywhere else—we had kept our home near Hartford. After the divorce, she moved back to Boston with our four kids, and we agreed to a custody deal under which I would have them every other weekend.

People laugh when I tell them what the NHL's Department of Player Safety looked like when I took the job.

The short answer is that there really wasn't one. Brian O'Neill had handled supplemental discipline before I arrived. He was a real gentleman from the old school, and he told me that he would always support my decisions, even if he disagreed with them. That was a great gift, and when I eventually handed the job over to Colin Campbell, I told him the same thing.

But there was no formal system in place beyond what was written in the NHL rule book. Shortly after joining the league, I called one of the top guys at the NHLPA, Ian Pulver, and asked him to help me brainstorm some kind of system. The first thing we did was get rid of the requirement to hold an in-person hearing to suspend players for four games or fewer. Players hated flying all the way to New York to receive a short suspension. Next, we agreed that a tie went to the player—if I was undecided on whether or not a player should be suspended, he'd walk. If I was undecided between a three- and a four-game suspension, it would be three. And we decided that we needed to build a catalogue, a video library that we could show to teams and players, outlining what was a suspendable offence and what wasn't, as well as the *degrees* of various offences, which would help us establish consistency in how we doled out punishment. Eventually, I started doing an annual tour of all the teams to explain the process.

Those are the foundations of the system that's still in place all these years later.

But what's changed, dramatically, is the technology and the man-power that the league devotes to player discipline.

It was a pretty lean operation in those days—by necessity. There was no high-tech war room, no player safety room. One of Gary's challenges as commissioner was that he had to increase revenues before he could beef up the staff at the league office. To start with, it was just me, Dave Nonis, Bryan Lewis (who was the head of officiating and a great person) and Jim Gregory, who was the league's longest-serving employee, and in some ways both the NHL's memory and its conscience.

At our disposal were four VCRs. That's not a misprint. *Four* VCRs. Glenn Adamo from the broadcast side would come down and set them to record—for games in the East, starting at 7:20 p.m. Puck drop was actually at 7:10, but there was almost never any trouble in the first few minutes of a game, and we had to conserve recording time because those machines had a two-and-a-quarter-hour limit. Obviously, we could record only four games a night, so we'd try to pick the ones where it seemed there would most likely be trouble. Then I'd head out to a Rangers game or a Devils game or a Flyers game and we'd hope that if anything controversial happened, the VCRs would catch it. If a game wasn't covered by those machines and we needed to review something, we'd have to get tapes couriered from the broadcasters to the league office. There were many times when I was home with my kids, or in a hotel somewhere, and a tape would arrive that I'd have to review.

I'll give you some examples of how the system worked in those days.

In 1998, during the playoffs, I was in Philadelphia for a game. My routine was to watch the first period with one team's general manager, the second period with the other GM and the third in the referees' room, where the standby official was otherwise going to be sitting for two and a half hours all by himself.

The game ended, and I hung around for a little while, waiting for the traffic to thin out on the New Jersey Turnpike. I was driving back when I got a call from Pierre Lacroix, the general manager of the Colorado Avalanche. They were two hours behind us, and their playoff game against the Edmonton Oilers had just ended. Let's just say that Pierre was a little worked up.

"Billy Guerin just tried to behead Peter Forsberg!" he yelled down the phone line. "It's worse than the Kennedy assassination!"

There had indeed been an incident during what had turned out to be a nasty game. Colorado had pulled their goalie. Forsberg was standing in front of the net, trying to jam in a rebound, when Guerin chopped him on the bicep with his stick—just like you're supposed to do, trying to disrupt the shot. But the stick came up and clipped Forsberg in the face, cutting him for nine stitches. There was a lot of blood.

"Hang on, Pierre," I said. "Calm down. I taped the game. I'll go back and watch it."

Five minutes later, Gary called, asking me what was going on in Edmonton. This was starting to sound like a big deal.

I called Dave Nonis, who had been watching a game on Long Island that night and who had already heard from Lacroix. I told him he needed to meet me back at the office right away. My biggest worry was that the VCRs might have screwed up and we wouldn't have the game on tape. It was one in the morning by the time I met Dave at the office. We turned on the machine. "Holy fuck," I said, "I hope we've got it."

It was all there—and it was nothing. We call anything less than 10 stitches "a shaving cut." That was part of our deal with the union—anything less than 10 stitches, unless there's a bad foul, doesn't require supplementary discipline.

I called Gary and told him what I thought, and that I'd show him the tape in the morning.

Then I called Lacroix.

"I hope you're calling me to tell me that Billy Guerin is suspended for the rest of the playoffs," he said.

"He's not getting anything, Pierre."

"Fuck you."

That's when I hung up on him.

Sometimes you had to improvise a bit. The Rick Zombo suspension was one example. He was playing defence for the St. Louis Blues against the Dallas Stars one night. The Stars won by a couple of goals, and there were no incidents reported to the league. But the morning after, I got a call from Bob Gainey, the Dallas general manager at the time.

"I'm not trying to get anybody in trouble," he said, "but you had better take a look at what happened at the end of our game last night."

So I went to the tape—not the broadcast tape, because they missed it on television. I had to look at the Dallas coaches' feed, which was shot from the end of the rink.

The Blues had pulled their goalie in the final seconds, trying to tie the game. Zombo, a right-hand shot, was playing the left point. The linesman on that side, Kevin Collins, was positioned two or three feet inside the blue line. He was supposed to be *outside* the blue line, and that mistake set things in motion.

The puck rimmed around the boards to Zombo, but as he tried to get it, he got tangled up with Collins. The puck squirted by and went out over the blue line.

Zombo was understandably frustrated. But what he did next was inexcusable. First, he chopped Collins across the calf with his stick. Dallas scored into the empty net and put the game away. Zombo reacted by skating over to Collins and cross-checking him across the shoulder blades.

You just can't do that to an official. It's written in black and white in the rule book. Each of those incidents required a minimum 20-game suspension. There was no wiggle room. But no one saw it, and our own official hadn't reported it.

After alerting Bettman, I called Kevin to find out why he hadn't written it up. He said he felt bad that his mistake had cost St. Louis a chance to win the hockey game. He added that Zombo was a good guy—which he is—and that nobody else had seen what happened, so he decided to just let it pass.

This was going to require a creative solution. I called Ron Caron, who ran the Blues then, and gave him a heads-up as to what I was thinking. He'd seen the tape, and he knew that something was coming down.

Then I called Zombo.

"Listen to what I'm about to say, you dumb fucker," I said. "And when I'm finished, you say, 'Thank you,' and we'll be done with it.

"You're looking at a 40-game suspension for what you did—and you'd already be serving it if Kevin had written you up. We have the best officials in the world. Kevin was out of position, but your response was completely unacceptable. And if you're ever in front of me again for abuse of an official, you're getting 40 fucking games. This time, you're getting 20, and you're getting off easy."

"Thank you," Zombo said.

The worst incident I dealt with was probably Claude Lemieux of the Avalanche on Kris Draper of the Detroit Red Wings in the 1996 Western Conference final. Dave Nonis and I were watching the game from the press box in Denver. We had already had an incident earlier in the game that happened while I was visiting with Don Adam in the off-ice officials' booth. The phone rang there. Don spoke to whoever was on the other end briefly, and then hung up.

"Who was that?" I asked him.

"That was Mr. Lacroix on his direct line to me," he said.

That would be Pierre Lacroix, the GM of the Avalanche.

I ripped the phone out of the wall. General managers weren't supposed to have contact with minor officials (the men and women who track ice time, hits, shots on net—it's an important role). I told Don the phone had better not reappear.

The Lemieux hit on Draper happened right in front of us. In real time, from where we were sitting, it honestly didn't look that bad. Bill McCreary was refereeing the game, and as far as I was concerned, he was the best ref in NHL history—definitely the best during my career. While Bill huddled with his linesmen, Dave and I were trying to figure out what the right call should be. A deuce? It was a two-minute minor, for sure. Or a nickel? (We called five-minute majors nickels.) Honestly, we weren't sure it merited a five-minute major.

Then we saw the replay. It was a full-fledged hit from behind, an absolute cheap shot delivered by a guy who, on merit, had a reputation as one of the worst cheap-shot artists in the league. And the consequences were horrific. Draper's face was rammed into the boards. It caved in on one side. He suffered a broken jaw, a broken orbital bone and a broken cheekbone.

We called Lemieux in for an in-person disciplinary hearing and suspended him for four games, which included games in the finals—the first time a player had been suspended from the finals since Clarence Campbell suspended Rocket Richard in 1955, which set off the infamous Richard Riot. (In the playoffs, the number of games in a suspension are weighted more heavily with each subsequent round.) Not everyone was happy with our decision because of the terrible injuries Draper suffered, but our job was to punish Lemieux for the act, not for the consequences.

Without Lemieux for those four games, the Avalanche still went on to win the Stanley Cup.

That summer, I received two boxes from Kris Draper's family. They contained a petition, with about 5,000 signatures on it, demanding that Gary fire me. It went right in the trash.

Later, Kris's uncle called me and asked if I had received it. I said no.

"Well, it was signed for," he said. "Someone at the NHL office signed for it, so it was received."

I promised him that I would keep looking for it.

Fuck them.

Being the public face of player discipline meant that someone was always mad at you—players, coaches, general managers, owners and especially fans. I got death threats because of that job.

After I suspended Alex Kovalev of the Rangers for breaking an opponent's hand with a slash, I came to work the next morning and the message light on my phone was lit up: two messages, two death threats.

One was from a drunk, so that was easy to ignore, but the other one was more disturbing. This guy knew where I lived, my walking route to work, even that I went in very early. He said he'd come up behind me and put a bullet in my brain before I even knew what was happening.

Gary was concerned. He wanted a police detail, the whole works. I refused. They killed four presidents, I figured, so if they really wanted to, they could get me no matter who was protecting me. But I did promise to vary my routine for a week.

Gary backed me up on everything. He never interfered and never once said, "I don't think this is enough games." And he's always hired a hard hockey guy. We had Colie Campbell after me, then Brendan Shanahan and now George Parros. He's always got a guy who understands that the physicality of the game is important, and we have never lost that.

My other job with the league involved collective bargaining. When I was hired, I knew we were about to negotiate new contracts with both the NHL Officials Association and the NHLPA, and that both of those negotiations were going to be contentious.

Gary Bettman understood the situation the league was in the day he was hired. He knew it was bleeding red ink. And he knew he wasn't going to be able to expand, fix the franchises that were in trouble and find new owners where they were needed if he didn't find a way to control player salaries. It was going to be a war—more than one, as it turned out—but in the end, he got the salary cap and revenue-sharing system the NHL desperately needed.

The negotiations with the officials came first, and they were like a dry run for what was coming with the players. The referees and linesmen were looking for a huge raise—something like 60 percent—but the league wasn't going to budge on its final offer. They worked without a contract for the first two months of the 1993–94 season and then walked out. We were ready for that—we had held a camp for replacement officials in Indianapolis and we didn't miss a beat. The replacement refs and linesmen weren't perfect, but they did well enough, the games were being played and the fans seemed to hardly notice the difference. We agreed to a contract on December 1, when they accepted what the league had been offering.

We knew it wasn't going to be so simple with the players. The league was bleeding money and we needed a new economic system. So we locked the players out before the beginning of the 1994–95 season and slugged it out. The timing wasn't ideal—the league was on a high after the Rangers beat the Canucks in that great seven-game Stanley Cup final. *Sports Illustrated* had that famous story about hockey being hipper than basketball. But if we didn't find a way to control player salaries, none of that was going to matter.

We had a great team, all smart and tough: Jeff Pash, David Zimmerman, Bob Batterman, Shep Feingold. At that time, the courts in the US were still trying to figure out the proper balance between the Sherman Act and the National Labor Relations Act. Antitrust litigation was still very much a viable tool in labour negotiations, and that was our group's bread and butter.

On the players' side, you had Bob Goodenow, backed by Bob Riley, Ian Pulver and John McCambridge. They had the players ready to fight a salary cap at all costs. Well, it cost all of us half a season—we played a 48-game schedule that year. And the next time, it cost a full season.

Early in the lockout, all the league's vice-presidents and managers were assembled in a boardroom. Gary told us we would have to accept a voluntary pay cut or start laying people off. I spoke up immediately. Hockey ops, I told him, was not going to be laying anybody off (there were only six of us), but we would take as deep a pay cut as was required. Rick Dudley spoke up next—not the Rick Dudley who played in the league and went on to work in management, but a different guy with the same name who was on the business side of the league office. He said he was worried that he would lose guys if he cut their pay, and he might actually have to give out some raises to retain his guys. There was some truth to what he was saying—"suits" have skills that are transferable between sports, so some of his people might have left. But he was willing to lay people off to protect his guys, and that annoyed me immensely.

"Who is going to be the first to go?" I challenged him. "Some single mom working in the office? If you were my teammate, I'd fight you at practice tomorrow."

We agreed to pay cuts and no layoffs.

Part of Goodenow's strategy during the lockout was to refuse to agree to meet, and then, when he did agree to a meeting, to always show up late. He would also play bait-and-switch. One of our early meetings was at the Marriott hotel at the Eaton Centre in Toronto. It was supposed to be attended by negotiating teams only—no owners or players involved.

When I got to the hotel, I went to the meeting floor first, to check things out before I went to our suite. I ran into Pat Verbeek, who had been my captain in Hartford and is a great guy. "Hey Patty," I said. He saw me, was obviously surprised and quickly slunk away while muttering something.

I peeked around the corner and looked into the meeting room. Goodenow was sitting at a table with his executive. Behind him, there were 30 or 40 players. It was a complete set-up. The NHLPA had flat-out lied to us about who would be attending the meeting, and by running into Verbeek, I had spoiled their big surprise.

I went up to our suite and told Gary what was about to happen. He didn't hesitate for a second. "Okay, it's players," was all he said, and then we marched into the room and took them on fearlessly.

Those negotiations were tense and gruelling from start to finish. We met in Boston, New York and Chicago.

The most bizarre moment of the lockout took place in Manhattan. It was 10:30 or 11 o'clock at night when we got a call at the league office. Goodenow said he was ready to make a deal and asked us to meet with him at the Plaza Hotel. Bettman, Jeff Pash and I made our way to his suite. The league was shut down and we had been negotiating for weeks, and we all felt like, finally, this might be the breakthrough.

Goodenow started rattling through the terms of this theoretical agreement.

"Free agency after seven years of service or at age 25," he said.

"What?" Gary said.

"Free agency after seven years or at age 25."

At that time, the age of free agency was 32. We hadn't agreed to anything different. That number came right out of the blue. To this day,

I have no idea what the NHLPA was thinking. Our guys were so careful in negotiations. Everything is documented. There's no way an offer like that would ever be extended casually. There would be lawyers involved.

It sounds crazy, but the truth might be that they just made it up and hoped we'd agree to it.

"I've never agreed to that," Gary said, "and I won't agree to that."

This is where things got strange. It was like an out-of-body experience. Goodenow froze. He went white. Then he grabbed the hotel phone, picked up the receiver and started frantically punching in numbers—randomly, it appeared.

"Stop the world!" he shouted. "Stop the world!"

I guess the idea was that he had told the players he could get a deal at that number, as though we had already agreed to it, and now he was acting as though we had moved the goalposts, which was absolutely untrue. Eventually, one of his guys, Bob Riley, had to take the phone away from him.

We got up and left. It was three or four in the morning, and we couldn't find a cab, so we walked back from the Plaza to the league offices. We had gone into that meeting all excited, thinking that the lockout was going to end and everyone would be going back to work. Now we were walking through the streets like a bunch of beaten dogs. No one said a word, but we were all thinking the same thing: "What the fuck? What do we do now?"

Gary is so sharp. He knew what to say: "All right, guys, it's a setback. But we haven't changed our position. We'll just keep negotiating. No one get excited. No one talk to the media. It's business as usual."

We ended up making a deal a couple of weeks later, and the season resumed in January 1995. It wasn't perfect. There was no salary cap, but there were brakes on salary escalation that we thought might work, but ultimately they didn't. The next time around, the labour war would be longer and more destructive, costing the full season and the Stanley Cup playoffs. It also cost Goodenow his job. So, in the end, it took two lockouts and many millions of dollars lost, but we got the economic system we needed.

———

In 1998, the National Hockey League participated in the Olympics for the first time. It was a tough decision to shut down the league for 17 days so that our players could go to Nagano, Japan. The owners weren't enthusiastic. But Gary felt we had to be on that stage, and he sold them on it. I became the league's advance man, making five trips to Japan before the Olympics, including when the Canucks and Mighty Ducks played a series of pre-season exhibition games there. I checked out the buildings to make sure they were up to our standards and talked to the players, giving them an idea of what to expect—and of what we expected of them.

"We don't need negativity," I told them. "The beds are going to be too short for some of you. I don't want to read about that in the papers. The food is going to be different. I don't want to read about that. Remember that you're ambassadors for the league."

Almost everything went smoothly during the Olympics. Nagano was a great experience. Everyone in Canada thinks it was a disaster because Team Canada didn't win. But the Czechs won the gold medal, and they went home and had a parade in Prague and there are kids in the league now who were inspired by that. The same holds true for Torino in 2006, which Canadians also think was a disaster because they didn't win. The Swedes won the gold, and there is a generation of Swedish players who remember watching that tournament as kids.

Being in the Olympics was a crucial part of the league's growth strategy, and I think NHL players should still be there—but only on the terms that we had in Nagano, Salt Lake City, Torino, Vancouver and Sochi. The players' contracts need to be insured and the league's risk should be mitigated. The IOC needs to charter everyone over. That didn't happen in South Korea in 2018, and that's why the NHL didn't go.

Of course, an incident happened in Nagano that many people think was a black eye for the NHL. I was in the middle of it, and I can tell you that it was wildly overstated, even though it's true that it reflected poorly on the US team and I was embarrassed as an American. But it was nothing close to what people came to believe it was.

The general rule for athletes at the Olympics is that, as soon as you lose, you get the fuck out. You clear out of the athletes' village and leave the place to those who are still competing. But after the US team got knocked out of the hockey tournament, they stuck around and had a blowout party in their rooms in the village. They made a lot of noise, and they were right next to the dorms where the Canadians were staying. Their biggest crime was they kept Canadian kids up late that night, which might have cost them a medal.

But the story that got out was that they had destroyed their rooms and offended our Japanese hosts.

As soon as we heard that something had happened, Gary, Bob Goodenow and I went to the village. We were let into the rooms to assess the damage. I wish I could show people just how "horrible" it really was.

There were some broken chairs—one of them was broken when Paul Holmgren, who was coaching the US team, sat in it. They were built to hold Japanese men, and Paul was a big guy. There were a few other broken chairs, and there were some little divots in the plaster, and some water on the floor from where someone had let off a fire extinguisher.

That was it. The damage was very slight and very limited. No big deal at all.

"I can clean this up in a half hour," I told Gary. Both Bob and Gary agreed with me, but Gary still wanted me to get to the bottom of what had happened.

I talked to the players who were in the room. They didn't have time to sync up their stories. They told me who was involved. A couple of players had too much to drink, made some noise and did some minor damage. Someone threw a bicycle over the railing and into the courtyard. All minimal stuff, but because it was the American team and everyone loves to hate the Americans, the whole thing blew up.

Gary was ready to suspend players on my recommendation. If they had really trashed the room, we would have fined them and then given the Japanese the money. But there was nothing like that, so there was no need to take any disciplinary action.

RAIMO SUMMANEN

WHEN I GOT BACK from Nagano, I knew my time working for the league was done. I had put in the five years I'd promised Gary, and now it was time to move on.

The Olympics themselves were a great experience, but that's just when it crystallized for me. I talked to Dave Nonis about it almost every night.

"I've got to get out of here," I told him. "I go to hockey games now and I don't care who wins. I just hope my officials don't screw up and I hope I don't have to suspend anyone. For a competitive guy like me to not have any skin in the game is tough."

When I got back from Japan, I told Gary I was done, that it was time for me to work for a team again. He wouldn't let me rush into it.

"Go to Florida for a couple of days," he said. "Go fishing. Drink some beer. And then decide. But if you come back and tell me that you're leaving, I will start looking for your replacement immediately. This isn't a place where you can shop for jobs and then come back to me on July 1 and tell me you're coming back for another year. I'm not doing that."

I went down to Tampa with Nonis and we chartered a fishing boat. The skipper called me the night before to tell me there was going to be really bad weather offshore, and suggested we cancel the trip. I told him I wanted to go anyway. I didn't care if I got sick.

"Sure," the skipper said. "Why don't you come down to the dock at six in the morning? I will fire up the engines so that you can breathe some diesel fumes. I'll cut up some bait and throw it at you. I'll rock the boat until you puke, and that way, you'll have an idea of what the trip is going to be like before we set out."

"Okay," I said. "I'll stay home."

Fishing or no fishing, the time in Florida didn't change my mind. I returned to New York and told Gary I was leaving. I had to go somewhere where I could care about wins and losses.

An expansion team, in Atlanta, was joining the league the following season. I'd always wanted to work to build a franchise from scratch. I met with Harvey Schiller, the president of the Thrashers, while the NHLPA was having a meeting in Atlanta. He showed me some of the things they were planning, including their uniforms (I told him he had to change the pattern on their socks, because the way they had it, it would hide the puck too much from the goalie).

"Where are you on this search for a GM?" I asked him. "I gave you three references, and you haven't talked to any of them. I think you've already got your guy in mind, and you're making a mistake if it's not me. I told you to talk to Bettman, I told you to talk to Lou Lamoriello and I told you to talk to Pat Quinn. I've talked to them all since—you haven't called them. I'd like you to call them before you make your decision."

Harvey promised he would.

In the meantime, I got a call from the Vancouver Canucks. They had fired Pat, and they asked me to meet with Stan McCammon, owner John McCaw's right-hand man. (McCaw had purchased the team from the Griffiths family.) I met with Stan at the Plaza Hotel in New York during the Stanley Cup final. Gary told me that, out of respect for the league, I couldn't announce that I was going anywhere until after the playoffs were finished.

McCammon was very honest. He said the team was swimming in red ink. In the fiscal year that was just wrapping up, it had lost $36 million. The parent company's stock was publicly traded, so that number was absolutely real. They didn't manufacture it. The season-ticket base had shrunk to about 9,000. "It's a big job," he said. "You have to understand that if you come here, this is a financial disaster that you will have to fix."

The meeting went very well, and a few days later, Stan called and told me that they planned to offer me the job. I told them I wasn't going to accept anything until I had met the owner in person. Other than at league meetings, I had never laid eyes on John McCaw, and I had learned from my experience in Hartford that knowing the owner and knowing his intentions was an absolute necessity.

Washington, coached by Ronnie Wilson, and Detroit were meeting in the finals that year. The Red Wings wound up sweeping the Capitals to win the Cup. I flew out to Seattle between Games 3 and 4 to meet with McCaw.

He was out on a catamaran that day, and they asked me to go to the marina and wait for him to return. He was late getting back, I had a flight to catch that night and it was hot and rainy. Here I was, sitting on a fucking dock in Seattle in a three-piece suit, soaked to the skin. Finally, McCaw's boat arrived, and I climbed on board. I'll never forget that first meeting. John had ruptured his Achilles tendon and his leg was in a cast. He had a little clicker in his hand, and every time he clicked it, a servant would appear and ask, "What do you need, Mr. McCaw?"

"Getting summoned with a clicker's not part of *my* job, is it?" I asked him.

The interview lasted for about an hour. He asked me why I wanted to meet him, and I explained that I wouldn't take a job working for someone I didn't know. He told me how his family had made its money, and how his brother Craig was kind of the brains of the outfit. They had sold their cellular business to AT&T for something like eight billion dollars. So money wasn't going to be an issue.

I laid out my vision for him. I explained how my teams play and how I was going to attack the financial losses. "We are going to run this team like a business, which you haven't done before. We are going to play a style that is entertaining—and with Mike Keenan coaching, you haven't been doing that. And we're going to be more active in the community than the next two teams combined."

My three pillars. He seemed to like that.

I remember that the flight back east from Seattle was really rough. When I got to the rink, Gary asked me how it had gone.

"Good," I said. "I think they're going to offer me the job."

"Not until after the finals," Gary reminded me.

The Red Wings wrapped up the Cup the next night. When I got back to my hotel room, the red message light on my phone was flashing. It was Steve Bellringer, the president of McCaw's company, Orca Bay, telling me they were going to make me a formal offer at 10 o'clock the next morning and to be sure I was available to answer the phone.

I got up early and went for a run. I have always found Washington to be a very confusing city to navigate. And I got lost. I was late getting back to my room, and when I opened the door, I saw that the fucking message light was on. I'd missed the call.

I called them back immediately.

"Thank God," Steve said. "We thought you were somewhere negotiating with Atlanta."

"No," I said. "They haven't made an offer yet. Right now, it's just you and me, but that could change."

We made a deal over the phone.

The plan was for me to fly to Seattle the next day and drive up to Vancouver—that way, I could avoid having to deal with any reporters who might have staked out the airport.

Gary called me the next day on my way to Vancouver.

"How come you won't call Harvey Schiller back?" he asked. "He said he's left you a bunch of messages."

That's when I told Gary that I was about to take the Vancouver job.

"I think Atlanta is willing to offer you more," he said. "And you'd be closer to your kids."

"It doesn't matter," I told him. "I made a deal."

We held the press conference and then I went back to New York to tie up any loose ends at the league office. From there, it was off to Buffalo for my first draft as the general manager of the Vancouver Canucks. That's where I ran into the guy I had inherited as head coach: Mike Keenan.

I was first exposed to Mike when I was in the agent business. He won a Calder Cup with the Rochester Americans of the AHL, and it was one of the best-coached teams I've ever seen. They executed all their systems beautifully, they changed lines on time, they did everything right. If you were evaluating their coach, you would give him straight A's. And Keenan was a great coach in the NHL early in his career. He won a Cup with the New York Rangers. But he's not my style of coach, and his teams didn't play my style of hockey. And later in his career, his ego took over and he started bullying people. By the time I got him in Vancouver, he was no good.

We were having our pre-draft scouting meetings when Mike asked if we could have a minute to talk. We headed up to his room.

"Have you looked at my contract?" he asked.

"Mike, I've been on the job for four days. I've been in New York. So, no, I haven't looked at your contract."

"Well, you should," he said. "Because it says in that contract that I have input on player personnel decisions."

"I know," I said. "They told me that. And have you looked at *my* contract?"

"How the fuck would I see your contract?"

"Well, you should," I said. "Because it says that I hire and fire the coach. So, you've got two choices when I leave this room. You can call the owner in Seattle and bitch. Or you can try to make this work. For my part, I'm going to try to make this work with you."

I left the room. He immediately called Seattle.

So, the clock was ticking from day one. He had no interest in working with me.

Stan McCammon begged me to work with Mike. "We brought him here because he's a big-name coach. He talked Mark Messier into coming here. We want you to try and make it work. We would like you to move heaven and earth to get along with Keenan. It will look bad if we fire a coach that we brought in with so much fanfare."

"I will try my hardest," I said, honestly, "but I'm not predicting good things."

And I did try. That first summer, we went through the expansion draft. Mike wanted to protect Peter Zezel and I wanted to protect Scotty Walker.

"I need Zezel," Mike said.

"You don't need Zezel. You're talking about the Zezel of four years ago. Scott Walker can play forward, he can play defence. He's tough—and we're going to get tougher, Mike. My teams are tougher than yours are. Scotty Walker is a Brian Burke player."

Mike wouldn't budge, so I called Seattle and asked them what they wanted me to do. I knew this was just the first of what would be a constant string of tests.

"Let Mike have his way on this one," I was advised.

So, I did, but I knew it was a big mistake. We let Walker go, and he ended up being a much better player than Zezel was at that point in his career. I was sick over it. But I took one for the team—or, more accurately, for the owners.

That first summer back in Vancouver, I personally called every season-ticket holder who had given up their subscriptions over the last two years. I started with the ones who'd had four seats, then the ones with two seats. I talked to probably 700 different people, trying to persuade them to renew. And I heard the same thing over and over again. "We like you, Brian. But you [meaning the organization] fired Pat Quinn. You traded away Trevor Linden, the most popular player in the history of the franchise. And you've got Mike Keenan behind the bench. We're not coming back."

That went on for weeks. At the same time I was trying to make trades to improve the team, I was driving to Surrey to meet with people like the guys from Lafarge Construction and try to talk them into keeping their luxury suite. I'd tell them what our plans were, tell them how we intended to turn the team around.

Eventually, the hard work paid off. In ballpark numbers, I steadily reduced the team's losses from $36 million, and the fourth year we broke even.

On the balance sheet, it was one of the greatest turnarounds in the history of professional sports.

The other thing that happened that summer in Vancouver was that I met my second wife, Jennifer Mather.

The first time I ran into her, I was going into CKNW to do a radio interview. She was in the newsroom, and we said hi to each other. Jennifer was already a well-respected media person in the city by then, but I didn't know her at all.

Not long after that, I was fishing with Dan Russell and Scott Woodgate, and they told me I should ask Jennifer Mather out.

"Who's Jennifer Mather?" I asked them.

They helped me put two and two together. In general, I don't like blind dates—maybe because I've had very poor luck with them. But they told me that Jennifer was separated, and they encouraged me to ask her out.

"Why would she go out with me?" I asked them. "She's beautiful."

Finally, I got up the nerve to do it. We went out and we immediately hit it off. But for a long time, we kept our relationship under wraps—Jennifer was famous in her own right, but aside from the players and other people around the team, nobody knew about us. That changed when we went to Sweden with the team for training camp the next year. One afternoon, we took a boat tour to see some Viking ruins, and then we took a team picture. Jennifer and I were both in the picture. The next day, the *Vancouver Province* ran the photo with the two of us circled and the caption "Swede-Hearts." So, the story was out.

After my first divorce, but before I met Jennifer, I was visiting my brother Bill in Chicago. We were sitting at his kitchen table, drinking beer, and I told him straight up that I was never going to get married again. And then I met Jennifer—and I was getting married. We had the ceremony in the Bahamas, and the only people there were my four kids.

We had some great years together, and two wonderful kids. Then the strain of the job took its toll. I'll take full blame for the job and my kids coming ahead of my marriage. That job puts a real strain on a lot of marriages—especially the losing part.

In the end, it just didn't work out. We still get along great. I'm happy to say that we are good friends, we still do stuff together with our girls, and we take our parenting responsibilities very seriously.

Back to that first season as the general manager in Vancouver.

Markus Naslund asked if we could have a meeting. He hadn't yet become the great player that he would, and he was hardly playing because Keenan hated him. I had a pretty strong sense that he was going to come in and ask me to trade him.

There have been a few instances when young players have demanded that I trade them and I've told them to fuck off. I told them something along the lines of "You're on your first contract. We don't know what you're going to be, but we're not quitting on you this soon, so shut up and keep playing."

But with veteran players, my view has always been that when they ask for a trade, you trade the player. If a player tells me he doesn't want to put on the sweater anymore, he's going, and he's probably not playing another game for us. I'd rather have him sit in the press box until I can deal him. That was Pat Quinn's rule, too—once a guy says he doesn't want to be here, you get rid of him, and you take the first trade that makes sense.

I didn't want to trade Markus. I could see how much potential was there. So when he came into my office and closed the door, I cut him off before he could make a sound.

"Don't say anything," I said. "Don't say a word. Because I have a feeling I know what you're going to say—and once you say those words, I will trade you. I don't want to trade you. I think you're going to be a really good hockey player. The coach isn't playing you. He hates your guts. So we need to figure this out.

"You're going to be here a lot longer than Keenan is going to be here. I want you to be part of the solution once we figure out the coaching situation.

"But Markus, you're fucking stealing money right now. You're not working hard enough. You're not scoring goals. You're not backchecking. You're a liability defensively.

"I will commit to you being part of the solution, but you've got to give me something back. You're playing like a piece of shit and you should be our leading scorer."

Markus told me later that he went home that day and sat down at his kitchen table with his wife, Lotta, who is both beautiful and really nice.

"He's right," he said. "I'm not keeping up my end of this."

They talked about it as a couple. And the next day, everything was different—the practices were better, the games were better. He was a different player. He played another nine years in Vancouver and he was a star. But I had to hit him with a shovel right between the eyes to get him going.

And of course, it never would have worked out that way if Mike Keenan were still the coach.

The experiment with Keenan and me was doomed to failure because he was never going to work as part of a tandem. He had to be the only horse in the race. He had to be the boss.

Mike's got a very charming side to him. He can fool you. The code in hockey is that you're nice to everyone's family. When my kids would come in to visit, he couldn't have been kinder to them. But he's a chameleon who thrives on conflict. You know those insurance commercials with the mayhem guy? That's Mike. If things are going well, he'll start a fight.

The way he manages a team is by picking out a couple of guys and bullying them. That's what he did to Trevor Linden in Vancouver before they finally traded him. I told Mike that that wasn't how my team was going to operate. I wanted a family atmosphere. But he couldn't—or wouldn't—change. He stayed true to his nature. Mike eventually self-destructs by tearing the dressing room apart.

And it's not like he's a tactical genius. Technically, his practices were like hockey school drills—rudimentary stuff. They were fucking hard—his teams are in shape, and his players finish all their checks, even the skill guys. They work hard and they're hard to play against. But all he had were those seven simple drills, and he never practised the power play. You look at how complex practices are these days. We were back in the '50s with Mike.

One time, I went to him and told him I wanted him to practise the power play.

"We don't practise the power play," Mike said.

"I know," I said, "and it sucks. So, tomorrow we are practising the power play."

The next day, he called the players together and said, "Management says we have to practise the power play, so we're practising the power play."

And they did. For two minutes. Then he went back to his usual drills.

I was sitting there in the rink, watching as my own head coach symbolically gave me the finger.

My only regret when I finally fired Keenan was that I had told him I would give him a chance to work with any players we got back in a trade for Pavel Bure, and it didn't work out that way.

When it came to dealing Bure, I didn't have any choice. He came in to see me with his agent, Mike Gillis, before training camp, and they both told me unequivocally that he wasn't going to play for us again, that he would hold out until we traded him.

I guess I was breaking my own rule, to a degree, because at first I tried to talk him out of it, reminding him of our history together.

"I got you out of your contract with Red Army," I told him. "I drove you across the border. You owe me more than this."

"Burkie, it's not about you," he said. "I do owe you. But the way this organization has treated me, there are things that can't be fixed."

"Tell me what they are," I said, "and I'll try to fix them."

"No," Pavel said. "They can't be fixed and I'm not playing."

There were other things Pavel didn't like about playing in Vancouver—he had no privacy; photographers were stalking him outside his apartment, and gossip followed him around. There were rumours of ties to the Russian mafia. Never once was this verified. I think he wanted to get out of Canada and go to a place where hockey stars don't have to deal with that.

But his big issues went back to a story that came out during the 1994 Stanley Cup final suggesting that Bure had gone to management and said he wouldn't play in the playoffs unless he was given a contract extension.

I have no reason to believe that was true—and if a player ever did that to me, I would have sat him out, no matter how good he was. Pat Quinn would have done the same thing.

But the problem was that the Canucks never really went out of their way to deny the story.

I asked Pat later if there was any truth to it.

"Of course not," he said. "If a player said that to me, I wouldn't have put him on the ice."

"So, why didn't you angrily refute it?"

"I didn't think it was anyone's business," Pat said, and that was that.

Pat was great when it came to defending his players in the media. He always had their backs. But in that case, I guess he thought that the story was so false, so outrageous, that he wasn't going to dignify it with a response—and in the end, that was part of what cost the team Bure.

If I wasn't going to talk him out of demanding a trade, I was going to at least try to protect our interests as best I could.

"Pavel," I told him, "if you hold out, I still won't be able to deal you until January, because there won't be a GM desperate enough to give me what I need until we're that far into the season. That would mean you wouldn't play at all for three months. I'll make you a deal. You come in and play the first two months for us, and if I haven't made a trade by the first of December, then you can hold out. If you're playing, I have a way better chance of getting value."

"No," he said. "I'm not playing."

So we started the season without him.

Early in the year, we were playing a game at Maple Leaf Gardens. Keenan wasn't happy that he didn't have Pavel, and he wasn't thrilled about the players who were available to him. But he knew the deal, and he knew I wasn't going to trade Bure until I could get something close to fair value for him.

I was sitting in a box with Dave Nonis, watching the first period. We were down 3–1 a couple minutes into the third period when I noticed that our goalie, Garth Snow, was on the bench. Our net was empty.

"Davey," I said, "what's going on? The referee doesn't have his arm up. There's no delayed penalty."

"No," Dave said. "It looks like Mike just pulled him."

Keenan was trying to show me up. We played with an empty net for a full minute, though somehow the Leafs didn't score.

"When they blow the whistle, every camera in this building is going to be on you and me," I told Dave. "So let's act like we don't have a care in the world. Act nonchalant."

That's exactly how it went. The cameras found us during the break in the action, and people watching the game on television saw Dave and me smiling and chatting away as though nothing unusual had happened. In reality, I was thinking that I couldn't wait to get downstairs and kick the shit out of Keenan.

A few minutes later, we were on the power play, and Keenan did it again. This time, Dmitri Yushkevich scored by banking the puck off the boards from his own blue line to make it 4–1.

After the game, I confronted Keenan.

"What the fuck was that stunt?"

"You've got to get rid of Bure and get me some fucking players so we have a chance to win," Mike said.

"Two things, Mike," I said. "One, I'm going to trade Pavel Bure when I can get value for him. I told you when he held out that it would take until January to trade him. I need a GM who's desperate, and I don't have one yet. I'll trade him at the right time.

"And the second thing: if you ever pull a goalie again in the middle of a game other than on a delayed penalty, I'm going to come down to the bench and beat you within an inch of your life in front of the crowd and the players and everyone else. I'm going to throw you down the hallway. I'm going to coach the rest of the game myself and I'm going to fire your ass as soon as it's over."

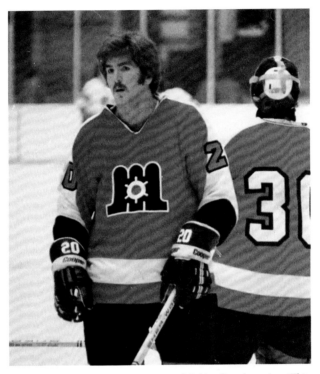

1977–78 Maine Mariners, great team and Calder Cup champions! This is my reward for lots of hard work: my tenth year of playing hockey.

People will judge you in large part by your family. I am lucky to have had six great kids. Family time is always important, especially travelling with your kids.

Two tours of duty in Vancouver. No grey hair in the first photo, tie properly tied. The twins were the product of the hardest I ever worked on a trade in all my years in the NHL. What great kids!

One of my best breaks. Working for the Big Irishman, Pat Quinn. Smart, tough, fair and an innovator. What a wonderful mentor! He is sorely missed.

Reaching the summit of Mt. Everest! June 2007, what a wonderful team of players and coaches. The best professional year of my life!

Ron Wilson, my friend, teammate and my coach for a while in Toronto. Toronto took its toll on Ron, and I had to make a change. Dion was a great captain and a warrior. We could have had a good run together.

I was lucky to have three great mentors: Lou Lamoriello, Pat Quinn and this guy, Gary Bettman. The National Hockey League has turned into a powerhouse due entirely to Gary's leadership. Brilliant man, great executive and an even better person.

My last skate with Brendan, Fenway Park, January 2010. Brendan was a great gift to the LGBTQ community. He certainly opened my eyes to the cause, and he has changed and improved lives all across North America. Pride Parade in Toronto! Eight was his special number!

On the left, holding me, is my mom, a great, sweet lady. And five of my six wonderful kids: Patrick, Molly, Gracie, Katie and Mairin. I am so proud of all of them!

There wasn't really any coming back from that with Mike. I wanted him gone and the players wanted him gone. The owners didn't want to pay him out, but there was no way the situation could continue.

We finally traded Bure to the Florida Panthers on January 17, 1999. The deal actually started to come together at the World Juniors, which were held in Winnipeg that year. I was sharing a cab with Bryan Murray, who was running the Panthers.

"I need a superstar," he told me. "We're dying at the gate."

"Well, I've got a superstar," I said. "So, let's talk."

In theory, I was willing to wait until March to get a reasonable deal. But we were losing games that we could have won if we had Bure in the lineup, and it was time to make a move. I was mad at Pavel by the time I traded him because of what he was doing to our team. It was as though we had a nuclear weapon that we couldn't use.

In the end, I'll admit I didn't get full value—not even close—but it was the best I could do. We got defenceman Eddie Jovanovski, who had been the first overall pick in '94; Mike Brown, a tough guy; Dave Gagner; goalie Kevin Weekes; and a first-rounder. We sent Brent Hedican, Brad Ference and a third-round pick the other way along with Bure.

Now we were heading into the All-Star break in Tampa, and it was time to make the coaching change. Not that I have a lot of sympathy for Keenan, but I will admit that it was really unfortunate for him the way it all played out.

The day before the game, Gary Mason, who was then a columnist for the *Vancouver Sun*, sat down with me and we drank a couple of beers together.

"For tomorrow's column," Gary said, "I'm writing that you've got to fire Mike Keenan before we come out of the break and that you ought to hire Marc Crawford. There are two or three other teams looking at Crawford, and if you don't hire him now, you're going to lose him.

"But before I write that, I need you to tell me if I'm way off base. I don't want to look like an idiot."

"You're not way off base," I told him, "but I haven't fired Mike yet. It's not fair if he reads it in a newspaper first."

Gary went ahead and wrote the column. He didn't quote me, and he proposed the Crawford hiring as though it was his idea, but a lot of people read it and assumed I had tipped him off. (Gary is a good guy, and a smart guy, and I like him, but I didn't talk to him for a long time after that.)

What Gary didn't know was that I was way ahead of him. I already had Crawford stashed in a Tampa hotel under an assumed name.

(The name was Raimo Summanen, which was a bit of an in-joke between me and Marc. Marc had been an assistant coach with our Fredericton farm team, and Raimo was one of his players. He was the kind of guy who would tell the coaches he didn't feel like playing in a Friday night game, but that he might deign to play on the Saturday. Raimo was driving them nuts. But for some reason, when I arrived to watch the team, he assumed I was there to bring him back to Vancouver. "Burkie, I am so glad to see you," he said. "Because these fucking guys—"

I stopped him right there. "Raimo," I said, "I'm sure you're wondering what your future is, but right now I'm trying to decide whether or not to punch you in the fucking head." Then there was silence. And then I really laid into him. Hence, the alias.)

The next day, Gary's column came out.

Keenan called me, frantic and furious, wondering what was going on. "I'll talk to you when I get back," I told him. "I'm not doing this over the phone."

By the time I got back to Vancouver and fired him, everyone in the world already knew what was happening. I had flown back on a commercial flight with Crawford, and people saw us together. Mike was furious.

"I'm sorry that happened," I told him, "but I'm making the change."

Marc Crawford did an amazing job coaching that team. Crow was good with the young players, he was good with the veterans, he was good with the media. He did an excellent job and the team just kept getting better.

And my life got so much better, minus a coach who spent all his time complaining, undermining my authority and picking on players.

One guy I knew might not be thrilled with the coaching change was Mark Messier.

People are constantly asking me what Messier was like in Vancouver, and I tell them that I've got all the time in the world for him. He was a leader for us. He did everything a captain should do. And he was a really good player—not a star anymore, but he was still an amazing athlete.

Keenan was Mess's guy. They won a Cup together in New York in 1994, and Keenan was a big part of the reason Mark decided to sign with the Canucks as a free agent.

Not long after I fired Keenan, I called Mess in to talk. The trade deadline was approaching, and our team wasn't going anywhere that season. I offered to send him somewhere where he would have a chance to win another championship.

"Burkie," he said, "I came here to do a job. The job's not done. I don't want to go anywhere else. I made a pledge to Mr. McCaw and I want to see some success here before I go."

I thought that was admirable.

As the end of that season approached, he was seriously thinking about retiring. I met him at a place in Yaletown and told him to take a couple of days off, go somewhere warm and think about it some more—we'd tell the press that he'd pulled a groin or something so he'd have cover.

"You've got lots of hockey left," I told him. "Don't make this mistake. Don't retire now. You're making six million a year. You've got this year and another left on your deal. Don't retire now."

He took some time, thought about it, and decided he wanted to keep playing.

Let me tell you another Mess story.

Kevin Weekes, who came over in the Bure trade, was a backup goalie on our team, and let's just say he wasn't the most popular guy in the dressing room.

Our starter was hurt, so Weekes was in net and we called up a kid named Alfie Michaud from our farm team in Syracuse to back him up. But we had no plans to put Alfie anywhere near the net.

The game started, and about six minutes in, Weekes started shaking his knee as though he'd hurt something. Then he skated over to the bench. Everyone on the team knew he was pulling the chute.

(It wasn't the first time we'd had an issue with him. There was a prior incident when Weekes had shown up late for a game and claimed it was because he had been robbed at knifepoint. His story was full of holes. None of his teammates believed him, and neither did I.)

Our trainer, Mike Burnstein, met him at the bench door.

"No fucking way, Weekesie," he said. "Get the fuck back out there."

"But I felt a tweak in my knee," Weekes said.

Burnstein didn't move an inch. "Get the fuck back out there," he said. "There's no way you're making this kid go in."

"I felt a tweak," Weekes said again. "I want to get it looked at."

Finally, Burnstein relented, Weekes went to the dressing room to get his "injured" knee looked at and Alfie came into the game. He tried to have a drink from his water bottle before play started, but he was so nervous that he started shaking like a leaf and poured the water all over his head.

Mess skated over to him.

"Look, kid," he said, "you do your best and we'll do what we can for you."

We lost the game, 4–1, but it wasn't Alfie's fault. We weren't very good, and it was just another losing night in what turned out to be a losing season.

After the game, Weekes went to the trainer and told him that, miraculously, his knee was feeling a whole lot better.

"Oh, no," Burnstein said. "You're going through all the tests, starting with an MRI."

Burnstein was going to do his best to torture him.

I was sitting in Crow's office, having a beer after the game, when there was a knock at the door. It was Mess.

"Burkie, can I talk to you for a minute?" he asked.

I went back into the training room, where he had kicked everyone else out. Then he closed the door behind us. Mess was stripped to the waist and he still had his skates on, so he was towering over me. He leaned in with that look in his eyes.

"Trade him or I'll fucking kill him," he said, and then walked out.

So needless to say, I traded Kevin Weekes. Kevin has gone on to a great broadcasting career, and we get along just fine.

Later that season, coming up on the trade deadline, we had a decision to make again. We had an option with Mess for a fourth year at $6 million. If we didn't pick up the option, we owed him a million bucks in a buyout.

We weren't good enough to justify bringing him back. Plus, we had the Sedin twins on the horizon and the West Coast Express Line (Markus Naslund, Brendan Morrison and Todd Bertuzzi) was coming together, so we had other guys we were going to have to pay. We needed that money.

I called Mess into my office two weeks before the trade deadline, told him we weren't going to pick up his option and asked him if he wanted a trade to a contender.

"Nope," he said once again. "I came here to do a job, and the job is not done."

The next year, he went back to the Rangers and played another four seasons for them. I have lots of respect for Mess.

CROSS-COUNTRY DAD

WHEN I TOOK THE Vancouver job, I took my kids out for lunch and promised them that, despite the distance, they were not going to lose one day with their dad. In my divorce agreement, I had them every other weekend. I told them we would keep the same schedule.

"You're really going to come back here every other weekend from Vancouver?" they asked me. I said yes—and I kept that promise. For the 11 years I was in Vancouver and Anaheim, until my four older children had all graduated from high school, I flew back to Boston every other weekend, no matter what.

I bought a house in Boston so that we would have a home base. Kids with divorced parents hate a long commute. I wanted to have a place close enough that if they forgot a schoolbook or a toothbrush, they could run over to their mom's house and get it.

I was pretty broke at the time. I remember that I approached the lady who was selling the house and told her I could give her 10 grand now, and if I couldn't get financing in six months, she could keep the money. I eventually got the financing, bought the house, fixed it up and then sold it when I found a condo even closer to where the kids lived.

It didn't matter what was going on with my teams. I always made the trip, and I paid for every flight myself. I missed a playoff game in Vancouver one year because my ex-wife wouldn't switch weekends with me, and I was in Boston with my kids, watching the game on television, the night that Marty McSorley hit Donald Brashear over the head with his stick.

My first couple of years in Vancouver, the travel was relatively simple because Air Canada had a non-stop flight to Boston. I'd try to see a game somewhere in the Northeast on the Thursday night and then pick up the kids from school on Friday and drop them off on Sunday night. When they dropped the direct flight, I had to fly through Toronto, switching terminals and clearing customs before connecting to Boston. All that flying probably took years off my life, but I wouldn't change a thing.

The point is, when all is said and done, who is going to come to your funeral, and what are they going to say? Do you think they're going to talk about how much money you made? Not a chance. They are going to talk about whether you were a good brother or good sister or good father or good friend. Did you do charitable work? Did you make a difference?

It's not about cars and country clubs and expensive vacations. The only thing that really matters is that you loved your kids, that you showed them that, and that you made a difference where you lived.

This is probably a good time to tell you more about them—my four kids from my first marriage and my two younger daughters from my second marriage. You'll note that they all have Gaelic names—and I'm not sure what it means, but I correctly identified the sex of all six of my children before they were born. I got them all right.

I'm really proud of them. The older ones graduated from university with no debt. They've all got my work ethic. They've all got my skills in the classroom. I think I did the right things as a dad and it paid off.

Katie, my oldest, is a lot like me—though she's a much nicer person, with a lot more personality. She's brilliant, beautiful, smart and intense. And she's tough as nails—tough, but fair. Katie was a junior in high school when my ex-wife moved the kids back to Boston after we split. She went to a new school, the Ursuline Academy, and the girls there were so mean to her, but she couldn't have cared less. She dated the star quarterback from the Xaverian Brothers school and she played three sports. She's super-intense and super-competitive. Katie was the first player off the bench in basketball—and she was just a goon. She would come in and take on the best player on the other team and just run her over. She wound up in foul trouble almost every time, even though she was only playing half the game. In volleyball and softball, she was a star.

She played hurt, she played when she was sick. I never missed a game in college hockey in the four years I was at Providence, and Katie is just like that. I'm proud to say she's a lot like me. But there's one way that we're very different: I'm a person who can sit and read for hours. Katie can't do that. She can't sit still. She's always moving and doing something.

She works harder at maintaining her friendships than anyone I've ever seen. Her friends from high school are still her friends today. After graduation, she went to Bates College, where she played volleyball for four years and was the captain the last two. Then she got her MBA from MIT. She's got a high-powered job now with a hotshot ad agency and PR firm, is making a great living and lives in downtown Boston in the shadow of Fenway Park.

My son Patrick started playing hockey when I was in Vancouver. He was not big and he was not physical, but he was tough and he was smart. Patrick also played Little League baseball, and I remember the dad who managed the team telling me it was really Patrick who was the manager. He was the catcher, and he would step out from behind the plate and bark orders at the other players.

On the first day he started playing hockey at Xaverian Brothers High School, I went to his practice to meet his coach.

"Hello," I said. "Do you know who I am?"

"Yes, Mr. Burke," the coach said. "I know who you are."

"This is my son. If he ever gives you a hard time, punch him in the head as hard as you can and then call me."

Even though he was a thinking athlete, and in general a really smart guy, Patrick didn't apply himself in school. He was the exact opposite of Katie that way. He did the bare minimum, got a B-plus average, and was happy with it. He was a popular student. The only time he really

CROSS-COUNTRY DAD   **161**

got in trouble in high school was for a fist fight. They were at a school dance, but he and the other guy went off the school grounds before they fought. The school still suspended him. I remember talking to Brother Dan, who ran the school, and bringing up that point, and he told me that even if the incident didn't violate the letter of their rules, it violated the spirit. Fair enough, I said.

After graduation, Patrick went to Notre Dame University. Dave Poulin was the hockey coach there then, and he was helpful in getting Patrick in. They put him in Alumni Hall, which at that time was the hardest-drinking dorm on campus, and he got in with a bunch of kids from Chicago who thought their mission was to party as hard and as often as they could. Those big football schools are different. Weekends when the team is home are just one big drunk.

Patrick was doing just okay in his classes. After his second year, he told me he thought he wanted to work in hockey.

"You sure don't look like you want to work in hockey," I said to him. "Look at your grades."

"I'm serious," Patrick insisted.

"Okay," I said, "if you're really serious, here's what your weekends are going to look like for the next two years: Friday night, you're going to be scouting a game at Michigan State. Saturday night, you'll be at Bowling Green. No more hanging around with your buddies and drinking all weekend. Now you're going to work."

He agreed to that. I paid him a hundred bucks a night, out of my own pocket. I was in Anaheim by then, but I wasn't going to put him on the team payroll.

"I'm paying you," I told him. "Don't let me down."

To his everlasting credit, he got right into it, sitting down with our scouts and learning how to grade players. When you're a rookie scout, you tend to grade players too high. I did the same thing when I scouted for the Flyers early on. The first game I saw, I was giving everyone sixes (the highest mark) for their skating when they were really threes—you have to grade them as potential pros, not as college players. Patrick made that adjustment and started giving us really valuable information on the kids he went to watch. And his grades in school came up.

He was doing really well until he hit a big bump in the road in his senior year.

One day, I got a call from my ex-wife telling me that she thought Patrick was struggling, and that I should go see him as soon as possible. It didn't make sense to me—his grades were good, his work was good. Still, I went to South Bend and took him out for dinner, just to make sure he was all right.

"Your mom called me about you—and you know she hardly talks to me. She's worried."

"Dad," Patrick said, "I'm okay. Don't worry about me."

I phoned my ex on the drive back to the airport in Chicago and told her that Patrick was fine.

The next morning, he couldn't get out of bed.

I will be the first to admit that I didn't know much about depression. I knew it was serious from everything veteran linesman Pat Dapuzzo went through when he worked for me at the NHL. Pat suffered from depression. But I did not really know this illness. My first reaction was that you should get your shit together and get out of bed and get on with your life. My point of view wasn't transformed overnight, but it was pretty close to overnight because this was my own kid and I could see how he was suffering. When I started to understand the disease, I understood just how insensitive I had been. I got on the internet, trying to find out everything I could about depression. I didn't realize how debilitating a disease it could be. People can be completely incapacitated, and suicide is a real risk. (We eventually found an excellent psychologist in Boston who got Patrick on medication, got him into therapy and then got him off medication.)

Patrick had to leave school halfway through his final term. He was just weeks away from exams. When he got home, he wasn't even able to do basic household chores.

One of the things I kept reading about was that physical fitness could play a positive role in battling depression. Patrick had always worked out, and I tried to encourage him to start again.

"Dad, I can't get out of bed most days," he told me.

I helped him come up with a plan.

"Tomorrow, you're going to walk to the end of the street—that's about 200 yards—and you're going to walk back. The next day you're going to go as far as the church—that's another 75 yards."

The exercise really helped him. Later, I'd encourage him to read a book and to go to the odd Bruins game with me. He had great support from his mother, and from his brother and sisters. I told him I loved him and that I would be there for him whenever he needed me. And eventually, he got well. He's become a tremendous advocate for mental health issues. He'll talk to anyone about it.

Patrick had to go back and complete his final term in the fall. After graduation, he got a full-ride scholarship to the New England School of Law. He also scouted for the Flyers six nights a week while he was in law school. After he got his law degree, he applied for a job in the NHL's Department of Player Safety. Brendan Shanahan, who was running the department then, talked to me.

"I want you to know that I'm interviewing your son, but I'm not hiring him unless he's a good fit," Shanny said. "As far as I'm concerned, his last name doesn't matter."

"That's the only way I want you to hire him," I said.

They hired Patrick on the spot, and he still works for the league. And we welcomed the lovely Caiti Donovan into our family when she and Patrick got married.

We go fishing together. We hunt together. When you're a dad, your daughters are special to you, but as your boys get older, they become your pals. For me, Patrick is more like a friend, a buddy.

I remember a day when I went hunting with Patrick and his brother Brendan at a club near Vancouver. The wind was blowing hard and the rain was pouring down. Brendan and Patrick each knocked down a couple of ducks. We were walking back to the clubhouse, and I heard Brendan and Patrick talking behind me.

"This is the best day of my fucking life," Brendan said.

And he was right. It doesn't get better than that.

———

I'm going to skip ahead here and talk about my other daughters.

Molly, the youngest child from my first marriage, is like her brother Brendan on steroids. She is sweet and beautiful, and she wants to make everyone around her happy. She will do anything for anybody.

When Molly was very young and I was working for the league, she was in the room when I was talking to Bettman. I always called Gary "Boss"—I still do to this day. "What does 'boss' mean?" she asked me. I told her that it meant Gary told me what to do. "So then I guess you're like my boss," Molly said. She's called me Boss ever since.

Molly was a very good athlete in high school, and she's really smart. After graduation, she wanted to go to Bowdoin College, a terrific school in Maine. The hockey coach there was a friend of mine. We visited the campus and were driving back when Molly said to me, "I love it, but I don't want to go there."

"Why not?" I asked her.

"Because I don't know if I can get in without your help, and I want to get in on my own merits."

I told her that all I could do for her was move her application from a bigger pile to a smaller pile—the same thing I did for Patrick at Notre Dame.

"I'm not going to give them any money, and I'm not going to make any phone calls," I promised.

In the end, she was accepted, went to Bowdoin and had a great experience there. You've got to pick a school where you're going to be comfortable and happy, the way I did with Providence College. It's really hard to do well academically if you're not happy. Molly had four great years at Bowdoin and loved every minute of it.

She works for Tripadvisor in Boston now. She'll always be a successful businesswoman because she's so smart and she gets along with everyone. She's the first person in to work every day and the last to leave.

My two younger daughters from my second marriage are Mairin and Fiona Grace—Gracie for short.

Mairin received the award as the top student in her class at Bishop Strachan School in Toronto last year. She's a very diligent kid, and really organized. Her room is neat. Her time-management skills are those of a 20-year-old and she's only 15.

And she's a sweet, beautiful kid.

Gracie is much more social. She reminds me in a lot of ways of Brendan. She is beautiful and extremely bright and she wants everyone to be happy around her. She loves music and loves to sing. She has her mom's gift—my second wife, Jennifer, can listen to a song once and then sing it note for note.

When Gracie was in the first or second grade, I would walk her to school, and the sixth- and seventh-grade kids would holler out, "Hi Gracie!" Everybody knew her.

They are wonderful kids, and I have been so blessed.

And Brendan . . .

He was born on December 8, 1988, and weighed eight pounds, eight ounces—all eights. It turns out that eight is a lucky number in Chinese culture. When he was in hospital after he was born, all the Chinese nurses would come over to him and rub his head.

"Very lucky baby," they would say.

From an early age, Brendan was the sweetest kid you ever met.

His older brother Patrick would get in fights at the playground. Brendan never did any of that. He tried to get along with everybody. He had this incredibly outgoing personality, even as a little boy. He would walk up to strangers and say, "Hi, I'm Bwen-dan Burke"—he had a little trouble pronouncing his R's as a kid—"What's your name?" He reached out to everyone around him.

Brendan turned out to be a huge kid, a hulking kid. Even in his baby pictures, you can see it coming. He wound up being 6-foot-4, where Patrick is only 5-foot-10. But he was so gentle. I called him Moose.

One of his grade-school teachers at St. John's in Canton, Massachusetts, Father Doyle, told me a story about Brendan. They had a dance at the school and Brendan asked the plainest girl in the school to dance. His friends were teasing him about it, and he said, "If I don't ask her to dance, no one is going to ask her to dance. Why wouldn't I do it?" And then the boys who were teasing him all did the same thing—they all asked girls to dance who wouldn't normally be invited. That's the kind of kid Brendan was.

One day when he was about 13, he came home and said, "I want to play hockey. I want to be a goalie." He hadn't played at all to that point. I signed him up for house league, and Molly and I went to one of his first games. His team lost, 7–1, and a bunch of the goals went right through him, but win or lose, he was thrilled. When he got out of school, he thought it was the coolest thing when beer-league guys would ask him to play goal and he didn't have to pay.

Near the end of high school, we started looking at colleges. Brendan was interested in Providence, but he didn't get accepted. He thought that was hilarious—his dad was supposed to be a big shot there, yet he couldn't get his own kid in. (The school called me afterwards and apologized. I told them I'd never assumed that the fact that I wrote them a big cheque every year meant my kid would get in automatically. And I never called them. They called me.)

We looked at other small Catholic schools, like Marquette University, and then Brendan visited Miami University in Oxford, Ohio, which is a much bigger place.

"I want to go there," he said.

I'll admit that I didn't get it, but I told him he could go wherever he wanted, wherever he would be happy.

When I took Brendan to Miami, I arranged to meet the hockey coach there, Rico Blasi, who is a great guy. Rico said Brendan wasn't good enough to play goal for him, but wondered if he might be interested in being the student manager of the team.

Brendan jumped at the chance.

When I was a kid, we had some family friends whose son never got married and was very effeminate. Remember, this was back in the early '60s, and ours was a very strict Catholic household. My mom tried to explain to us how some men didn't like women, but that everyone is special, everyone has gifts, and you have no right to judge them. We were raised in a family where you would never make a racist or a homophobic comment. But at school, we used all those slurs to describe gay people, and as a player I called guys "cocksuckers," just like everyone else. That's how we talked all the time. I was ignorant—we all were. I didn't have any gay friends. I didn't know any gay people—or at least I didn't as far as I knew.

I am so ashamed of who I was then. I had to evolve. But at least Brendan grew up in a house where he never heard a joke about "fags." That's the way I was raised and that's the way my kids were raised.

I had no inkling that Brendan was gay. My ex-wife said she suspected it, but not me. As far as I knew, he went to the prom with cute girls and that was that. I never thought twice about his sexuality.

I was the last one in the family he came out to. He had told his mother and his siblings. He told Patrick while they were moving a couch together.

"Okay, you're gay," Patrick said. "Now pick up the couch."

He finally came out to me when he and Molly were visiting us in Vancouver.

"Dad, I need to talk to you," Brendan said.

It was 11 o'clock. That's late for me. I'm an early-to-bed guy. I said we could talk in the morning.

"No," he said. "I want to talk to you now."

"Okay. What's up?"

"Dad, I'm gay."

"Are you sure?" I said. Maybe that sounds like a strange response. But there is a questioning phase that some people go through.

"Yeah, I'm sure," Brendan said.

I hugged him.

"You've given us a million reasons to love you, Brendan," I said, "and this doesn't change any of them."

Really, in a lot of ways, it was a non-event in our house. It's not like you choose these things. It's who you are. As Brendan said to me once,

"Do you think I would choose to be part of a hated minority?" That's why I have such a hard time with families who are tough on their kids when they go through this. It's just despicable to me. I used to rant and rail at those people. Now I just feel sorry for them.

I remember telling Brendan that his life as a gay man was going to be so much easier than it would have been if he had been in my high school. There were no gay kids in my high school, I said.

"Of course there were, Dad," he said.

"I know," I said. "That's my point. You would have been taking your life in your hands if you came out back then."

After he got back to school, he was on a gay website where someone called the guys on the Miami hockey team a bunch of fucking homophobic assholes. Brendan wanted to make a point: he was part of that hockey team, he was gay, and that wasn't true. And to do that, he would have to come out to his teammates.

Brendan called me and told me what he planned to do. I initially tried to talk him out of it unless it worked for his team.

"You have to talk to the coach," I said. "You're part of a team. If this will disrupt the team in any way, you wait and come out at the end of the year. I'm not ashamed of you coming out. I will be there for the announcement. But you make sure the coach is fine with it."

Brendan came out to the coach first, and Rico hugged him and told him he was fine with whatever Brendan wanted to do, that it wouldn't change a thing as far as the team was concerned. Then Brendan came out to his teammates. They were totally supportive.

It was Patrick who first understood the impact it could have—that if Brian Burke's son came out as gay, it would be a big deal in the hockey world. He was the one who encouraged Brendan to go public. We approached John Buccigross from ESPN to write the story, and it blew up.

I went on TSN with Brendan to do an interview, and I let him do just about all the talking. He made a lot of young men's lives easier because of what he did. I was so proud of the way he handled it.

But now, suddenly, everyone in the world seemed to be talking about Brendan Burke, and I will admit that I was concerned.

"You've got to keep your head on a swivel for the next few weeks," I told him. "You're a target. Some guy somewhere is going to see you and say, 'There's that faggot Brendan Burke.' Be careful. Don't go out alone."

Isn't that embarrassing? Doesn't it say something about the world that I felt like I had to give my kid that advice?

12   DRAFTING THE TWINS

MY MODUS OPERANDI HAS always been to do something big at the end of my first year in a job. I like to get to know the team for a full season and then make a dramatic move. At the end of the first year in Hartford, I drafted Chris Pronger. At the end of my first year in Toronto, I got Phil Kessel.

As for one of the most important—and most complex—deals of my career, I was in Boston, visiting my kids, when I set the wheels in motion.

During training camp heading into my first year back with the Canucks, Thomas Gradin, who was our head European scout, came to me and told me we had to find a way to draft a pair of identical twins out of Sweden named Daniel and Henrik Sedin. By all accounts, they were terrific young players, but there were a couple of pretty significant roadblocks in the way. The twins had already let everyone know, through their agent, Michael Barnett, that whatever happened, they'd be returning to Sweden for at least one season after the draft. They felt that they needed another year before they were NHL-ready, and as it turned out, they were correct. Some teams are a little afraid of using a top-three pick on a player they won't have right away, but that part didn't bother me.

Their second condition was a bigger issue: the Sedins said they wouldn't come to North America at all unless they were drafted by the same team. They were a package deal, and to get them both, you'd need two picks close to the top of the draft—probably in the top four—which was just about impossible.

"You've got to find a way to get them both," Gradin said.

"Have you lost your friggin' mind?" I said to him. "Nobody has ever picked twice in the top four. How am I supposed to get two top picks?"

"I don't care," Thomas said. "But you've got to get them."

I was ready to send Thomas for a psychiatric evaluation. We knew we weren't going to be great that season, so we would likely have a pick in the top five or six, at the very least—but just that one. We didn't have a second first-rounder.

But because Thomas was so insistent, and because I normally trusted his judgment, I talked to Dave Nonis and made sure we had a couple of scouts go over to Sweden at the beginning of the season to take a close look at the twins. The reports we got back said that they were definitely good enough to play in the NHL, but that they might not turn out to be stars.

The World Junior Championships that year were held in Winnipeg—the same tournament where I started the ball rolling on the Bure deal with Bryan Murray. I remember that it was minus-40 the entire time. It was so cold my teeth hurt when I walked out to the car.

Daniel and Henrik were playing for Team Sweden, and they finished third and fifth respectively in scoring, but they got a lot of their points against also-rans like Belarus and Kazakhstan. Against Canada, in the semifinals—the game everyone in hockey really watched—they got knocked all over the place. They were tall, but they were skinny and looked fragile. I joked to our scouts that they spent more time on the ice surface than the Zamboni. It was hard to imagine them being impact players in the NHL.

After the tournament, I told our scouts that we were probably going to trade our first-round pick. Outside of Patrik Stefan, who was going to go first overall—and I didn't think we were *that* bad—it was going to be one of the worst first rounds in the history of the league. Might as well get something for the pick rather than drafting someone like Pavel Brendl, whom we didn't like all that much. Now that I had seen the twins in person, and came away unimpressed, I wasn't inclined to try and move heaven and earth to get them.

You break your scouts' hearts when you tell them you're trading away a high draft pick. They work so hard all year long leading up to that moment, and now you're going to take it away from them. But I had to be honest. I told them to keep working as though we were going to pick, but chances were I would deal the first-rounder away.

The season moved along, and we weren't getting any better. It was clear that we were probably going to be picking in the top three or four. I was talking to teams, hoping to make a trade, but I wasn't getting any traction. We weren't the only ones who knew how weak the first round was going to be.

The draft lottery determines the draft priority every year. That year, Tampa wound up with the first pick. Atlanta was second, and we were third.

The twins had spent the 1998–99 season playing for Modo, the top team in the Swedish Elite League, but after what had happened at the World Juniors, the buzz around them had really died down. Then, in April, they announced the rosters for the World Championship, which was being held in Oslo that year, and the twins were listed as part of Team Sweden. I remember looking at the press release and wondering, "Who got hurt?" That's a men's tournament. You don't take kids to the World Championship. If you look back from that day until now, you can count on one hand the number of 18-year-olds who have played.

I called Thomas for an explanation.

"Nobody got hurt," he said. "They made the team. You've got to come over and watch them."

I told Thomas I'd make the trip on one condition—I'd come over and watch the twins play in the Worlds, but then he had to drop this nonsense.

"But you'll come over with an open mind?"

I promised.

Sweden was playing in a pool that was based in Hamar, a two-hour drive from Oslo that has to be one of the most beautiful trips in the world. I hitched a ride with the Blackhawks' front office—Bob Murray, Trent Yawney and Dale Tallon. Chicago had finished out of the play-offs and had the fourth pick in the draft, right after us.

We watched Team Sweden play three games in all, and from the first two shifts of the first game, you could see it—I'm not sure what else to call it other than the Twin Thing. Hank would throw the puck into an area where it didn't look like there was anyone within 20 feet, and then Daniel would suddenly skate to that spot and the puck would be right on his tape. It was like they had hockey telepathy.

I became a believer almost instantly. I knew then and there that these kids were going to become really good players—I wouldn't say I knew they would be stars at that point, but they were going to be really good players.

On the drive back to Oslo, I tried to downplay my excitement when I was talking to the Chicago guys. Murray is one of the best talent evaluators of the modern era, so he knew what he was looking at. But I did my best to play coy.

"Those twins are pretty good," Bob said.

"Aww, I don't really like them that much," I replied, though I'm not really sure how convincing I was.

When I got back to Vancouver, I told Dave Nonis we were going to have to find a way to draft both of them.

"How are you going to do that?" he asked.

"I don't know, but we're going to do it. I've got to have them."

Bob Murray called me three weeks before the draft and asked if I was interested in trading our third overall pick to the Blackhawks.

"No," I said, "but you're going to trade me the fourth pick."

This is what I was thinking: Tampa was probably going to take Daniel first overall because he was the higher rated of the two, and take their chances that he'd play for them without his brother. Atlanta would then take Patrik Stefan at No. 2.

But if I could somehow get two picks in the top four, I'd be in the driver's seat, the only one with a chance to draft *both* Sedins, providing everything fell into place. It wouldn't be easy, and it was risky, but I was willing to try because I liked them so much.

Bob remembered what happened in the Pronger draft back in 1993. "I know you can make things happen," he said. "But this time it's going to cost you."

He put his cards on the table. In return for the pick, he wanted a first-rounder the following year, plus defenceman Bryan McCabe.

McCabe was a player that I loved. At 24, he was in the prime of his career. He was physical, he moved the puck well and he was a great teammate. I didn't want to give him up.

I spent two weeks trying to talk Bob out of it. "What about this other defenceman? What about this forward?" He wouldn't budge.

The draft was held in Boston that year. The Sunday before was Father's Day, which is always a special occasion in our family, because it lines up with Katie's birthday on June 19 and Molly's on June 17. I took the kids out for lunch at a place called Finian's in Norwood, Massachusetts.

The rule was that when we got together as a family, I turned my phone off—this was our time, not hockey time. But just this once, I told the kids I had to keep the phone on. There was just too much riding on what would happen over the next few days.

Bob Murray called in the middle of our lunch (my oldest daughter, Katie, says she's still mad that I left the table to talk to him). I had been thinking long and hard about his offer. It was becoming clear that he wasn't going to back down, and I was absolutely determined to do whatever was necessary for a chance to draft the Sedins. I finally accepted his deal over the phone: McCabe and a first for Chicago's pick.

"But there's one condition," I explained. "We're not going to register the trade with the league until Friday afternoon."

"Why?" Bob asked.

"Because I think I've got a better chance of pulling this off if Tampa doesn't know I've got four."

Rick Dudley was running the Lightning then, and I thought that if he knew I already had two picks in the top four, he would know what I was trying to pull off and he'd demand a much higher price to flip his No. 1 pick for one of mine. He still had leverage—provided he was willing to take Daniel with the first pick and then take his chances on signing him.

Bob and I are very close, so he had no problem holding off on registering the deal until the day before the draft.

Now I had the No. 3 and 4 picks. At one point that week, I thought we actually might be able to wind up with the first, second *and* third, which no NHL team has ever done. We liked Patrik Stefan a lot (he was a really good pro until he got concussed), and we thought Atlanta, being a new team, might bite on something in return for their pick. But Donnie Waddell, their general manager, never wavered.

"We're picking," he said.

"Have you looked at the draft?" I said, trying to change his mind.

"I know," he said. "But we're picking."

So that was the end of the 1–2–3 dream.

On the Wednesday night before the draft, I talked to Dudley.

"We're not moving the pick," he said.

I talked to him again on the Thursday night.

"We're not moving the pick," he said.

On the Friday, Barnett met with Dudley and reiterated that if the twins weren't drafted by the same team, they wouldn't be coming to North America. Michael's recollection is that we went to the meeting together, but I don't remember it that way. What I do remember, clearly, is Dudley calling me after the meeting and screaming at me.

"You can send your trained pony over here all you want to threaten me, but I don't give a shit about him or you," Dudley said. "I'm going to go ahead and pick whoever I want."

Duds is a tough man. We were cursing and swearing at each other and I was just grateful he wasn't in the same hotel, because I think he would have come upstairs and beaten the crap out of me. I'm a pretty good fighter, but Rick Dudley is a scary guy.

Now it was time to play my card.

"Duds, hang on a second. Just so you're clear, I've got four."

"What are you talking about?"

"We just registered the trade an hour and a half ago. I've got three and four. No one is leaving here with the twins but me. I'm the only guy with two picks in the top four. You're going to pick a guy who's not going to come, or you're going to trade that pick to me."

As you can imagine, Dudley wasn't very happy hearing that news. It took a few hours for the reality of his situation to sink in. He called me back that night and said he would be willing to flip picks in return for a second- and fourth-round pick, which was an exorbitant price to move down two places in the draft.

"Fuck you," I said. "To move two places? I'm not giving you a second-round pick. I'll give you two thirds."

Dudley hung up on me.

I'll never forget what it felt like when I crawled into bed that night. Jennifer, who was with me at the draft that year, was waiting in the hotel room for me.

"Do you have a deal?" she asked.

"No," I said, "and now I'm getting fired. I just traded Bryan McCabe and a first-round pick for Pavel Brendl. Unless Rick Dudley shows up tomorrow and changes his mind, I'm screwed."

Dave Nonis and I sat down at our table three hours before it was going to start. We were the only people in the place.

"If Rick Dudley doesn't walk over here the minute he arrives," I told Dave, "we're fucked."

It was a long wait—or at least it felt like one. When Dudley finally came in, he put down his stuff and then came directly to us.

"All right, I will do your deal—two thirds," he said.

"You fucker," I said. "You already traded the pick, didn't you?"

He had. The Lightning had conditionally traded the No. 4 pick, which he didn't have yet, to the New York Rangers, who wound up picking Brendl. Duds had made the best of a tough situation.

Dave Nonis and Jay Feaster, who was the Lightning's assistant general manager, went back to register the trade with the league. Now we had picks one and three, which meant that as long as the Thrashers did the expected and took Stefan, we had the Sedins. But now I wanted the cherry on top.

I walked over to the Atlanta table and sat down beside Don Waddell.

"Donnie," I said. "Do you want to be the star of this draft?"

"Fuck you," he said. "I've seen you walking around. I have a pretty good idea who is going to be the star of this draft."

"Do you want to pick first overall?"

"Why would I give you anything when I can still get the player I want?" Don said. "You're taking the Sedins and I'm taking Stefan."

"I don't want to go up there twice," I said. "The magic of the moment will be when they're both on stage together. And I've been spending picks like a drunken sailor. I need one back. Plus, your boss, Ted Turner, is here watching."

Donnie thought about it for a few minutes.

"Okay," he said. "We'll do it."

They gave us a third-round pick to move up from No. 2 to No. 1.

I went back to our table and told our guys that we had two and three and that we were taking the twins. Thomas Gradin was like a kid at Christmas. He couldn't contain himself.

While Dave Nonis and Larry Simmons, Atlanta's assistant general manager, were registering that second trade, I found the twins in the crowd and made a little gesture at them, like I was firing a pistol. They knew now that we were picking both of them, and they were obviously excited, but they had to try to maintain poker faces so they wouldn't give it away.

Now it was time for the draft to start. Gary Bettman came out on stage—and got booed, of course, because he always gets booed.

"I have some trades to announce," he said. The building went dead quiet. It wasn't just trade, singular—it was *trades*, plural.

"Vancouver trades Bryan McCabe and a first-round pick in 2000 in exchange for Chicago's first-round pick, that's fourth overall."

Now there was a buzz in the room, as people started to realize that we had the third and fourth picks.

"I have another trade to announce," Bettman says.

The building went quiet again.

"Tampa Bay trades its first-round pick, first overall, to Vancouver in exchange for the fourth pick overall in 1999 and two third-round picks."

Now everyone knows I've got No. 1 and No. 3.

"I've got another trade to announce," Bettman says. The noise died down once again.

"Vancouver trades to Atlanta the first pick overall in exchange for the second pick overall and a conditional third-round pick in 2000. So, the order of selection is Atlanta, Vancouver, Vancouver, Tampa."

(After that, he announced that Tampa had traded the fourth pick to the Rangers.)

Now everyone in the building and watching on television knew what was going on. It was a big deal—arguably the most dramatic series of trades in the history of the draft.

The Atlanta guys went up on stage, with owner Ted Turner in tow, and announced that they were selecting Stefan first overall. Then it was our turn. I'd had two sweaters made up, both with No. 99, for the draft year. The nameplate on one read D. Sedin, the other H. Sedin. I went on stage and announced the picks, and then the twins came up. But I couldn't tell them apart. I just held out the sweaters so that they would each pick the right one.

I was exhausted after that. I went back to our draft table, slumped into my chair and put my head down. I had nothing left. Dave had to nudge me to get me back in the game. "Hey Boss," he said. "We've still got work to do here. You've got to snap out of it."

I sent a runner to get me a big cup of coffee, and somehow I managed to get through the rest of that day.

Looking back, pretty much everyone in hockey acknowledges that we did brilliant work, finding a way to draft what turned out to be two of the best players of their generation. But if you look back at the media coverage then, it was lukewarm. There was a lot of skepticism about the twins, and it took a while for it to fade.

And I have to admit that there were moments when even I had my doubts.

That summer I was in Penticton, teaching at the Okanagan Hockey School, and the twins came over to train there for a few days. I brought them up to my hotel room and took one last shot at convincing them to come straight to Vancouver.

"Are you sure you're going back to Sweden?" I asked them.

"We're going back," they said.

"Nothing I can say to talk you out of it?"

"Nope."

So, that was that. I wasn't going to twist their arms if they really felt like they needed one more year in Sweden.

They returned to their club—Modo in Ornskoldsvik in northern Sweden, arguably the most famous team in the Swedish Elite League, one with a long history of producing great players. I flew over to watch them play a game there that fall. They were terrible. Absolutely awful. Of course, Thomas Gradin was with me. "I'm getting fired over this deal unless there's a good reason that they looked that bad," I told him. "And before I get fired, I'm firing your ass because you're the one who told me to do this."

Thomas went downstairs to talk to the twins after the game. (I was so mad, I refused to see them.) When he came back to see me, he had a huge smile on his face.

"You'll like this," he said. "The reason they were terrible was because they were up all night. They had a calculus exam, and they stayed up until four in the morning studying for it."

That's right. They were still in high school.

It took the twins time to establish themselves once they came to Vancouver, and they took a lot of flak in the local press in the process. They were doing some things well, but it wasn't showing up in the scoring stats, and they were still developing physically.

The late Neil Macrae, who was one of the top sports radio guys in Vancouver, started calling them the Sedin Sisters. There was no way I was standing still for that. I called Macrae and told him that if he ever uttered the words "Sedin Sisters" on his show again, I was pulling everyone off his station, CKNW. I wouldn't let any Canucks personnel appear, and I'd drop my own show on the station.

So, that stopped pretty fast.

Marc Crawford deserves a tremendous amount of credit for the Sedins' success, because he saw their greatness right from the beginning and just kept playing them. I remember after one game, the media guys were quizzing him about why he continued to give the twins so much ice time despite what were perceived to be their struggles.

"What game are you guys watching?" Crow asked them. "They don't get scored on. They wear out the other team's second pair on defence. By the end of the second period, the second pair have their tongues dragging on the ice. And the offence is going to come."

He was right about that. They turned into great players. But they were also more than just great players. They changed the way the game was played. The faceoff plays—back then, no one used faceoff plays, but the twins did. The slap pass—no one was doing it, and these guys perfected it. The cycle plays they made. The area passes. It was a clinic. Every night, they did something different. Fans were buying tickets just to see what the twins would do next.

They had the benefit of playing on a good team—we had a great No. 1 line, the West Coast Express, to take some of the pressure off them. And they had the benefit of playing with Markus Naslund and Mattias Ohlund, two wonderful Swedish players who were their mentors.

But it was Crow who pushed them. If they got scored on—which was rare—or if they got knocked down, they would come to the bench and Crow would tell them, "You're going right back out."

I give Marc and Thomas the lion's share of the credit for what the twins became. And, of course, the twins themselves.

All I did was draft them.

Off the ice, it took me a while to really get to know Henrik and Daniel—not to mention tell them apart. When they first came to Vancouver, you could have a better conversation with a snowman than you could with the two of them. They were so quiet and so polite.

"How's it going, Hank?" you'd ask.

There'd be a long pause because they always wanted to appear thoughtful. Three seconds . . . four seconds . . . five seconds . . .

"Fine," Hank would say. And nothing more.

"How are your parents doing?"

The same pause—three . . . four . . . five . . .

"Fine," he'd say.

But their work ethic was remarkable. They trained harder than anyone. And they were magnificent in the community. As rookies, they would volunteer for every school and hospital visit. They did all kinds of stuff that no one even heard about. The only reason people know about the million and a half dollars they gave to the Vancouver Children's Hospital was that the hospital convinced them that publicizing the gift would help them raise more money from others.

In just about every way, they're perfect people. There's not one flaw in either one of those kids. They're not selfish, they're not jealous, they don't have tempers. They're exactly what you would aspire to be if you hoped to be a good person and wanted to be fun to be around and wanted to have a lot of close friends. That would sum up the Sedins.

13 ▼ "THAT'S NOT HOW WE PLAY"

THERE AREN'T THAT MANY days in my life that I wish I could take back. In fact, there's really only one—the night of my son's accident. But career-wise, there are two incidents I wish had never happened: the night Marty McSorley hit Donald Brashear over the head with his stick, and the night Todd Bertuzzi attacked Steve Moore. Both involved my team—though in the first instance, our guy was the victim, and in the second, everything was not as it seemed and our guy was treated extremely unfairly.

I'll admit that, for a time, I wondered why this stuff seemed to keep following me around. Was it a function of the way my teams played? In my head and my heart, I knew it wasn't, but it sure seemed like some higher power had decided that for a few years, the Vancouver Canucks would be at the eye of the storm.

On February 21, 2000, the night that McSorley–Brashear turned into an international incident that extended way beyond hockey, I was in Boston once again, visiting my kids. It was one of our weekends together, and as I mentioned before, I never missed those, no matter what was going on with my hockey teams. The Canucks were playing the Bruins in Vancouver, and I watched the game on television.

Brash had fought Marty earlier in the game—and won—and then he got into it a bit with the Bruins bench. Later in the game, he collided with Boston goalie Byron Dafoe, and Dafoe went off on a stretcher with a knee injury. So, needless to say, emotions were running high. Marty tried to get Brash to fight him again, but Brash refused. None of us believed Brash owed him that second fight. It was a lopsided game.

With a few seconds left in the third period, Marty clubbed Brashear in the head with his stick, and Brashear fell to the ice. His helmet came off and he suffered a seizure. Stick-swinging incidents weren't that uncommon earlier in NHL history—the most infamous was between Wayne Maki and Ted Green in 1969, and it was a whole lot worse—but this one, on national television, really shocked people, and then all hell broke loose.

With the time difference, it was very late at night when the game ended, but I found out from our people that Brash was going to be okay, though he did suffer a concussion.

Stan McCammon called me to ask me what would happen next. I told him that there would be a league disciplinary hearing for McSorley in the next few days. In the meantime, we would see how Brash was in the morning. And then I went to bed—I've always had trouble staying up late.

The next day, the Vancouver police showed up at the rink, wanting to interview our players. I told Steve Tambellini, who worked in our front office, to tell the police I'd be back the next day, and then we would give them everything and anything they needed. But I didn't want them interviewing players until I got there.

BCTV sent a camera crew to the rink that day, and they did a report that suggested we weren't cooperating with the cops, capping it off by saying they tried to interview me, but I had refused to talk. Of course that was a lie—I wasn't even in the city.

(I sued BCTV for libel—the first, but not the last time I've sued the media and won. There was no way I was going to let it pass. In the end, they settled—they paid my legal fees and made a small charitable contribution.)

Bill Daly called me while I was at the airport in Toronto, waiting for my flight back to Vancouver.

"Why are you stonewalling the investigation?" he asked.

That really pissed me off.

"Fuck you, Bill," I said. "I'm on my way back. I had my kids this weekend. I've told the police I'll meet with them this afternoon when I get back."

He started laughing.

"That's the delay? Sorry about that. You're all good. Don't worry about it."

There were two cops waiting at the rink when I arrived. I told them we would delay our practice so they could interview whoever they wanted. But they admitted to me that they really didn't know where to start.

So, I helped them out.

"The two closest players on the ice were Mattias Ohlund and Matt Cooke. Why don't you start by asking them if they heard anything? Did they hear McSorley threaten Brashear?"

(They both came in and told the police they didn't hear anything.)

"The next two people you want to talk to are the linesmen. Here are their numbers from the league, and here's the referee's number. And you can talk to any other players on our team. And you should talk to the head coach."

Brashear had been released from hospital by then. They had kept him overnight for observation.

To me, it was pretty clear what had happened. The two heavyweights had fought earlier in the game, and Brashear won. McSorley is a good guy, and he thought Brash owed him a rematch. We were winning big, and Brash wouldn't even look at him when Marty tried to challenge him again.

Marty said he meant to hit him on the shoulder. I don't know if I accept that, or if he just snapped in the moment, but in any case, he did club him on the head, and Brashear's helmet came off when he hit the ice, which is when the damage happened.

I think I have every frame of the video memorized. It's one of those clips I've watched a few too many times.

Under normal circumstances, at that point, the league's disciplinary system would have dealt with the matter, and that would be it. There would be a hearing and a suspension. We take care of our own business in the NHL.

But in Vancouver, anyone can file an assault charge by claiming they have witnessed an assault. Three different fans who were at the game called it in, the police were forced to investigate, and it became a matter for the courts. This wasn't just a sports story now—it was an international crime story with lots of uninformed knee-jerk reaction to the "violence" in hockey. I was even interviewed on CNN by Greta Van Susteren.

McSorley was charged with assault with a weapon. The police wanted me available to be called as a witness, and McSorley's team also wanted me in case they needed me to testify about the league's policy of supplementary discipline. I wound up sitting in the Crown's office in the courthouse because I wasn't allowed to hear any of the testimony in case I was called by either side. In the end, I wasn't called, so I didn't see a minute of the trial.

Marty was convicted and sentenced to 18 months' probation. But it never should have been in a courthouse in the first place.

Brashear was back playing before the end of the season. McSorley was suspended for a year by the NHL, but that turned out to be the end of his career. He never played another game.

There are a lot of ways to assign blame, and there was more than one bad decision behind each of the two disasters that rocked the Canucks and the league while I was in Vancouver. Todd Bertuzzi was no Marty McSorley, and Steve Moore was certainly no Donald Brashear. But the two cases have something in common. McSorley's career ended because Brashear wouldn't fight him. And Moore's ended because Moore wouldn't fight Todd.

Todd Bertuzzi was a unicorn. I've never had a player with that kind of size and those kinds of hands. The things that he could do with the puck, the goals he could score while protecting the puck and leaning in with the defenceman draped all over him—I've never had a player built like him who could do that. He could change a game all by himself. He was truly a multidimensional player. In terms of the physical part of his game, Todd didn't hit a lot, but when he hit, it was usually to back up a teammate, and he hurt people. Every once in a while, he'd decide that he'd had enough and run someone over and you'd say, "Jesus Christ, it looked like that guy just got hit by a truck."

Todd is also a good guy and was a popular teammate. He was absolutely coachable. We all liked him. He is a quality person. He played for his country. He is nice to everybody. He is a dedicated father, absolutely devoted to his kids. The notion that people in Canada think of him as some kind of villain because he showed poor judgment for one and a half seconds is just not right.

Looking back at what happened, you can't just start with the part everyone remembers. That was the culmination of what developed over a series of three games between the Colorado Avalanche and the Canucks in February 2004.

In the first game, Steve Moore, who was a minor-league call-up, cheap-shotted our captain, Markus Naslund, who was the leading scorer in the league at that point. There was no call on the play, and the NHL decided not to suspend him for it. But we were certain it was an intentional dirty hit directed at Naslund's head.

Afterwards, one of our players, Brad May, said there was now a bounty on Moore's head. When I heard that, I was enraged. I yelled at Brad for that one, and so did the coach. The league wasn't amused, either. We don't talk like that in our sport, and that's not my idea of retaliation. I explained to Markus afterwards that we wouldn't be going after Moore. We *wanted* him on the ice. He wasn't a good hockey player. We didn't even think he'd still be with the team the next time we played. He had been called up due to injuries, and we thought he'd go right back.

My idea of retaliation for the Avalanche targeting our captain was to go after *their* captain: Joe Sakic. They get our best player, we're going after their best player; they get our No. 19, we get *their* No. 19—but cleanly and legally. I'm not going to trade a king for a pawn.

The next time we played them, the game was in Denver. Gary Bettman and Colin Campbell were both in attendance, which was no coincidence. Gary came over to see me in my box before the game.

"Are we going to have a problem?" he asked.

"Gary," I told him, "if we were going to do something, we'd wait until we played them again in Vancouver in two weeks. Then we'd have the last change and we'd send somebody onto the ice and he'd beat Steve Moore into another lifetime. But we don't care about Steve

Moore. So, there won't be any problem tonight and there won't be any problem in Vancouver."

We played that night, and the game ended in a tie. Moore was in their lineup, but there were no problems at all.

Two weeks later, we had the third game in Vancouver. Matt Cooke challenged Moore to a fight before an early faceoff, and they squared off. As far as I was concerned, that meant Moore had paid his tab and we were done with it. I thought it was over.

But the players saw things differently down on the ice. Cooke had said "We're going" to Moore before the faceoff, but the players felt that Moore had jumped him, that he started the fight before Cookie could get his gloves off. They were yelling at Moore on his way to the box that the tab wasn't paid, that he'd have to go again.

Now we were into the third period, and the game was way out of reach—Colorado was winning, 8–2. But the Avs' coach, Tony Granato, kept throwing Moore out there. Up in the box, we couldn't figure out why he would do that. He knew what the situation was. He knew the first fight had happened. Why keep putting him out there when the game was already won?

We had heard that Moore was an unpopular teammate in Colorado. Maybe Tony wanted him to take his medicine. Maybe he didn't like what he did to Naslund. (Later—this was reported by the *Vancouver Province*—we learned that Moore said to the ambulance driver who took him from the rink to the hospital, "I don't know why Tony kept putting me out there.")

The guy who set off the final chain of events was Sean Pronger, who we had just called up. He had absolutely no orders to do anything other than play hockey. He got on the ice, saw Moore, figured, "All right, here's the guy who cheap-shotted Nazzy and jumped Cookie, and I'm going after him." He threw Moore up against the glass and then stepped back to give him a chance to fight. Moore declined and skated away.

Bertuzzi's line was in the process of changing. Pronger was out there because he had already come on for Brendan Morrison. Todd saw Pronger go after Moore, he saw Moore skate away, and then he went after him, chasing him, tapping him with his stick.

If you're going to send someone after Steve Moore, you're not going to send Sean Pronger and you're certainly not going to send Todd Bertuzzi. We don't want Todd breaking his hand in a fight. But Todd saw what had happened with Pronger, and Nazzy was his best friend.

What he did was dumb, and however well intentioned, you can't condone it. There's no code that says you avenge a teammate by sucker-punching a guy from behind. That was unforgivable. But he paid an awful price for it. It changed the way he played. It changed his career. It changed his life. And it cost him a fortune.

The coaches were yelling at Todd to come off on the change. Upstairs in the box, we were screaming, "No! No!" I knew Todd was going to cross-check him or something.

Moore wouldn't even turn to look at him, and that's when Todd grabbed him by the sweater and sucker-punched him in the back of the head. Then it looked like he jumped on him and hit him again, but Bertuzzi actually stepped on his stick and tripped and fell on Moore. As he fell, he threw the second punch, which landed after Moore was down.

Bertuzzi landed on Moore, then Pronger landed on him. Moore's teammate Andrei Nikolishin landed on him, Mattias Ohlund landed on him—Moore ended up under about 800 pounds of hockey player.

If you go back and look at the tape, you'll see that they were initially sliding along the ice, and you'll see that Moore's neck looked fine. But he ended up with all those bodies on him, and that's when his neck got twisted. I will believe until I die that the injury happened during that pileup.

Moore didn't get up. He didn't move. The building went dead quiet. We were all stunned. They took him off on a gurney and put him in an ambulance. While we were waiting for information on his medical condition, we were all nervous wrecks—whether it's your fault or not, when you see a guy motionless, being wheeled off the ice, you feel sick.

Bertuzzi was a mess. He knew right away how serious it was. After the game, he apologized to me, to the coach, to his teammates. He wanted to apologize to Steve Moore and wanted to go and see him in the hospital.

"No, not tonight," I told him. "We don't want you anywhere near this kid tonight. Just go home and try to get some sleep."

All we cared about that first night was the kid. The only thing we talked about was how we hoped he was okay. We saw how his neck was twisted. We didn't know if he was concussed, if he had a broken jaw. Then a rumour started circulating that he had a broken neck, and the only thing I could think was, "Jesus Christ, I hope this kid walks again."

The next morning, I tried to contact Moore at the hospital, but he wouldn't take my call. So I called Bob Goodenow and asked him to pass on a message: "The kid won't take my call. I understand. He probably thinks I had something to do with it. But I just want to know if he's okay. I'm just calling to see how he is."

Goodenow called me back later and told me that Moore was fine. He wouldn't take Bob's call, either, because he had been bombarded with emails and he was busy checking them.

So, he's sitting up in his hospital bed, checking his email—what the fuck?

Later that morning, Pierre Lacroix, the Avs' general manager, held a news conference where he announced that they were transferring Moore to a rehabilitation hospital in Colorado, where he would receive the best possible care and hopefully make a full recovery.

So, they sure made it sound like it was serious.

Iain MacIntyre, who was working for the *Vancouver Sun* then, called the neck hospital and asked them if they had been told to make room for Moore. They said they hadn't—that it was a long-term care facility, not an emergency facility. (I was mad at Pierre for that. I thought it was dirty pool. I wouldn't have done it. But Pierre is still a friend. It didn't end our friendship, but we had a pretty heated debate about it. Among other things, I told him using an injured kid to try to influence a suspension was just wrong.)

I asked our trainer how someone could have a "broken neck" and still be sitting up checking his email. He told me that we've all got flanges on our vertebrae, and that he had probably broken off one of them—which is painful, but not dangerous. He said that, because I was a former rugby player, he could probably find one or two broken flanges in my back if they were to take an X-ray.

We went from concern for the kid, wondering if he would ever play again—if he would ever walk again—to wondering if we were getting played by the Avalanche. Were they trying to milk this to get the biggest suspension they could?

Which is exactly what they did. To this day, I'm convinced that the injuries weren't severe enough to end his career. I think he could have come back and played if he'd wanted to.

The league scheduled an in-person disciplinary hearing, and I flew to Toronto with Todd. The media frenzy around the story was crazy, so I didn't want anyone finding out we were there. We checked into the Westin Harbour Castle Hotel under the names Fred Flintstone and Barney Rubble. (I remember that when I got my wake-up call the next morning, I picked up the phone and the voice said, "Good morning! It's seven o'clock, Mr. Rubble.")

I knew the cards were stacked against us. The story wasn't just all over the sports networks, it was all over the Canadian news and all over CNN. The play seemed to be getting replayed constantly in every bar in the country. It was a terrible look for the league. And some of the writers and commentators were saying that this kind of incident was bound to happen with a Brian Burke team because of the way they played. More than one person took a cheap shot like that at me.

The worst came from Larry Brooks at the *New York Post*, who wrote a story saying that I had gone into the dressing room after the Naslund hit and challenged the team, and that's why Todd went after Moore. It was absolute fiction. I've never gone into a dressing room during a game in my life. I sued the paper. I wasn't in the courtroom the day of the suit, but as I understand it, the lawyer for the paper stood up in court and said, "Your Honour, this Canadian court has no jurisdiction over the *New York Post*." Then my lawyer produced the *Post*'s sales video, which said the paper was published in 140 countries and reached 17 million people outside the New York area. The judge watched the video and said to the *Post*'s lawyer, "I think you should talk to Mr. Burke's lawyer." They published a full retraction and apology, paid my legal fees and made a donation to the charity of my choice.

I have lifelong contempt for Brooks, who—like Steve Simmons in Toronto and Tony Gallagher in Vancouver—is the worst of the hockey media business, a true weasel. More on that subject to come.

The truth is, my teams have never had big suspension problems. That's not how we play. We play tough from whistle to whistle within the rules, and we fight. We talk about not taking major penalties, not getting suspensions. So, that bothered me a little bit. A Brian Burke team was going to send Todd Bertuzzi out to fight a minor leaguer? Really?

When we walked into the hearing, I was thinking that Todd would get 20 games. Maybe the rest of the regular season. I never envisioned it would be more than that.

Todd was a mess that day. He was blubbering so hard, he could barely testify.

Colin Campbell and Bill Daly were handling the hearing for the league. When it was over, Colie asked if they could speak to me privately for a minute. The three of us went to Colie's office.

The first thing they asked was whether I had done anything to bring the temperature down before the incident. That was the first time it occurred to me that it wasn't just Todd who was under investigation—it was me as well. It's like the cops starting to interrogate you without telling you that you've been charged.

"You guys are a pair of assholes," I told them. "You're telling me that I'm under investigation? I met with the coach, I told him to have a meeting with the players. We gave Brad May hell for the bounty thing."

"Get Crawford on the phone," they told me.

Marc picked up the phone, thinking it was just me, only to find out that Bill and Colie were also on the line and that he was also being interrogated. He wasn't prepared at all.

I said, "Think back to the first incident, Crow. Do you remember how I asked you to talk to the team and calm things down?"

Crow hesitated just a little bit.

"Yeah . . . I guess so," he said.

I repeated the question, and he said, "Oh yes," and went on to describe what happened.

Daly took that first hesitation as proof that we weren't telling the truth.

"You guys should have got your story straight before the hearing," he said.

I was furious. "Our stories *are* straight," I told him. "This is what happened. We didn't prepare for this. I told Crow to talk to the players and talk to Brad May. I talked to Brad May. I thought we brought the temperature down. How did we play a game in Colorado without incident if we were out to get Steve Moore? If we wanted to get Steve Moore so badly, we would have gotten Steve Moore then. He's a minor leaguer. We want him on the ice."

They chose not to listen to that argument.

The league suspended Bertuzzi for the rest of the season and the playoffs, and he would have to apply for reinstatement the following season before he would be allowed to play again. And they fined the Vancouver Canucks a quarter of a million dollars.

I learned that day that there was no loyalty to me. There was no loyalty to our team. They were going to get that story off CNN no matter what it cost, and the only way to do it was to take Todd out for the balance of the year. For the most part, it worked.

The public reaction was mixed. Some people thought he should have been banned for life. Some thought the punishment was too severe—mostly Vancouver fans. But most people thought the punishment wasn't severe enough, so I never felt I had a really firm pedestal to stand on to rail against the league, even though I definitely did not agree with its point of view.

I remember saying to Dave Nonis that the suspension was like killing a fly with a bazooka. The remedy was so much broader than it needed to be. If the injuries didn't occur from the punch, then it was pretty hard to argue that Todd should be responsible for them. But the league maintained that all the consequences that flowed from the original punch would have to be taken into consideration—no different than in the law, where if you shove a person and they whack their head on the sidewalk and die, you're responsible for the outcome.

But the fine was something else entirely. They had absolutely no evidence that the team had done anything to create the situation. It just looked good in the press release. It was a PR exercise and it was grossly unjust. I told Daly, "All you've done is make me look like an asshole, and guarantee that I'm going to get sued when Todd gets sued."

I held a grudge against the league for at least a year after that—we Irish people are good at holding grudges.

But eventually, I came to realize that Gary was just doing his job. He was always going to do what he thought was best for the league, even if it cost me. The fact that I had worked for the league and had been Gary's right-hand man didn't matter. I was sour about it for a while, but then I asked myself what I would have done if I were the commissioner. The answer was: probably the same thing. I just didn't see it coming at the time.

Moore sued Todd, and he sued Crow and me as well, but I was never really worried about that. First off, I always thought the case would get tossed. Second, I had an indemnification clause in my contract, which meant that the club would have to pay any judgment levied against me. But most important, I knew I had done nothing wrong. When I think back on the incident, I wish it had never happened, but I wouldn't change anything that I did.

Later, the suit against Crow and me was thrown out, and then Moore refiled against Todd alone. They eventually settled.

From the minute I knew that Moore was physically okay, what I was most concerned about was the impact on my team. We lost Todd, who was Second Team All-Star, and after that, his line, the West Coast Express, pretty much dried up.

The truth is, even after he came back from the suspension the following season, Todd was never quite the same player again. He wasn't as committed physically. I think he was afraid of hurting somebody. For a player who plays that style, losing that edge can really affect him.

It also hurt his relationship with his teammates. He was more quiet. It devastated him. People close to me say I was never the same after my son's accident, and I think Todd was never the same after the Moore incident—he would probably say that he didn't change that much, but he did. Major events like that change you, and Todd changed as a hockey player and as a person. (He is all the way back as a person now, I'm happy to say.)

We still had a good season. We finished with 101 points—our second straight 100-point season. The building blocks were all there for the team that went to the finals in 2011. If you look at that team, almost all of the players were ones that I brought in or Dave Nonis brought in.

But we lost to the Flames in the first round of the playoffs—a seven-game heartbreaker.

And then I got canned.

"I WON'T BEG FOR MY JOB"

THE SEEDS OF MY firing were actually planted the previous fall, and it had nothing to do with the way my team was performing on the ice, and everything to do with Bertuzzi's contract. Those negotiations were the beginning of the end for me.

Todd had a year left on his deal, for which he would be paid $4 million. One of the methods I used to hold down payroll was to go to our guys when they had one season left on their contracts and offer them a big signing bonus if they were willing to extend.

I asked Todd's agent, Pat Morris, what he thought Bertuzzi would be paid if he had arbitration rights in the coming season. He said $7 million. So I offered him a $3 million bonus, which would top him up to $7 million that year as long as he was also willing to sign for the following two seasons at the same $7 million salary. (He was 28 years old then, and in the system in place at the time, NHL players weren't eligible to become unrestricted free agents until age 31.) It was a good deal for him and a good deal for us, at a time when some of the big stars in the game were earning $10 million or more a season.

We agreed in principle. But to get it done, I still needed the approval of our owner, John McCaw. I explained to him over the phone what I wanted to do, and he was all for it. But he still wanted me to come to Las Vegas and make a formal presentation.

We had just played our last pre-season game in Tucson. The team flew back to Vancouver while Dave Nonis and I headed to Las Vegas. I insisted on having Dave there—I wanted someone else in the room to back me up. So there were four of us—me, Dave, McCaw and Stan

McCammon, the president and CEO of McCaw's sports company, Orca Bay, who was no friend of mine.

I set up an easel, wrote out the numbers and was explaining how the deal would work.

"I want the signing bonus to be as small as it can be," McCaw insisted, which was logical, but of course would defeat the whole purpose of the exercise.

"John, this is the number," I told him. "This is what the agent has agreed to. This is how we get him to the seven million that he thinks he deserves. It's going to be three million to sign. It's not coming down."

Finally John said, "Okay, go ahead and make the offer."

I picked up my briefcase, and Dave and I headed out the door.

"But just remember," John said as we were leaving, "I want the signing bonus as low as it can be."

I put my briefcase down and stopped in my tracks.

"John, I'm not leaving here with any uncertainty. This is the deal. If you're approving this deal, you're approving this deal the way I explained it."

"Okay," he said. "Go ahead and present the offer."

We had a half hour to kill before heading to the airport, so Dave and I went downstairs to the casino and played a little blackjack. I was still a bit uncertain as to what had just transpired.

"He *did* just sign off, didn't he?" I asked Dave.

"Absolutely."

"Let's go ahead and make the offer."

That was on a Thursday. The next day, we called Pat Morris and officially made the offer.

Meanwhile, the process took a turn internally. It was a tense 48 hours. I will spare you the details. There was conflict over this offer. John and I had words. We did the deal, but the confrontation gave McCammon the ammunition to convince John that I wasn't a "team player," which is what they told me when they declined to renew my contract at the end of the season.

But there was also one other factor in that decision. My second contract with the Canucks included a clause that would protect me if

McCaw decided to sell the team. The day he first interviewed me on his boat in Seattle, one of the first questions I asked him was if he had any plans to sell. He said he didn't, and that was the truth then. But I knew that John had started losing interest in the Canucks after he met his wife, Gwen. When he bought the team, he was single, had all the money in the world and was living the life. But then he fell in love with that lovely lady (she is amazing) and moved to Los Angeles. That day in Las Vegas when Dave Nonis and I laid out the offer we were making to Bertuzzi, John's wife had come in and told us that she was pregnant with their first child.

The way my second contract was structured, if the team was sold for $80 million, I'd get a bonus of $1 million. If it was $85 million, I'd get $1.5 million—all in US dollars.

When we negotiated it, I told John that if he wanted out, I could put together an ownership group in a heartbeat that would pay him $80 million for the team.

"No, we want you on our side," he said. "You're an asset. When we sell the team, you're going to be one of the assets we sell with it."

Somehow, it didn't quite work out that way.

During my final year with the Canucks, McCaw quietly received an offer for a whole lot more than $85 million. But he knew that if he put the sale on ice until my contract expired at the end of the season, they could save themselves $1.5 million. Then the process became public—McCaw was negotiating to sell the team to Francesco Aquilini, Ryan Beedie and Tom Gaglardi. So, that became the plan—they didn't want to pay me out, so they decided to get rid of me. There's documentation to prove it. When he and his partner later sued Aquilini over the way the sale finally went down later that year, Gaglardi said in his sworn deposition that he had been told by McCammon that they had intentionally stalled the deal in order to get my piece out.

At the end of the 2003–04 season, McCaw flew all the senior management people down to Beverly Hills for a post mortem. We had lost the playoff series to the Flames, but other than that, it really couldn't have been going better. We had the twins. We had the West Coast Express. The building was sold out every night.

But by then, McCammon and I were dysfunctional. Stan was resentful of anyone who got credit for anything on the hockey side or the business side—especially if it was me. I'm happy to share credit. I'm famous for it. But I felt that Stan had very little to do with our success, and I wasn't shy about treating him that way.

John spoke to each of us individually.

His first question for me was: "Tell me why I should bring you back."

"John, I will fight for my job, but I won't beg for my job," I told him. "If you don't want me to come back, I won't be out of work for long. But I fear we won't have hockey next year, and that means I'll be out of work for a year."

I was looking ahead to the labour war that was coming. I knew there would be a lockout, and I was correct in believing that it would mean shutting down the league for at least a year.

John couldn't have cared less about my job prospects. He's a nice guy, but he was taking all his cues from Stan.

I knew then that I was finished, so I decided to throw a grenade on my way out the door.

"If you're going to make a change, let's end the suspense here," I said. "Everyone knows you're not bringing me back, and this is a charade. I'm supposed to beg for forgiveness and beg for my job? It ain't fucking happening. But if you're going to start getting rid of people who aren't producing, you'd better get rid of Stan, too, because he's useless."

(As it turned out, Stan would be gone three months later.)

"I'll get back to you," McCaw said.

"You don't have to, John," I told him.

I knew what was happening. It was only a question of when.

The day I got the news, I was driving my daughter Katie to the airport in Vancouver. My secretary, Patti Timms, called and whispered through the phone that Stan was in the office. Patti arrived at seven every morning, and Stan wasn't normally there before 9:30. But that day, he had come in early and was huddled behind closed doors with Loring Phinney, a guy from an outside PR firm.

"This is what happened the day they fired Pat," Patti whispered. "They're trying to figure out how to spin it."

I told her I'd be in as soon as I got Katie to her flight. Then I turned to Katie and said, "I guess it's today."

She started crying.

"Don't worry," I told her. "I'll just go somewhere else and work. It will be fine."

After dropping Katie off, I called Jennifer and told her what was happening.

"What are you going to do afterwards?" she asked me.

"I'm going to stop at the liquor store," I said. I knew what was coming. My staff was going to show up and hold a wake in my honour. Jennifer wasn't crazy about having the house filled with people on the day her husband was fired, but that's one of the charming traditions in hockey. There's always a wake, and everyone shows up at your place and gets hammered.

When I got to the office, Stan told me that they weren't renewing my contract—which by then was the worst-kept secret in Canada. Then, bizarrely, he tried to give me a kind of pep talk.

"Stan," I told him, "I don't need a pep talk from you. I am going to come back here with my next team and kick the living shit out of this one."

They let me keep the truck that was part of my deal until my contract expired on June 30. "You can do anything you want until then," Stan said, "but you're not welcome here."

In the meantime, the TV trucks had already started pulling up in front of my house. I let Jennifer tell them I'd talk to the media in a couple of days, after the dust settled, but that I wouldn't be saying anything that night.

Dave Nonis turned up at the house around 3:30 in the afternoon—which is early for a wake. He was sobbing like a baby. Jennifer met him on the front porch and hugged him.

I came out and asked him what he was doing out there, crying.

"They offered me your job and I don't know what I should do."

To this day, I'll never forget how bad Dave felt for me, despite the fact that it turned into a huge opportunity for him. That tells you what kind of a guy Dave is.

"You're taking the job," I told him. "You don't want a stranger coming in here and finishing what we started. We've just had two 100-point seasons. We're a contender. We just need a goalie."

(Dave went out and got a goalie—Roberto Luongo—and that team went to the finals two years after he got fired.)

Marc Crawford arrived next, along with his wife, whom I really liked, and the assistant coaches. By the end, we had 40 or 50 people there, and the booze was flowing.

There is one more chapter to the story.

After the team was sold, I was prepared to fight McCaw for what I was owed, and I went as far as having my lawyers send a demand letter. But I asked them to tell me honestly if I had at least a 75 percent chance of winning. They couldn't do that—they told me it was more like 50/50. When you're suing people who have a lot more money than you do, they can just pile on depositions and stall for time and bleed you dry.

So, I decided to let it go.

But it's funny how what goes around comes around.

When Mark Messier signed with the Canucks—a deal that was done by Pat Quinn and George McPhee before I came back to the team—his contract included a clause that guaranteed him a percentage of the increase in the value of the franchise over the three or four years of the contract. McCaw sold half of the team and the arena for $150 million in 2004, and then the other 50 percent for another $100 million two years later (these are rough numbers reported in the media). Naturally, Messier expected his payout, but the Canucks refused, arguing that those figures were misleading, and that the team itself was not actually worth more than when Messier signed. I didn't know how you could make the argument that the hockey team didn't appreciate in value over the whole time he was there. On the books it might have looked as though the building made all the money, but that was just an accounting trick.

The case went before an arbitrator and Messier's lawyers called me as a witness, because I knew as much about the inner workings of the Canucks' finances during those years as anyone did.

When Victor de Bonis, who was the Canucks' CEO at the time, saw my name on the witness list, he confronted me.

"You're testifying?"

"Absolutely," I told him.

"But your contract had a confidentiality clause."

"Feel free to raise that with the arbitrator," I said to Victor. "But the rules of evidence are much more lax here than they are in court. And by the way, I'm pretty sure the league would support my decision to waive it."

"What are you going to testify to?"

"The truth, Victor," I told him. "This is karma. You guys screwed me out of a bunch of money, and it was unfair and it was wrong and it was dishonest. And now I'm going to tell the truth. I'm not going to say one thing that's not true. This isn't about revenge. This isn't about getting back at you guys. But I find it interesting that I'm in a position where, by telling the truth, I can make Mark Messier a lot of money—a lot more than the million and a half you guys screwed me out of."

We met in a boardroom, and I didn't say a word that wasn't true. I wouldn't do that. I'm an officer of the court. I'm a member of the bar in Massachusetts. I take the rules about telling the truth under oath, and even when you're not under oath, very seriously.

In the end, the arbitrator awarded Messier millions of dollars.

And one postscript.

The day before my Anaheim Ducks played the Ottawa Senators in Game 5 of the 2007 Stanley Cup final—that would be the night we won the Cup—I got a call from John McCaw. (And I should clarify here that, despite the way things ended in Vancouver, I still like John. He's a nice man. But just like Richard Gordon in Hartford, there are some guys who are suited to own teams and some who aren't, and John is one of those who aren't.) It had been three years since they let me go and then stiffed me out of my bonus, and I hadn't spoken to him in the interim.

"Hey Brian, John McCaw here. Congratulations on all your success. I've been following you very closely."

"That's funny, John," I said, "because you live in Beverly Hills and I'm just down the road in Anaheim, and we haven't talked in three years."

He skipped right by that.

"I think it's great how well you're doing. And by the way, can you get me eight tickets for the game?"

"John," I said, "you know the league takes over ticketing in the finals. I can't get you tickets. But I can tell you that if I had eight tickets, I still wouldn't give them to you."

I found out later that he called Bettman and made the same request. Gary offered to sell him two.

"But I'm a former owner," John protested.

"Yes, you're a *former* owner," Gary said. "I'd be happy to sell you two."

DOWN THE ROAD FROM
DISNEYLAND

▼ **15**

I WAS OUT OF a job for the first time in a very long time, and with a labour war looming, I knew that my chances of getting hired by a team right away were going to be slim. I decided to take some time for myself and do something I'd always wanted to do: take my Harley and ride it from coast to coast.

But before I got to that, TSN called and asked me if I'd be interested in working on their draft telecast. They also asked if I'd be interested in signing a contract for the rest of the year. But if I was going to work in television, what really intrigued me was the upcoming World Cup, and that was being broadcast by the CBC. I approached the people at the CBC to see if they might be interested in hiring me—they were—and then I set out on my motorcycle adventure.

My plan was to ship the Harley to Boston and then ride it back home, but the local dealer in Vancouver explained that shipping it across the border might be complicated. He suggested that I pick it up in Montreal instead, and then ride it down to Boston.

I called a Harley dealer in Montreal to set it up. The guy who answered the phone had a thick Québécois accent.

"I'd like to ship my bike from Vancouver to Montreal," I told him.

"What's your name?" he asked.

"Brian Burke."

There was a long pause.

"*The* Brian Burke?"

"That's me."

"Mr. Burke," he said, "we are very sad for you. It's not fair what happened to you in Vancouver."

The draft was in Raleigh that year. I arranged for the bike to be delivered to the Bell Centre on the Sunday morning, after it was over. I sent my bags back to Vancouver with one of the Canucks' scouts, and then flew to Montreal with nothing but my leathers, my helmet, my gloves, my boots and my passport.

The Harley was waiting for me at the rink, as promised. I rode it to Boston, threw a few T-shirts and an extra pair of jeans into the saddlebags, and then hit the road. Riding across the northern United States, I didn't run into a soul who recognized me. I'd hit the road at dawn, cover four or five hundred miles in a day, pull into a motel somewhere, then have a few beers and something to eat. It was a gas.

Five days after I set out, I rolled up to Canadian customs at the Peace Arch on my way back into Vancouver.

"Are you bringing anything back, Mr. Burke?" the border officer asked me.

"Yeah," I told her. "A sunburn and a sore ass."

The lockout began immediately after the World Cup ended. Mark Milliere at TSN asked me to come back and be part of their panel and talk about the labour situation, based on my experience working in the league office during the previous lockout. I flew from Vancouver to Toronto every Tuesday, checked into a hotel, taped the show on Wednesday afternoon and flew home Thursday morning. I found out that I really enjoyed the hell out of television. It was fun, and TSN is a very good employer.

My wife and I went to meet with our banker, and we told her it was possible that I'd be out of work for at least a year. She told us that with the equity we had in our home, we wouldn't have to change our lifestyle in the short term—we could still travel, eat where we wanted and continue to pay for my two kids who were still in university. Anything more than a year, though, and we'd have to talk.

By the time the lockout ended and it was clear that the 2005–06 season would begin on time, there was just one NHL front-office job open. Bryan Murray surprised a lot of people by deciding to step down as general manager of the Mighty Ducks of Anaheim and move to Ottawa to become the head coach of the Senators.

To be honest, I really didn't think Anaheim was a place I wanted to work. Disney had made such a shitshow of that franchise—shitty uniforms, shitty name, the whole movie tie-in thing. I wasn't all that interested. The Mighty Ducks had made a Cinderella run to the Stanley Cup final in 2003, carried by their goalie, Jean-Sebastien Giguere. The next season, right before the lockout, the magic had worn off and they'd missed the playoffs.

But I realized that it might be the only job available. And at least Disney was on the way out and the Ducks would have a new owner.

As luck would have it, I had the inside track.

There is a guy named Jac Sperling who is kind of an international man of intrigue around the NHL. He's from Minnesota, and he's been involved in the purchase or sale of 10 or 12 different teams. He helps to find buyers and find the financing. One of the deals he helped broker was the Minnesota Wild coming into the league as an expansion franchise. For a while, he was the Wild's CEO.

I had advised Bob Naegele, the owner of the Wild, when he was putting together his hockey operation, and I was one of the people who suggested he ought to hire Doug Risebrough, who is a great guy, as his first general manager.

When Henry Samueli bought Anaheim from Disney, Jac Sperling helped put the deal together. Samueli didn't know anything about running a hockey team, so Sperling suggested that Henry send his right-hand man, Mike Schulman, to meet with Risebrough and get some advice.

Once again, karma was in play.

"I don't know why you're interviewing anyone other than Brian Burke," Riser told Schulman. "He's the best guy available. He works like a dog. He's tough as nails. He knows how to build winners. Look what he did in Vancouver."

(Susan Samueli, Henry's wife, told me later that after they heard that, the job was mine to lose.)

When I went for the interview and met the Samuelis, I knew that this was a job I really, desperately wanted.

They were the smartest owners I have ever worked for and the nicest owners I have ever worked for. Brilliant people. They're fantastically wealthy, but every dime they have, they made for themselves. This isn't someone spending Daddy's money. Henry came from a working-class family that ran a liquor store, earned his Ph.D. in electrical engineering and was a professor at UCLA before he founded a company called Broadcom with one of his students. The business made him rich.

The Samuelis own a beautiful home overlooking the Pacific, and they have a private jet, but otherwise they are very modest and very family-oriented. Susan drives a beat-up Mercedes station wagon that's got to be 15 years old. I remember saying to her, "For God's sake, with the money you guys have, you can afford a new car. I'll take you to the dealership and help you pick one out."

"Why?" she asked. "Why would I buy a new car? This one is perfectly fine." She was dead serious.

That's Henry and Susan Samueli for you. They're special. I'm glad that I got to meet them, let alone work for them. (It reminds me of the time when I was running the Leafs and told Johnny Bower that I could find him someone to cut his lawn so he wouldn't have to do it himself at age 80-whatever-he-was-then. "Why would I do that?" Johnny asked.)

Henry really likes hockey, and he used to go to Ducks games before he bought the team. He bought the lease on the arena first (it was the Arrowhead Pond then—now it's the Honda Center) and then approached Disney about buying the franchise. There was a threat of litigation at one point, because Disney wasn't willing to guarantee the team would stay in the arena, which would have violated the lease. But in the end, the sale of the team was amicable. The announced price was $75 million. As a straight business investment, it probably didn't make a lot of sense for Henry, but he's like a lot of wealthy people who get into professional sports. Jerry Jones was just another rich guy until he bought the Dallas Cowboys; now he's famous. Owning a team gives you some notoriety, and in the case of the Samuelis, it also gave their kids something to which they could aspire. Plus you can operate profitably in Gary Bettman's NHL, and you can usually make good money when you sell the team.

In the interview process, I was classic Brian Burke. Between Hartford and Vancouver, I'd had my fill of interfering owners, and so I laid it on the line. "If you hire me, there are two hands on the steering wheel, and they're both mine," I told Henry and Susan. "If I look and there's a hand on the steering wheel and it ain't mine, we've got a problem. If you don't want to give that much autonomy away, I'll step back right now and help you hire the right general manager—because it's not me." Susan told me later that they really liked that approach.

Neil Smith was the other finalist. It was just the two of us. After the interview, I went home and stared at my phone, hoping it would ring, thinking, "Fuck, I have to get this job."

And I did.

The hockey landscape in Southern California was a little different then than it is now. Obviously, the Gretzky trade in 1988 was the biggest thing that ever happened to the sport there. It was a seismic event, and it made the Kings the biggest hockey game in town, even long after Gretzky was gone. The Mighty Ducks were a distant second, kind of an amusing little circus toy that played their games far off the beaten track. The fan base in Anaheim then wasn't that different from what it is today—they had, and continue to have, a hard core of between 8,000 and 10,000 people who are there for every home game. These are not Toronto Maple Leafs season-ticket holders who go to six or eight games a year and then sell off the rest of their tickets. These are passionate regulars who go to at least 30 games a year. They have their routines, and if you're around the team, you get to know the regulars.

After Gretzky, the next seismic hockey event in Southern California was the Samueli family buying the Ducks, though not very many people realize that. They single-handedly changed the culture of hockey at the grassroots level. They bought roller rinks, built a practice facility and founded the AAA Ducks, with bantam and peewee teams that travel all over the place. They started high school hockey in Southern California—now there are something like 113 teams. They've made hockey matter in that whole area from the Mexican border to the southern fringes of Los Angeles.

The rink in Anaheim was actually built for basketball, so it's not an ideal place to house an NHL team. The lower bowl is too small, which makes it nearly impossible to make money—we didn't even make a profit the year we won the Cup—but the other events in the building keep the business in the black. It is a beautiful facility, though. When they were building it, it was actually under budget, so they took the extra money and put it into things like marble floors and cherry wainscotting. There isn't another arena quite like it in the NHL.

For the hockey players, the lifestyle in Anaheim is great, as long as you love beautiful weather and you're happy being anonymous. (I actually got tired of all those warm, sunny days. I like red leaves in the fall and cold mornings. In Southern California, it's Groundhog Day every day.) I remember we used to shop at the same grocery store as Scott Niedermayer and his family. We'd see Scott and Lisa and their four kids pushing their cart down the aisle, and not a soul would speak to them. Nobody knew who they were. In Canada, he couldn't walk three steps without getting stopped for an autograph.

The only downside for me was that I couldn't do as much charity stuff as I was accustomed to doing, because I didn't have the same platform. In Canada, I'm Brian Burke, and people will listen to me and send in money to a good cause. In Anaheim, not so much. But otherwise, it was great working there.

On the hockey side, my first task was to honestly evaluate the team that I had inherited. It had been only a year since they'd gone to the Stanley Cup final, but it was clear to me they weren't going to do that again anytime soon.

They'd had a really good draft just before I arrived, picking up Ryan Getzlaf and Corey Perry in the first round. I loved both of those kids. I wish I could take credit for drafting them. But beyond them, the Ducks, to me, were an average hockey team and a soft hockey team. That last part had something to do with who was coaching them.

I like Mike Babcock, and I think he's a good coach. But he's a Greenpeace guy, and I knew it would never work with him coaching my team.

After I got the Anaheim job, Mike called to congratulate me.

"I'd like to talk to you about an extension," he said. "I only have one year left on my deal."

"Mike," I said, "I'm trying to decide if you're coming back or not. So, we're not talking about an extension. We need to see if there's a fit. I think you're a good coach, but I don't think you're a Brian Burke coach. I like a chain-gang mentality on my teams, and I don't think you do.

"I know that Detroit has already reached out to you. I think you should call Kenny Holland and make a deal with him."

So, that's how Babcock wound up in Detroit. I knew they had tampered with him, but I didn't mind because I knew it wouldn't have worked out if he'd stayed with the Ducks.

I didn't fire Mike, and I wouldn't have fired him, but I wouldn't have kept him over the long term, either. I respected him, so I would have figured some other way out. But in the end, the parting was amicable. He got what he wanted. It certainly turned out very well for him in Detroit. And I got what I wanted—a chance to hire my own guy.

My first move was to bring Bob Murray over from the Canucks to be my assistant general manager.

Dave Nonis didn't want to lose him in Vancouver. "I know what you're calling for," Dave said when he picked up my call. "Don't take Bob Murray. Is there any way you can leave him here?"

There wasn't, and it was a promotion, so they really had no choice but to let him go.

If you look at the Stanley Cup, you'll notice that they include the assistant general manager's name in the inscriptions, along with the players and coaches and GM. There's a reason for that—but I honestly don't think an assistant GM has ever had as much to do with a team's success as Bob Murray did with ours. He pushed me on Shawn Thornton. He pushed me on Travis Moen. He's the one who pushed for Francois Beauchemin, whom I didn't like at all. (I told Bob that when I phoned Doug MacLean, who was running the Columbus Blue Jackets, and told him I wanted to trade for Beauchemin, he was going to say "Done" before I even finished his name. It was going to be embarrassing. "That's the guy I want," Bob insisted. So I phoned MacLean, and before I had finished saying "Beauchemin," he said yes to the deal. I was fucking sour about that one for a long time. But Bob was absolutely right. Francois was great for us.)

Bob and I both sat down separately and made a list of our preferred head-coaching candidates. As it turned out, there was only one name on both of our lists: Randy Carlyle.

Randy had spent the previous season coaching the Manitoba Moose, Vancouver's farm team in the American Hockey League. So I had to call Dave Nonis again to ask for permission to talk to one of his guys.

"I won't take anyone else," I promised him, "but I've got to have Randy."

Randy Carlyle comes from nothing. He grew up outside of Sudbury, where his dad was a janitor in a nickel mine. He used to shoot rabbits on the way to school for the family dinner. If Randy has a flaw as a coach, it's that he can't stand privileged kids. He can't stand players who come from dough. And he particularly doesn't like Americans— which he'll deny, but he doesn't. So you can imagine how he feels about entitled Americans.

In terms of the way his teams play, he was the perfect match for me. He loves black-and-blue hockey. You never had to tell Randy to play the game tougher because that's how his teams always played. He liked it as crude as I did. My three pillars were Randy's three pillars. We were going to entertain you. We were going to gamble. We might give up more chances than other teams, but we'd be exciting. We could dazzle you with the puck and we could run you out of the building and onto the street. We were going to be tough as nails. We weren't going to take any shit from anyone. And we were going to have great goal-tending—and with Jiggy in net, we were already set there.

We announced Randy's hiring a couple of days after the draft—and what a draft that turned out to be. Because of the lost lockout season, the date was pushed back from late June to July 30, after the new collective agreement had been ratified. And because there hadn't been a season, they couldn't use the normal system for determining the order of picks. Instead, the league came up with a weighted lottery based on playoff appearances over the past three seasons and whether or not teams had claimed the first overall pick in the past four drafts.

The bottom line was that each team wound up with one, two or three Ping-Pong balls in the lotto machine. The Ducks had two.

And the stakes? Just the opportunity to select the best player of his generation, and one of the greatest who has ever lived, Sidney Crosby.

I remember talking to our scouts before the lottery, and how anxious they were for us to at least get a pick in the top 10—I had to explain to them that there was no skill involved, and there was nothing I could do to improve our odds.

They broadcast the lottery on TSN that year. The balls started dropping, and we were still there in the last eight, and then in the last seven, until finally it came down to the last two: the Ducks and the Pittsburgh Penguins.

With the big moment at hand, they put the Penguins' president, Ken Sawyer, and me on stage to represent our teams. Ken is a really low-key guy, but if we had won, I was ready to dance and do the whole Rocky thing.

It was tense. I really thought we were going to win.

And then James Duthie, who was hosting that night, announced, "We'll be right back after a commercial break."

I could have fucking killed him in that moment for making us wait.

After the longest commercial break in history, Gary Bettman stepped to the podium. He had a silver envelope with a big number 1 on the outside. Inside was the logo of the team that would claim the first overall pick.

"The No. 1 overall selection in the 2005 entry draft belongs to . . ."

For just an instant, I saw a flash of colour—there's yellow and black in both teams' logos—and I really believed we had it. Then Gary crushed those dreams.

". . . the Pittsburgh Penguins."

I shook Ken Sawyer's hand, and that was that.

When I see Sid now, we talk about what could have been, and he's always gracious about it.

"Well, it worked out well for both of us," he says. "You got your Cup, and I got mine."

But if we had gotten Sid that day, we definitely would have won more than one.

Even without him, we liked our options with the second pick. I really wanted to take Jack Johnson. We already had Corey Perry and we were going to bring back Teemu Selanne, and I was clear with Chuck Fletcher, our head of amateur scouting, that I thought we could use another defenceman. But he and Tim Murray, our director of player personnel, thought we needed a scoring forward, and they won the argument.

That led us to Bobby Ryan. I like Bobby immensely. He's a great kid and a great player. I pushed to select him for the American Olympic team in 2010. As you probably know, he had a very tough childhood, living on the lam under an assumed name (his birth name is Bobby Stevenson) after his father assaulted his mother. The family wound up in California, where Bobby became a legendary roller hockey player as well as a great ice hockey player. We didn't really consider the California connection when we made the decision to draft him, but we certainly sold him that way in Anaheim after we picked him.

The one thing that pissed me off was that I knew nobody else had Bobby rated as highly as we did. We should have been able to trade down to four or five, pick up something for making the switch, and still get the guy we wanted.

But the Sedin deal kind of wrecked draft day for me. I was radio-active after that. Guys wouldn't even talk to me. Carolina had the third pick and Minnesota had the fourth. The Hurricanes wound up taking Jack Johnson. I asked Doug Risebrough if Minnesota would consider trading down, and he said no way. "I've seen your draft day act before," he said. "We're keeping our pick."

The Canadiens were at five, and they wanted Carey Price there. So, we were stuck picking Ryan at No. 2. Seems to me it's a general manag-er's job to maximize assets, but that day, my argument fell on deaf ears.

With Randy in place, Bob Murray and I could start to take a hard look at our roster. The Samuelis gave me full control over player moves— with one exception. They knew what they knew and they knew what they didn't know, which is a great quality in an owner. They were help-ful, but they deferred to me on personnel decisions.

That exception was a big one, though. At the end of my first year, we had the chance to trade Bobby Ryan for Keith Tkachuk. The Samuelis vetoed it because it would have cost us an extra million and a half dollars that wasn't in our budget. "I'm never going to overrule you on a hockey deal," Henry said, "and if you can make the money work some other way, go ahead and do it." I couldn't, so the deal didn't happen.

I hated the idea of trading an 18-year-old, and Ryan was a blue-chip prospect. But we might have won another Cup if we'd gotten Tkachuk.

Our big move that first summer was landing Scott Niedermayer in free agency. His brother, Robbie, was already with us, and had a year left on his contract. Lou had called me from New Jersey, asking if I'd trade him Robbie—I laughed and said no chance. He was thinking the same thing I was thinking, that having Robbie would give him the upper hand in keeping Scott.

I flew up to Cranbrook to see Robbie and talk to him about an exten-sion. The first thing I asked him was what he thought we needed to do with the team. "I'm sick of us getting pushed around," he told me. "I know your teams don't get pushed around, but we do, and I'm sick of it."

I told him to keep an eye on the transaction wire. We got Todd Fedoruk. We brought in Thornton. We just kept adding toughness, and Robbie had to notice that. Later, we brought in Brad May and traded for George Parros. The Ducks weren't going to be intimidated by anyone.

I went back up to B.C. on July 1 and met with Scotty. It was his first shot at unrestricted free agency, and I asked what his goals were.

"I want to play in the Western Conference," he told me. "I think it's more wide open than the Eastern Conference. I want to play with a contender. And I want to play with my brother."

"There's only one person who can tick all those boxes, and that's me," I told him. "And I'm not trading your brother. If that last part was an oblique reference to a trade and you guys have another team in mind, the answer is no. You're coming here or you're not playing with Rob."

We signed them both the same day, but I insisted on waiting and doing them a half hour apart to keep the two situations distinct. Everybody says Robbie got overpaid and Scott took a little bit less. Maybe a little bit. But both of them got what they wanted, and we had added a true elite No. 1 defenceman who was also a freak of nature in terms of all the minutes he could play.

Scott Niedermayer is also a tremendous leader. I know that can be a cliché, but let me give you an example of exactly what I'm talking about.

During my first season with the Ducks, we were playing a game in Boston. Our AHL farm team, the Pirates, was based in Portland, Maine, which isn't far away, so we brought them in to watch.

Corey Perry was a rookie on our team, and Joffrey Lupul was in his second year. The morning of the game, they were late for the bus that was taking the team to the rink for the skate. The bus was leaving at nine o'clock and they arrived at one minute to nine, so they weren't late, but they were *late*—when you're playing for one of my teams, if you're barely on time, you're late. They showed up breathing hard and with their hair a mess. Obviously, they had slept in and someone had called them to tell them they were about to miss the bus.

Scott was waiting for me in the hotel lobby when the team came back from the arena after the game-day skate.

"What are you going to do with them?" he asked me.

"I'm sending them back to Portland with the Pirates," I said. Randy Carlyle and I agreed that a little trip to the minors would get their attention.

"Don't do that," Scott said. "Let me handle it."

"Okay," I said. "If you're willing to stake your reputation on these two fuck-ups, I'm going to make this interesting. If I have a problem with them of any kind at any point this year, you're going to sit out a game."

"Fine," Scotty said. "I'll handle it."

Perry and Lupul came to see me with their bags packed. They knew they were getting sent down and they were white as sheets (well, Perry is white as a sheet all the time, but that morning he looked like Casper the Ghost).

"There are 20 kids coming down in a bus from Portland to watch us play tonight," I told them. "They would all give their left nut to be in your spot. And you two can't make it to the bus on time. Not only that, if you're sleeping in on a game day, it means you were out last night. NHL players don't go out the night before a game.

"I'm glad you brought your bags, because you're going back with the guys to Portland."

I paused for a minute to let that sink in. Then I let them off the hook.

"You're not going back. You know why? Because our captain thinks you're salvageable. I don't. So I'm leaving your fate with Scott. You guys need to understand what's at stake here. If you fuck up one more time this year, if you break one more team rule, he sits out a game."

We never had another speck of trouble with those kids. They both turned into very good NHL players.

That's Scott Niedermayer.

The other important move that first summer was bringing Teemu Selanne back to Anaheim. Don Baizley was Teemu's agent, and he wanted a ton of money. But Teemu had had his knee completely redone. I loved him as a player, but I wasn't sure he was going to come back as a 30-goal scorer. Baizley and I finally reached a number we could both live with, and Teemu scored 40 goals that season and 48 the next.

As a person, Teemu is the anti–Chris Pronger. He's never in a bad mood. He brings his enthusiasm and positive energy to any room he enters, which has great value in hockey, because this is a business filled with grumpy people. It's like sunshine fills the room when Teemu arrives. He was a great player, but he was also a great teammate. Everybody loved him, and I'm convinced we wouldn't have won the Cup without him.

I especially remember one night in Dallas. We had lost a game to the Stars, and everybody was on the bus, which was supposed to leave at 10:45 for the airport. Everybody but Teemu, that is. "Why the fuck are we sitting here?" I asked our PR guy, Alex Gilchrist.

"Eight Ball," he said—that was Teemu's nickname.

I looked outside, and there was Teemu, signing autographs and having his picture taken. There could have been 200 people out there, and he wasn't going to skip any of them. Finally, he climbed onto the bus.

"Fucking Finn making 35 of us wait while he runs for mayor," I muttered as he walked by my seat.

"Fans, Burkie, fans," he said, giving me a big smile. He couldn't have cared less.

How can you stay mad at a guy like that?

Once the season began, the first real issue I had to deal with was what to do with Sergei Fedorov.

He was a great player who had a great career, and I don't want to shovel dirt on him here. But he was really a problem for us.

When Bryan Murray brought him to Anaheim from Detroit the year before, he envisioned that Sergei would be a star for the Ducks the way he had been for those great Wings teams. But somewhere along the way, Sergei lost interest. He was spending a lot of time in LA. He wasn't a big drinker, so it wasn't that kind of a lifestyle issue, but he loved the nightlife, and he'd be riding back in limos at three or four in the morning, even on days when we were playing a game.

Randy turned on him right away, and I turned on him pretty quickly after that. We both thought Sergei was a bad influence in the dressing room. He had no interest in being part of what we were trying to do, and I felt like other players were starting to follow his lead. That's one of the reasons I sent Getzlaf and Perry down to our AHL team in Portland, and I was straight with them about that. "This is really unfair," I told them. "You've done nothing to warrant this. You don't deserve this. But you can't learn at the knee of a guy who is so self-centred. If you go down and go through the motions, you'll be down there all year. If not, I will solve this problem and then I will bring you back." (To their credit, they went down and tore it up in the AHL. Kevin Dineen was our coach there, and he loved them.)

Fedorov played only five games for us before I traded him to Columbus in the deal that brought Beauchemin to Anaheim. And Perry and Getzlaf came back and both had terrific rookie seasons.

We had a nice team that year. Joffrey Lupul was there. Vitaly Vishnevski. Rusty Salei, who was a wonderful kid. Sandis Ozolinsh was on that team—we traded him at the deadline. It wasn't a Brian Burke team yet, but we got as far as the conference final, where we lost to the Oilers. I think we could have beaten Edmonton that year (I don't know if we could have beaten Carolina, who wound up winning the Cup). We didn't figure out until the fourth game that we were as good as they were, and that was too late. Plus, Chris Pronger was just an unstoppable force for the Oilers. It was as though he had declared, "You're not winning this series," and then backed up his words with his play.

After the season, Bob, Randy and I held a full staff meeting where the first order of business was to answer one big question: "Is this team for real, or did we just get hot and ride Jiggy?"

We all believed that we were for real, that we had the foundation of something special, but we still had to find a missing piece—a true shutdown defenceman. Salei was close to that, but we knew we were going to lose him in free agency. All of us agreed that there was one guy out there who could put us over the top: Pronger. Chris wanted out of Edmonton, and his wife *really* wanted out of Edmonton (she had actually left town the previous Christmas). If we could make a deal for him, it would be a game changer. Take a look at his career. His direct impact on a team's playoff success is a matter of record.

At the draft, Edmonton's assistant general manager, Scott Howson, walked over to four tables, including ours, and dropped off a piece of paper: Pronger trade proposals for each team. They asked us for Lupul, Ladislav Smid and our first-round pick the following year. I didn't hesitate for a minute. "Okay, let's do it," I said to our guys.

We couldn't finalize the trade at the draft because we had to clear up a tagging issue tied to the salary cap. But I assured Kevin Lowe that we had a deal. Lupul had been fantastic for us in the playoffs that year, and we loved Vladdy Smid, who was a first-round pick. (I'll never forget calling Vladdy in the Czech Republic to tell him about the trade. He was in a noisy bar when I got him, and didn't quite get all the details straight. I remember hearing him holler to his buddies, "Hey guys, I just got traded for Chris Pronger!") But it was worth it.

I called Kevin after July 1 to finalize the deal. He was in his car on his way to his place in the Shuswap.

"I'm punching your ticket to the finals," he told me.

"I think you are," I said, "and if we make it, I'll throw in another first-round pick."

Kevin offered to pull over and call the deal in to the league right there, but I told him it could wait until tomorrow.

The day we got Pronger was the day we started talking openly about winning the Stanley Cup. Hockey superstition says you're not supposed to do that; everybody thinks it's bad luck. But we started talking about winning a championship in training camp. I remember telling the players to look around the dressing room. "Look at who's here. Anything less than a Cup is a blown opportunity. Some of you assholes may not get another chance. Scott, you've got three Cups already, but Teemu, you don't have one yet, and Prongs, you don't have one yet. Look around this room. This is your best chance."

It was a fun year. We didn't lose in regulation until the seventeenth game. Scotty Niedermayer is the best puck-moving defenceman I ever had. A quiet leader. A confident guy. And Chris Pronger is the best first-pass defenceman I ever had, plus the ultimate warrior. We had one of those two on the ice all the time, and once in a while when we were scuffling, Randy would put them out together and we would have the puck the whole time. I felt sorry for some of the teams we played.

Early in the season, we played Chicago and we got our forecheck going. We had the Blackhawks pinned in their own end and we changed all five of our skaters—*twice.* The defencemen changed, the forwards changed, the defencemen changed again, the forwards changed again, and we never gave up the puck. The only thing that would have made it a better story would be if we had scored—we didn't.

We also kicked the shit out of teams. It was hilarious. We'd play you any way you wanted to play. You want to fight? We're pretty good at that. We like that. You want to skate? We're pretty good at that. We like that. There was an arrogance around our team, but it was earned. We walked into buildings and you could see the opposing players get nervous.

In the playoffs, we beat Minnesota in five games, and then the Canucks in five (though that second series was harder than it might look now—two of the games were decided in double overtime, and a third in overtime). There was still one hurdle we had to get over. Buffalo and Ottawa were playing in the Eastern Conference final, but I knew we could beat either one of them. We were facing the Red Wings in the Western Conference final. "This is our Stanley Cup," I told our captains.

It wasn't easy. They chased Jiggy in Game 3, and Pronger got suspended for a game for a hit on Tomas Holmstrom. We split the first four games. The big turning point was our overtime win in Game 5 in Detroit. The Wings were leading, 1–0, heading into the final minute. Then Scott Niedermayer took a shot that deflected off Nick Lidstrom's stick and beat Dominik Hasek to tie it with 47 seconds to go. In overtime, Andy McDonald made a steal off Andreas Lilja, passed the puck to Teemu, and he buried it right in the middle of the net (Hasek was overplaying the puck, as usual). Then we came back home and took care of business in Game 6.

No slight to the Senators, our opponent in the finals, but we won the Cup right there.

What a team. What a year.

After the big team party, there was one more celebration. I drove the Stanley Cup down to Camp Pendleton and presented it to a bunch of wounded warriors. These were all US soldiers who had come back missing limbs, suffering from post-traumatic stress disorder. Some of them were in really rough shape. I was in a room full of real heroes, and I'll never forget watching those guys looking for their favourite teams on the Cup, a bunch of them in tears.

That Cup-winning team started to unravel that first summer.

Teemu Selanne and Scott Niedermayer announced their retirements. I tried to talk both of them out of it. I advised Scotty not to sign his retirement papers, suggesting that after he recharged his batteries, he was going to want to come back and play. I even worked on his wife, Lisa, who is a terrific person. They were living in a beautiful place in Newport Beach. "I love the lifestyle," she said. "I love the travel, I love the money. I want him to keep playing. But I'm married to this guy, I love him and I'm going to go along with whatever he wants." So much for playing that card.

What we should have done was assume that both guys would come back later in the season, and keep some cap space available for them. We might've stumbled a little bit for a while, but even if we had a shitty record in February or March, we'd have the band back together; then, all we'd have had to do was get into the playoffs, and we'd have marched to the sea like Sherman. But we didn't do that. We thought we had a standard to maintain. My first year in Anaheim, we played in the conference finals; the second year, we won the Cup. We weren't about to go back to being a third- or fourth-place team. So, we tried to fill all the holes, and that created salary cap issues, which caused all kinds of problems.

I brought in Mathieu Schneider, who just wasn't a good fit for our team. He clashed with our coach and with our captains. I didn't have any problem with him personally, but he just wasn't right for us. We signed Todd Bertuzzi, who I thought would be an effective player because we were a black-and-blue team and he'd fit in well with our group. Bertuzzi was good for us. But I let Sean O'Donnell go, which was really stupid. He was an important part of our team.

And then there was the whole Dustin Penner fiasco.

Penner had just completed his first full season in the NHL and was a restricted free agent. From the start, he was a problematic player for me and for Randy Carlyle. He battled his weight constantly. He was indifferent and lazy. He frequently made mistakes on the ice that were costly. He was grumpy. His teammates liked him, but they didn't love him.

I remember one day, Penner came into the weight room when Bob Murray, Randy and I were all riding exercise bikes before the rest of the players arrived. All of our players had to weigh in every day, and they also weighed in with our strength coach once a week, so we could make sure they weren't lying.

"Get on that scale, you fat fuck!" Randy yelled at Penner. "If you're not under 240, you're not playing tomorrow."

Penner got on the scale, but he kind of hid the number from us and then jumped off and said, "I'm good to go."

"Wait until I get off this bike," Randy said. "We'll check you, you fat fucker." He was screaming at Penner because he knew he was lying.

I thought, "If I have to threaten and beg guys to get in shape to play, I don't want them on my team." Frankly, if I had gotten a decent offer on Penner during the year, I would have traded him.

That said, he had some really good playoff games for us on the way to the Cup, and he's an incredible natural athlete. For a guy his size, he had great feet and great hands. He could dazzle you with his skill. He'd make two or three moves in a period and you'd think, "Christ, if only he could do that more than once a month."

After the season ended, we suspected that we were going to get an offer sheet on Penner. I know people think that the rarity of offer sheets on restricted free agents is evidence of collusion. That's not true. They don't happen because they don't usually work. If the guy is a good enough player, the team is going to match your offer, so why bother?

The reason we weren't willing to match on Dustin Penner was that we were going to be up against the cap, and I didn't think he was worth the aggravation or the money. This player? This money? You can have him. I'll take the compensation picks. Fuck it. We would be relieved to get rid of him.

But the first thing that pissed me off was that if Dustin Penner was worth that kind of dough, what were we going to have to pay Perry and Getzlaf, who were *real* players, *real* warriors, down the road? By overpaying a player, you're fucking up the whole league. You're making my job more difficult just so you can make a splash on free-agent signing day.

Then a breach of etiquette set off a feud between me and Kevin Lowe.

Kevin and I had always gotten along fine. We were friendly. We respected each other. We did the Pronger deal. So, under the circumstances, he should have at least given me a heads-up that the Penner offer sheet was coming. I was in Penticton, teaching at a hockey school, and as it happened, Kevin was in town at the time. He could have called me. Heck, he could have told me in person—he knew where to find me. Instead, I got a fucking fax from the league office. Jesus Christ almighty. That's why I snapped. I blew up. I wasn't picking a fight. I was honestly sour. I was really mad at him.

You have seven days to match an offer sheet, and I waited until the seventh day to confirm that we weren't going to match, even though we knew from the beginning that we weren't. I wanted to make him wait as long as possible.

Things escalated between us later that summer. Kevin did a radio interview in Edmonton and said something along the lines of "I'm so sick of Brian Burke. Tell him anytime, anywhere, we'll fight."

I don't pay attention to the media, but people will always alert you to what's out there. Someone sent me the radio clip, and when I heard it, I couldn't believe it. Kevin Lowe challenged me to a fight? What? Are we in high school?

I immediately called Glen Sather from our house in Newport Beach. The cell service there was better when you were standing outside, so I went out into the backyard. I thought my wife was upstairs, but she was in the kitchen, and she heard every word.

"Your buddy Kevin has just publicly offered to fight me," I told Slats. "That's not cool. So, now he's going to have to go through with it. We're fighting. You tell him that's not how you invite a guy to a fight. Here's how you invite a guy to a fight: I'm going to be at the Holiday Inn in Lake Placid on August 1, 2 and 3. USA Hockey is having a tournament there. You tell Kevin to get himself to Lake Placid, I'll rent a barn, I'll kick the shit out of him there, and then I'll drive him to the hospital."

Sather tried to calm me down.

"You guys are friends," he said.

"Fuck him," I said. "He challenged me to a fight. I've never let anyone challenge me to a fight and let it go."

And that's true. If you challenge me to a fight, fuck it, we're fighting. It's part of the code. It's what you do. If I die tomorrow, they can write on my tombstone that I never took any shit from anyone. So, I meant it: I wanted to fight him. And the cool thing about being a hockey player is that Kevin Lowe wouldn't be the least bit nervous about fighting Brian Burke, and Brian Burke wouldn't be the least bit nervous about fighting Kevin Lowe. If I *had* arranged it, he would have shown up on time. He's not afraid of me and I'm not afraid of him. And so all I was thinking at that point was, "Now I've got to find a barn in Lake Placid."

I got off the phone, and Jennifer was beside herself.

"Have you lost your fucking mind?" she said. "Do you know what Bettman is going to do if he finds out you guys are going to fight?"

"He doesn't have to know about it," I said.

Ten minutes later, Bettman called. To this day, I don't know if Slats called him and alerted him, or if my ex-wife did. But somebody did.

"I'm hearing rumours about you fighting Kevin Lowe," Gary said.

"Well, he fucking started it."

"I don't care who started it," Gary said. "If you two fight, I will suspend you for longer than your contracts. I'll keep you out of the league for two years after your contracts expire. I can't have two of our GMs in a fist fight."

And so, the fight of the century never happened.

After that, our paths crossed occasionally at league events. It was always polite—Kevin is a polite guy by nature. Polite, but not cordial. I was still mad at him. There were people out there who knew he had challenged me to a fight but didn't hear my response, and who thought I had backed down. It was important to me that people not think I backed down. I don't back down from fights.

One day, at my place in Boston, I was on the phone with someone, and Kevin's name came up in the conversation. I ripped him a new asshole. "That fucking, no good Kevin Lowe, etc., etc. . . ."

Brendan overheard my end of it.

"Are you bitching about Kevin Lowe again?" he asked.

"Yeah."

"Didn't you use to be friends?"

"Yeah."

"Didn't you take him on a fishing trip?"

"Yes."

"Then why are you carrying on this grudge years later?"

"Brendan," I told him, "we're Irish. We carry grudges for centuries. I expect you to carry on my grudges after I'm gone."

But Brendan made it pretty clear that he didn't approve.

After Brendan's accident, Steve Tambellini, who was the general manager of the Oilers by that time, called me to tell me how sorry he was.

"You tell Kevin that I have a fence to mend," I said. "I owe him a phone call."

That fence has been mended now, thanks to Brendan.

———

That last season in Anaheim, the magic just never came back. We still had Pronger, and eventually, Teemu and Scotty came back. But the pieces didn't fit anymore. I could sense that. We agonized over what to do. Bob Murray is a pretty smart guy, and Dave Nonis was there by then, too. All three of us struggled with how to fix the team. I think I've erased a lot of my memory of that year. I didn't enjoy it at all. After two seasons of riding high, it was no fun.

We lost to Dallas in the first round of the playoffs. We weren't very good, but I thought we'd beat fucking Dallas. I do remember that Stephane Robidas played out of his mind in that series for the Stars.

After we got knocked out, the focus shifted to my contract situation. I was entering my last year, and I had some decisions to make.

A lot of people think I ditched Anaheim in favour of the Toronto Maple Leafs, and that the Leafs tampered in the process, but nothing could be further from the truth. I loved my time in Anaheim. I loved the owners, I enjoyed living in Southern California, and my wife loved it there. Right after we won the Cup, Jennifer called a real estate agent and found a beautiful place in Newport Beach. She wanted to stay.

And the Samuelis very much wanted me to stay. In October 2008, the night after the Ducks played a game in Toronto, Jennifer and I flew to Minneapolis, where I was honoured to receive the Lester Patrick Award for service to the game of hockey in the United States. Afterwards, at a Chili's restaurant in the airport, I met with Henry Samueli's guy, Mike Schulman. I was just beginning the final year of my four-year contract, and he offered me a 10-year extension to stay with the Ducks. The Samuelis tried to make it easy for me. They told me I could even give up the general manager part of the job any time after the third year, while keeping the salary and keeping the title. It was an incredibly generous offer. I know there are a lot of people in my family and around me who think I should have taken it and stayed there.

But I just couldn't handle the travel anymore. Flying back and forth across the country every other weekend for my kids was killing me. Molly was the only one left at home, but there was no way I was going to break my promise to her, and there was no way I could keep making that trip.

Beyond that, I had to travel to every league meeting, which meant flying to New York or Florida—it seemed they were always on the East Coast. And the Ducks' AHL farm team was located in, of all places, Portland fucking Maine. You couldn't be farther from California and still be in the United States.

I told Mike that if I hadn't won a Cup, maybe I wouldn't feel like I had the right to choose. But I had delivered, I had fulfilled my obligation to the owners, and now, one way or another, I had to go. I was ready and willing to finish the final season on my contract, but after that, I was going to have to leave. I didn't know where I would land next, but I couldn't stay on the West Coast.

The Maple Leafs had fired John Ferguson Jr. the previous January. Cliff Fletcher was running the team on an interim basis. But no one from Toronto had contacted me, and I had never talked to anyone there about it. Richard Peddie and I spoke regularly because we're good friends, but we never talked about the job.

Not long after that conversation in Minneapolis, I was in Toronto for the PrimeTime Sports Management Conference—two of my favourite days of the year. I love the chance to get to teach again.

During the first day of the conference, I got a text from Schulman, telling me that he needed to talk to me right away. I was in the middle of a panel, but in a half hour or so I went up to my room and called him.

"We need you to fly back tomorrow," he said.

"Why?" I asked him.

"We're making a change. Henry wants a GM who is going to be here for the long term. If you're not taking our extension, we're going to make the change now, but we have one problem."

"What's that?"

"You're the executive vice-president and general manager. We can't name a new general manager unless you step aside or we fire you."

I told Mike to forget what it said in my contract. The Samuelis were wonderful people, and I was willing to do whatever they wanted me to do, but I wasn't going to go quietly unless it was to make way for Bob Murray. Mike assured me that the plan was to promote Bob, and so I agreed to come back and endorse the move.

I called Jennifer to tell her what was happening. The first thing she asked me was, "Is Toronto there for us?"

Honestly, I had no idea.

After the conference wrapped up the next day, I flew back to Anaheim for the announcement.

I had two requests of the Ducks. First off, I told them that I'd like to be at the podium with Bob to show my support for him.

"No," they said. "It's got to be the Bob Murray show, not the Brian Burke show."

Fair enough. I wasn't in the room for the announcement, and instead met with the press separately later that day.

I also wanted a chance to meet with the team and explain to the players why I was leaving. They said no to that as well—"It's not your team anymore, it's Bob's team now," they explained. I tried to argue that my players needed to hear from me what was happening; otherwise, it would look like I was bailing on them. The Ducks wouldn't budge.

The only beef I had with the Anaheim Ducks during my whole time there was that they didn't let me say goodbye to my team. That really pissed me off, and it really hurt my feelings. I didn't want them to think I walked out on them. And that is exactly what they thought. We had a team reunion party on the 10th anniversary of the Cup win. I was having a cigar with Teemu at his bar, and he made a crack about me bailing on them and going to Toronto. I took him outside and told him the story of what really happened.

"Burkie, the guys don't know that," he said. I told him to spread the word and make sure they knew that I didn't leave of my own volition, that the Samuelis pulled the plug on me.

That night, at the game, Bob and I sat in our usual box, but we switched places. He was sitting in the boss's seat now.

The next day, I flew up to Vancouver to get out of town, clear my head and spend a couple of days duck hunting. (The duck part is purely coincidence.)

16 ▼ THE VATICAN OF HOCKEY

WHILE I WAS AWAY hunting, the Leafs called Anaheim for permission to approach me, and the Ducks agreed—they were more than happy about the prospect of getting me off their payroll. From there, things moved quickly. Richard Peddie called me and asked me if I was interested. I told him that my contract ran through the end of June and that I wasn't worried about where my next job would come from, but I was very interested. One of my goals had always been to work for an Original Six team. We talked about terms and had a couple of good discussions.

The truth is, Richard was one of the biggest reasons I wanted to come to Toronto. I really respect him. He's been one of the best executives in all of professional sport over the past 20 years. He's a progressive thinker. When he was running the Leafs, they moved women into positions of power and authority, they gave young people opportunities, they promoted people of colour. Richard ran the organization brilliantly.

The next step was for me to meet Larry Tanenbaum and the people from the Ontario Teachers' Pension Plan, who co-owned the team. I had always liked Larry from afar. When you work for the league, some of the owners are happy to ignore you—even when I was Anaheim's senior VP of hockey operations, a lot of the owners didn't know my name. But Richard and Larry would always talk to me like an equal.

They wanted me to come to Toronto for the meeting, but I said no way—there isn't a chance I could fly there without being seen. So, we set it up at an airport hotel in Boston instead. In addition to Larry and Richard, the Leafs were represented by Dale Lastman, and by Erol Uzumeri from the Ontario Teachers' Pension Plan.

One of the first things they asked me was how long it was going to take to make the team competitive, and I was honest with them. I told them five years. "You've got an overpaid team with a lot of no-trade contracts," I told them. "It's going to take me two years just to shovel out the stable before I can bring the new horses in."

My main question for them was about ownership. After what I had been through in Vancouver, I wanted assurances that it wasn't about to change. "I got fired because a team got sold," I told them. "We're talking about a five-year deal. Tell me that Larry and Richard are going to stay involved, and tell me you're not going to sell this team. If that's not what the future holds, I want to know right now."

"This team makes $80 million a year for us," Uzumeri said. "It's one of our best assets."

"So, there's no chance it will be sold?" I asked.

"No chance."

Of course, by the end of my third year, Richard Peddie was gone, the team was on the block, and soon enough, I was on my way out the door. I don't think I was lied to. I think they intended to keep the team. In any case, that day, I could have been forgiven for believing that the Toronto Maple Leafs were the most stable organization in all of professional sports.

A few days after the meeting in Boston, we finalized the deal, and then I flew to Toronto for the press conference. That's where I first used the line that whoever finally wins the Cup in Toronto is going to have schools named after them—not just streets, but schools. It would be that big.

But no one had done it since 1967, and some of the people who had been in charge over the last half century (and then some) knew what they were doing. This isn't an excuse—I didn't get the job done in Toronto, and that's my fault. But for anyone who takes on the Toronto Maple Leafs, there are a bunch of hurdles to surmount that just don't exist in other hockey markets.

It's a combination of things. The sheer volume of the media coverage in Toronto is unlike anywhere else. When we were struggling in Calgary, there were maybe 20 media people in the dressing room after a game, looking for answers. In Toronto, it's 80 for a weeknight game against a soft opponent, and 100 on Saturday night or when the visiting team matters. Now add on social media, which I hadn't really had to deal with before I came to Toronto. You're under a microscope every day, and the coverage is overwhelmingly negative. When things are going badly, every one of those 100 people has a rock ready to throw. Whether they decide it's Brian Burke's fault or Ron Wilson's fault or Randy Carlyle's fault or Phil Kessel's fault or Dion Phaneuf's fault, they pick targets and they hammer away.

I told my players that when they retired and looked back at their careers, the best years would be the ones they played in Canada in front of people who loved them and loved the team and loved the sport. I said they should realize how lucky they were to play in Canada. That's why I worked in Canada every chance I've had—hockey isn't a sport here, it's a religion.

But some guys just couldn't handle the spotlight. We brought in Francois Beauchemin, who had been so good for us in Anaheim, and he just couldn't deal with the attention. It got to the point where we would have a discussion before we traded for a guy or drafted a guy— he might be an NHL player, but can he play *here*? Sometimes, we'd decide the answer was no, and we'd find someone else.

The flip side of that is the sense of entitlement that can creep in. When I was in Anaheim, I think two players had car deals—you make a couple of appearances a year for a dealership, and you get a nice Porsche or something similar. It's yours, for free, for the whole season. In Toronto, every player has a car deal. Every single player. And they don't pay retail for anything. You want a suit? They've got a guy who'll get you an Armani suit for three grand instead of five. You want a new stereo system? There's a guy who will install a $9,000 system for you for only five grand, just so long as you're a Leaf.

In a Canadian city, if you're playing well, they'll idolize you, and you can get a big head. But if you start playing badly, the same people will trash you mercilessly, and that's when the lack of privacy really kicks in. It's a horrible price to pay.

Canadian taxes are another issue. Players—including Canadian-born players—don't want to play here and pay our taxes. When I was in Calgary, I'd offer our players a modified no-trade clause where they could list eight teams they couldn't be dealt to. Invariably, every one of the Canadian teams was on the list. Even for the Canadian kids!

And in Toronto, you're also dealing with what I call the Ontario effect. There are so many players on visiting teams who grew up in and around Toronto. You don't think they're going to play as hard as they can in front of their family and friends? People don't generally acknowledge it, but it's very real. When the Islanders came to town, John Tavares used to put on a show for his family against us.

Add it all up, and in Toronto, it's not just about the team you put on the ice.

When I arrive in a new job, I don't start by cleaning house. I like to give everyone a chance. I've never gone in and fired a bunch of people, because I don't think it's the right thing to do. There are good people everywhere. And the reason a team fails is usually the decision maker at the top, not the people below them.

Aside from changing some things about the way we scouted and rated players, my first moves in Toronto involved adding talent to the organization. I brought in Dave Poulin, who's excellent. I brought in Dave Nonis, of course, because he's always travelled with me. I brought in Claude Loiselle, who's a smart, talented guy.

I also decided to keep Ron Wilson, my old college teammate, as the head coach. On one level, I knew that Ronnie wasn't the right guy for the way I wanted my team to play. As much as I like him, our philosophies on how to play are completely different. He didn't value toughness the way I do.

I remember early on, we had a disagreement about Colton Orr, who's a true heavyweight. I told Ron that he had to play Colton every night—and I added that I was embarrassed that I had to have a meeting about it so that I could order him to do something that I thought was obvious. It was the only time I've had to go to one of my coaches and tell him who to play.

Ron thought that if he had a forward who could make some plays and do things better than Colton, it would make us a better team. And no one will deny that in terms of skill, Colton Orr is a limited guy. But everyone was a little braver when Orr was on the bench. I believed we needed that intimidating presence.

But I wanted to give Ron a real chance, not only because we were friends, but because I think every coach deserves a chance. In hindsight, I stayed too long with him, and that was probably a big part of what cost me my job in the end. But I felt that you fire a coach when he can't win with a team that's good enough to win—and the team that was there when I arrived was not good enough to win. I wasn't going to make a decision on Ron until I had given him enough assets that he had a shot.

By the time I got to Toronto, Ronnie had already been beaten up pretty badly by the media. He had become jaded and sarcastic. I talked to him about it—I told him that sarcasm doesn't work in Toronto. But he'd been chewed up so much that he was already a shell.

Toronto can kill you that way. I know it aged Dave Nonis after he took over as the general manager. If you listen to the white noise, it can kill you, especially if you're not winning. But I don't think it had much of an effect on me because I honestly didn't care what the media said.

One day, Damien Cox from the *Toronto Star* came into my office to interview me. "I know you say you don't read anything that's written about you, but I know you really do," Damien said.

I led him out of my office to the desk where my assistant, Catherine Grey, laid out the media clippings for me each day. They put the date on the top corner, and the stack was about two feet high.

"Go through that stack," I said to Damien, "and if you find one day where I took out the clips and read them—*one day*—I'll apologize. Go ahead and look."

He looked at a couple and didn't find any evidence that I'd read anything.

"You know what I do when this pile gets too big?" I asked. Then I reached over and pushed the whole stack into a recycling bin.

"That's what I do. That's what I think of what you write about the hockey team."

Damien was a little bit sour about that.

When I took stock of the team I inherited in Toronto, it was pretty clear that there was a lot of work to be done. My model for success was the same as it had been going back to my AHL days in Maine: a top six up front with a high skill level, a blue-collar bottom six, lots of speed and lots of toughness. That Leafs team had some skilled players, mostly Europeans, who were a little past their prime. A lot of guys were over-paid. We had a lot of no-trade and no-movement contracts. And we had no toughness at all.

We didn't really have any quality defencemen. Ian White was serviceable, and we had Tomas Kaberle, who was serviceable but really on the soft side. His puck retrievals were really cautious.

The first thing I asked Ronnie Wilson was whether we needed a goalie. He was convinced that Vesa Toskala could do the job. I was skeptical about that, and as it turned out, I was right.

As I mentioned before, when I get to a new team, I like to take the first season to evaluate what I have, and then, at the end of that season, make a splash. I made an early deal to bring in Brad May—Mayday has kind of followed me around for my entire career. But the big, signature move was trading for Phil Kessel just before my second season with the Leafs started, in September 2009.

If you don't like Kessel as a player, you wouldn't have liked the trade in any case. I love Phil, but in Toronto, he never recovered from the label that we paid too much to get him. His demeanour didn't help him, either. He's one of those guys who doesn't care at all whether the media likes him, or even whether the fans like him—and fans like you to care whether they like you.

I remember one day, after Phil got ripped by the media, I went down and sat beside him at his stall in the dressing room. I asked him if he wanted me to blow something up, to pick a fight about something so it would cause a distraction and get the media off his back for a couple of days. "Want me to brush the flies off?" I said. "Want me to do a rant?"

"Burkie," he told me, "the only guys I care about are right here." He pointed around the dressing room. "Don't you dare start a shitstorm over me."

He was dead serious. He didn't care then and he doesn't care today. That's one of the things his teammates love about him. He doesn't give a shit about what's happening outside the rink. He just plays. But it hurt him in the Toronto market, and the money he was making hurt him. Canadians hate athletes they perceive to be overpaid and underperforming.

A big part of that perception didn't set in until it became clear exactly how much he had cost us in the deal, and that's where I'm not afraid to admit that I made a mistake.

To get Phil, we gave Boston a first- and a second-round pick in 2010, and another first-round pick in 2011. There's no arguing that the price we paid for him turned out to be way too high. Nobody was in the habit of "lottery-protecting" draft picks in trades in those days—it just wasn't done. But even if it was, I don't think I would have asked for it, because we were absolutely sure that we were going to be a decent team. We figured the pick would wind up being around 10th or 12th. We didn't foresee the 18-wheeler going off the cliff.

It's not like we didn't talk about it. Our biggest fear was missing out on Taylor Hall, who wound up going first overall. Not so much on Tyler Seguin, whom the Bruins took with our pick, which would end up being No. 2.

"Guys," I remember saying when we debated doing the deal, "there's no fucking way this is going to be a top-five pick. We're a good enough team, we finished strong last year, and with the changes we made and adding Kessel, we're going to be that much better."

I was wrong about that, and it cost us dearly. But the team I built in Toronto was heading in the right direction. We became the fastest team in the NHL and the toughest—not as good as my Stanley Cup team in Anaheim, but built along the same lines. The other team's defence would have to give up ice as soon as we got the puck because we were so fast with Kessel, Mikhail Grabovski and Nikolay Kulemin. And behind them we had a chain gang, guys like Colton Orr and Mark Fraser. The only player they added after I was fired in what turned out to be the season when they made the playoffs for the first time in years—was Frazer McLaren. All the other pieces were already in place.

We got rid of Toskala and brought in J.S. Giguere, who wasn't in quite the same form he was when we won the Cup in Anaheim, but still he was good for us. We traded Kaberle to the Bruins for a first-rounder and Joe Colborne.

That was a funny story. I remember calling Rick Curran, who was Kaberle's agent, and telling him I wanted to move Tomas. "He's a great kid," I told Rick. "He's smart. He's funny. But he's not committed enough to our program and I'm not going to sign him after his deal is up at the end of the year."

"He has a full no-trade and no-move clause in his contract," Rick said to me.

"I know that," I said. "The Toronto Maple Leafs gave him that. But I didn't."

"I don't think that's good faith," Rick said. "Fergie gave that to him in good faith."

"Well, it was a mistake. I've never given any player a full no-trade or no-move."

"He doesn't want to go anywhere," Curran said.

"Rick, let me explain how this works," I said. "One way or another, Tomas has played his last game here. I can't move him or trade him without his permission, but I don't have to dress him. Tell Tomas that unless I get a list of teams from him that he's willing to be traded to, he will spend the rest of the season sitting in the press box next to me. I'll start by putting him there this Saturday night, and we can both wave at the *Hockey Night in Canada* cameras together."

Rick called me back and told me Tomas was willing to go to Boston. That wasn't a list—that was one team. But eventually, we made it work.

———

Everyone remembers the Kessel deal, but I think the biggest deal I made was going out and getting the No. 1 defenceman we desperately needed, Dion Phaneuf.

I fell in love with Dion as a player the first time I saw him at the World Juniors. I thought he was everything you could want in a defenceman—big shot, physical, a vocal leader, a guy who could move the puck. He would be perfect for us.

It was January, and the trade deadline was more than a month away. As you may know, I'm not a deadline-day guy. I think that all it does is make teams overpay. Remember the blue-light special at Kmart—they'd set up a flashing blue light somewhere in the store, announce a great bargain, and all the shoppers would converge, in a frenzy, wanting to buy whatever it was. That's what it looks like at the NHL trade deadline. There are three or four players everyone wants, all the shopping carts surround them, and someone ends up overpaying.

All of those general managers are desperate to make a splash. Maybe they want to impress their owners by proving they're doing something; maybe they're in the fifth year of a five-year contract and haven't made the playoffs, and if they make the playoffs this year, it will save their job. That's a huge change since I came into the league. Guys now trade just to win a round in the playoffs. Not when I started. The result is a classic feeding frenzy, and a dozen or more teams might make big moves, even though the last time I checked, they hand out only one Stanley Cup every year, and there's only one parade. That's why more mistakes are made on trade deadline day, and on July 1 when the UFAs become available, than the rest of the days of the year combined.

I like to get ahead of that and get my work done before things get crazy. This story will give you a pretty good idea about all the things that can come into play before a trade comes together.

Darryl Sutter was running the Calgary Flames then. We were both doing our due diligence as general managers. As I remember it, it was a Wednesday when we first connected by phone.

"What are you looking to do?" Darryl asked me.

"I'm only interested in one guy off your team, and that's Dion," I said.

"I'm not moving Dion," he told me—and that was that.

The next day, Bob Murray called me from Anaheim.

"Are you in on Dion?" he asked me.

"They're not moving him," I told Bob.

"Well, that's funny, because they just offered him to me."

You can imagine how I reacted to that. As soon as I got off the phone with Bob, I called Darryl.

"What the fuck are you doing?" I asked him.

He told me to relax, that he had been just about to call me, that they had changed their minds and Dion was now in play.

So, this is on the Thursday. Earlier that same day, Ron Wilson had come to me and told me he wanted me to get rid of three guys on the team as soon as possible.

"I need you to move Nik Hagman," he said. "I need you to move Jamal Mayers. And I need you to move Ian White."

Hagman had stopped scoring for us and had gotten drilled a couple of times, and we thought he was avoiding contact a little too studiously. Mayers was a good player—my kind of player, in fact—but he was getting on Ronnie's nerves because he was a leader on the team and he wasn't always delivering the same message as Ronnie. Ron liked him— he had even considered him for the captaincy at one point—but he felt Jamal had started making too much noise.

"You have to get rid of him," Ronnie said.

Ron thought that Ian White was expendable. We liked his play. He was a small, right-shooting defenceman who could move the puck, but he could be a frustrating player, prone to big mistakes.

The truth is, we didn't *have* to move any of them—it wasn't as though they'd started to stink like week-old fish. But moving them and getting something back could help us get to where we wanted to be as a team.

Two of the first three players Darryl asked for were Hagman and Mayers. So, that part was going to be easy. The third player he asked for was Matt Stajan. Matt is a great kid. We didn't really want to trade him, but to get Dion Phaneuf, we would have thrown two Stajans in.

Then Darryl said, "You've got to take back some money to make this work—you've got to take Fredrik Sjostrom off our hands."

We liked Sjostrom, so I was okay with that.

"And I'm trading you a defenceman, so I need a defenceman back," Darryl said. "We want Ian White."

So, now all three guys that Ronnie asked me to get rid of were in the deal.

It was time for me to push back a bit.

"I'm not doing four for two," I told Darryl, "especially since the second guy I'm getting is a cash dump, so it's really four for one. No way I'm doing that."

I asked him to throw in Keith Aulie, whom our scouts really loved.

"There is no fucking way I'm doing that," Darryl said.

We hung up—politely.

I turned to my guys, who had been listening in on the conversation, and said, "If we are going to lose this deal over Keith Aulie, I'm going to fucking fire someone here. The guy we want is Dion. The pieces we're moving, other than Stajan, are guys we don't want. We actually like Sjostrom. What the fuck are we doing?"

But our guys were unanimous that they really wanted Aulie, so we left it there.

The next day—Friday—Darryl called back and said he'd give us Aulie. So, we had a deal. But there was a minor complication.

Darryl said he needed a day to sell his ownership on the trade. One problem—that day was Saturday, and all seven guys would be playing. What if one of them—or more than one of them—got hurt?

"I'll do it sight unseen," Darryl said. "Even if all the guys get hurt, I'll still do it. We can register the deal on Sunday." I agreed.

All of our guys got through our Saturday night game okay. Then, with the time difference, we had to wait for the Calgary game to finish. Dion and Sjostrom got through that one okay.

Aulie was playing in the AHL. His game was in Abbotsford, B.C. Our chief scout, Mike Penny, was watching him there, and it was about 1:30 in the morning in Toronto before he called to tell me that Aulie had gotten through the game unscathed.

We made the deal official the next day.

Dion Phaneuf may be the most dedicated athlete I've ever seen, especially when it comes to his off-season training. He works so hard. He is ultra-competitive, and he gets impatient and frustrated with teammates who aren't as competitive as he is. Dion would block a puck with his face to win a regular-season game. He would dive in front of a shot and never think twice about it. His physical strength is amazing. He is always the first guy on the ice and the last guy off. He'd drag his teammates into the weight room. After a practice, he'd go to the gym and ride the bike for 35 minutes, and by the time he finished, there would be a pool of sweat around him on the floor. He moved the puck well, had a huge shot, and would fight for his teammates.

The hardest thing for Dion in Toronto was being around guys who didn't care the way he cared. Later in life, I can imagine him playing in a beer league somewhere, and getting in a fight with somebody—maybe even with a teammate who isn't trying hard enough. He can't help it.

Dion loved being the captain here, and he certainly didn't mind being the centre of attention. It's not an ego thing, though. It just doesn't affect him. He's going to play his game with or without the C.

In Toronto, the crowd kind of turned on him after he got the big contract extension at the end of 2013. Canadians hate high-salaried athletes in general, and they invariably blame them when the team isn't winning. There was a TV piece around that time that certainly didn't help—they toured his house and he showed off all his suits and his collection of expensive watches. In terms of public opinion, Dion had a hard time recovering from that.

I was proud to run the Leafs. I wouldn't trade that for anything. But nothing is quite the same as getting the call to run the team that represents the best of the whole country where I learned the game.

After we won the Cup in Anaheim, USA Hockey approached me and asked if I would be interested in getting involved with international hockey. They offered me the chance to be the general manager of the American team at the World Championship in 2009, and then to do the same job with the Olympic team in Vancouver in 2010. I had contributed to the US program before, as general manager of the team at the World Championship in 1993, but I stepped aside after Doug Palazzari came in as executive director of USA Hockey. He didn't like pro hockey—he wanted it to be all amateur—so we didn't see eye to eye, and I didn't have anything to do with the program for about five years. I wasn't the only one—it was the same story for Mike Milbury and a lot of others. Some of us felt we had the wrong guy running the show. But when Dave Ogrean came back to replace Palazzari in 2005, it was a different story, and I was happy to get back in.

I suggested that, rather than it just being me and an assistant general manager, we ought to form a committee with all the American GMs from the NHL. We ought to make it bigger and better. So we brought in David Poile, Stan Bowman, Dale Tallon and Dean Lombardi. That's how we picked the team for the 2009 World Championship and that's how we picked the Olympic team in 2010. Those teams are all picked the same way today. We added maximum talent to the management teams.

Not long after I got the job, I called Jerry Colangelo in Phoenix. I didn't know him personally, but I had admired him from afar and wanted to talk to him about how he assembled the basketball Dream Team that went to the Barcelona Olympics in 1998. How do you take a group of highly paid professional athletes who are All-Stars in their own right, turn them into a cohesive group, and turn winning a gold medal for their country into a singular goal?

Jerry agreed to a meeting, but on the day I went to his office, he was dealing with some kind of crisis, so his time was really short—instead of 45 minutes, I had to make do with 15. So much for small talk. I got right to the point.

"What's the most important part of putting together an Olympic team?" I asked him.

"Don't make it about hockey, the way we didn't make it about basketball," he said. "Make it about being an American. The easiest way to do that is to build a tie with the military."

He talked about making sure the housing at the Olympics was appropriate, and about not putting together an All-Star team—it wasn't just about assembling the best talent, but about finding the right pieces that would fit together as a unit, which is exactly how we ended up selecting our roster. All great advice—and all delivered in 15 minutes.

The military part especially resonated with me. We held our Chicago orientation camp in the summer of 2009, and we brought in some American heroes to speak to the players. Joe Dias was an Army Ranger who got hit with a piece of shrapnel when they were attacking an oasis in Iraq. Chad Fleming lost a leg in Afghanistan. He had 20 surgeries and finally told doctors to amputate the leg, and then he went back and did three tours with a prosthetic limb. Mike Walton was a Medal of Honor winner, the most decorated Navy SEAL in the Vietnam War. When we got to Vancouver, another Army Ranger visited the team in the athletes' village. Had his nose shot off in an attack, then was shot in the abdomen, and still refused to get on a stretcher, walking to the evac helicopter on his own. Each of our players in Vancouver carried a personal memento from one of the wounded servicemen. Ryan Miller, for instance, received an ammunition round from a Marine vet who'd had it removed from his body.

The Winter Classic was played at Fenway Park in Boston on January 1, 2010, and that's where we announced the US Olympic team. Brendan, the girls and I had a chance to skate on the ice before the game.

Brendan was more enthused about the Olympics than all my other kids combined. He was so excited about the chance to go to Vancouver and see the Games, and he was following every country's selection process. He knew more about it than anyone I knew.

We all went out for dinner after the game. Afterwards, I said goodbye to Brendan and his sisters and we went our separate ways.

I never saw him again.

BRENDAN

BRENDAN WAS GOING TO go to law school. He interned with a US congressman the summer before his accident, and I think he would have gone into politics eventually. I know that he was furious to learn that, because he had been born in Canada—in Vancouver, when I was the assistant GM there—he was ineligible to become president of the United States.

He was considering the law schools at both the University of Michigan and Michigan State. On February 5, he had been in Lansing and was rushing back to get to a Miami University game. A friend named Mark Reedy was with him. Brendan was driving.

He was going too fast in a blizzard. He skidded through an intersection not far from the Indiana–Ohio border, narrowly missing a minivan. If he had hit the van, everyone would have walked away. Instead, he hit a reinforced pickup truck. He might as well have hit a brick wall.

When the first responders got there, they tried to revive him. They performed CPR until one of them finally said, "We can do this indefinitely, but he's not coming back." He had broken his neck. My son was dead. His friend Mark died, too.

(I later met with Mark Reedy's parents in Detroit, near their home, when the Leafs came in to play the Red Wings. They're nice people. Their son died in my son's car, and so they have every reason to hate my guts, but for some reason, they don't.)

I was in London, Ontario, watching Nazem Kadri play for the Knights when Patrick called me.

"Brendan's dead," he said.

I collapsed to the ground.

Trevor Whiffen, my friend and partner in the PrimeTime Sports Management Conference, was with me that night. He wanted to drive me home.

"No, I need to be alone," I told him.

"You can't drive," he said.

"Trevor, I'm fine," I said. "I just need to be alone."

All I remember about that drive back along Highway 401 was trying to make a deal with God. "I will drive this truck off the road and into a bridge and die right now if you will promise me my son comes back. I will bury this fucking truck. I want to trade my life for his." Waiting for a sign—and I would have done it. But the sign never came.

The Leafs were playing a game in New Jersey that night, and the team got back to Toronto before I did. Dave Nonis and Ron Wilson were waiting for me at the house when I arrived.

The next day, the blizzard that Brendan had been driving through hit Toronto. Larry Tanenbaum had arranged for a private jet to fly me to Indiana to get my son, and they had an air ambulance ready to fly him home to Boston. But I wound up stuck in the airport in Toronto all day because we couldn't take off in the bad weather.

My son had been alone that first night. I absolutely didn't want him to be alone for a second night. Finally, we got out late in the afternoon, and arrived just as the sun was going down.

I said I wanted to see Brendan. The guy there warned me that they had put all kinds of lanolin and creams on him to keep his skin fresh-looking. They cleaned him up a little bit before they let me see him.

When Brendan was puzzled, he would get this wrinkle in his brow—kind of a signal that something was not quite right. He had that look now—even dead, he had that look. Something's not right. And he had a scuff where the seatbelt hit him on his jaw.

The whole day, I was trying to find out more about the boy who died with him. I called Katie and asked her to find out more about him. I had to call his parents. I had to reach out to them. Their son died in Brendan's car.

The air ambulance brought us back to Boston—just me and my wife and Brendan. The funeral home picked up Brendan's mom and the other kids in a limo. When we landed, they put Brendan in a hearse and we all went back to the funeral home—Dockray & Thomas, run by a guy named Brian Fitzgerald. I need to mention them here, because they were great to us when we really needed their help.

"What would you like us to do?" Fitzgerald asked us.

"We will have a wake," I told him, "and then we will have a funeral Mass. But we are not going to bury him that day. We will have a reception for all the guests coming from out of town at the country club."

Going through all the details and planning helps you deal with it, or at least it did for me.

The Leafs sent their entire team, and so did Miami University. And the NHL is always great when one of its family is going through a crisis.

The day of the wake was bitterly cold. The viewings were scheduled for between three and five in the afternoon and seven and nine in the evening. By two o'clock, there were people lined up on the sidewalk, and at first I didn't understand who they were.

"What are they doing?" I asked Brian Fitzgerald.

"They are here to see your son," he said.

"Let them in," I said. "It's too cold to be out there."

There were people from town. People from Brendan's high school.

I stood in the same place the whole day. People streamed through from two o'clock to 10 at night without a break. In all, more than 1,000 people came.

At about seven o'clock, I asked my older brother Bill to go out and get us some beer. My wife, Jennifer, was horrified at the suggestion that we would bring beer into a funeral home. But this was supposed to be an Irish wake, and that's the tradition.

I gave Bill about 200 bucks, and the crowd went through the beer he brought back in about half an hour. So I sent him out and got more beer and some booze. We set up a makeshift bar with bottles and Solo cups. It turned into what a wake is supposed to be: a chance to mourn, but also to remember the good times.

The next day was the funeral Mass. A neighbour who had lived across the street from us when the kids were young sang Leonard Cohen's song "Hallelujah." To this day, I can't listen to that song. I hate that fucking song.

Molly was sitting with me and she said, "Dad, I can't stay and listen to this." We went outside behind the church and there were fucking photographers there. That really pissed me off. I guess I understand now that they were just doing their jobs. But seeing the media standing around snapping pictures of me . . .

Those fuckers.

We went back in after the song was finished, and after the Mass we went to the reception.

The next day, we buried Brendan. It was bitterly cold again. We didn't bring a big group to the cemetery. I didn't want a lot of people there.

In winter, after the ground freezes, they have to thaw it so they can dig the grave. They put burning charcoal on top of the grave to soften the soil, and then they bring the backhoe in. When we got there, there were still six or seven guys in overalls, standing around the gravesite. I didn't realize that they were there to get the grave and the coffin ready before we got out of the car.

"What are those guys doing at my son's funeral?" I asked.

They positioned the coffin so that he could be lowered into the grave, and then we buried him.

It was so fucking cold. I remember thinking, "He's going to be so cold in there."

We buried him next to his grandpa, which was nice. And he's in the only cemetery in the world that has a trolley line running through it. The trolley to Mattapan goes right through the cemetery. Brendan is in a nice, quiet corner, where there are always a lot of birds.

Those were the worst few days of my life.

I wouldn't wish the experience on my worst enemy. I hope it never happens to the person I hate most in life.

I called a family meeting the day after we buried Brendan. I took the older three kids out to lunch at an Irish bar and we talked. I remembered that I had a cousin who died young, and his dad never recovered from it.

"We have to talk about what we are going to do here," I said to the kids. "This is critical. We have two choices: we sit down on the side of the road with our heads down and mope, or we march ahead. And I am marching ahead and so are you. We are going to find a way to make Brendan relevant and remembered forever, but we are walking forward as a family. The four of us can do anything. And we are just going to keep doing what we do well. Keep doing our charity work. Keep all the values that you've learned from me and your mom. And keep marching.

"Anyone have a problem with that?"

We all made a vow that day to carry on.

The kids were worried about me. Here was this big, tough guy who was a wreck for weeks. But what saved me was work. The Olympics in Vancouver were coming up. The people from USA Hockey came to the funeral, and they told me that someone else could take over the team if that was what I wanted. They said they'd announced the roster, that they could take it off my plate, that I was free and clear.

I said no way. Brendan cared so much about the Olympics, and it meant so much to him that I was putting together the American team.

"I'm so proud of you, Dad," he told me.

I had to go—and I had to go on.

The Leafs were great to me. Richard Peddie was such a wonderful boss. He told me to take as much time as I needed. He offered to let me work from home, or work just a couple of hours a week. He asked me if I wanted to take a leave of absence and go away somewhere.

"I can't," I told him. "I just can't. I've got to stay on the hamster wheel. It's my therapy. I don't have a choice."

If I hadn't had both of those jobs to keep me busy, I know I would have hit rock bottom.

I came pretty close anyway.

———

Brendan Burke was a special kid. I'm convinced he would have been the first openly gay senator from the Commonwealth of Massachusetts, and even if he hadn't done that, he would have done something productive and meaningful with his life.

But he never got the chance.

He had earned enough credits to graduate posthumously with his class at Miami. I've set up a scholarship in his name at the school.

After Brendan died, his brother, Patrick, started the organization You Can Play. He used Brendan's example to help gay athletes with the coming-out process, and to let them know that they were welcome in sports. If you can play—you *can* play.

The response from the hockey community was mind-boggling. Players stepped up immediately. Zdeno Chara was one of the first. They did this great public service announcement, all these players shot in tight, in black and white, saying, "If you can shoot, you can shoot. If you can score, you can score. If you can play, you can play." The league immediately became official partners.

We are not going to let Brendan's memory die. He has already changed lives.

When you work in hockey in Canada, there is no privacy, but people are so kind. People would stop me and hug me in elevators and on the street—just random strangers. Everyone knew. I got probably 1,000 pieces of mail. People took the time to write these beautiful letters.

I remember getting a letter from a guy—handwritten, three pages long.

"Mr. Burke, I was driving my son back to university in Guelph and suddenly he said pull over, here, at this liquor store. I thought that was odd because my son doesn't drink. He said, 'Dad, I'm gay.' The thought that went through my mind in that moment is that if it's good enough for Brian Burke, it's good enough for me. So I said, 'No problem.' You have no idea how you helped me with this."

And I still get letters from boys I never met who say they came out to their parents a week after Brendan's death, or a week after he came out.

My son made a tremendous difference during his short life. When someone dies young and tragically, you always hear people on the news talking about how they were special. The truth of it is, most of us aren't special. Some of us are average. Some of us are assholes.

Brendan wasn't mean enough to make it in hockey—to succeed in hockey, you've got to be a bit of a prick—but he was handsome and smart and sweet and everybody loved him. I wonder what he would have accomplished by now if he were still here. I know that he would have been a star.

And we're going to make sure that his legacy continues.

"NOT TODAY" DAYS IN TORONTO

THE OLYMPICS BEGAN A week after Brendan died. Being there was the best possible therapy for me.

The captains of our team had dog tags made up with Brendan's name on them. They came into the coaches' office in Vancouver and gave me the dog tags and then left. I sat and sobbed for about a half an hour. Our coaches, Ronnie Wilson and John Tortorella, did their best to stay out of my way and went about their business while I had a good little cry.

Then I went back to the business of trying to win a gold medal.

I still carry those dog tags. I have two loonies that I had in my pocket when I made the Pronger deal, which are good luck charms. I have a medal that Kerry Fraser gave me that was blessed by the Pope. And I have those tags.

Our team started the tournament really well. We took the right group of guys there—just as Jerry Colangelo advised. Not necessarily the best talent, but the best team. We had guys like Chris Drury and Tim Gleason—Swiss Army knife guys. Gleason led our team in blocked shots and killed every penalty. We included some non–household names. We got heavily criticized for it before the Olympics, but we got it right.

We won the first two games in the preliminary round, and then we beat Canada, 5–3, to finish on top of our pool—and you could argue that that's what really cost us the tournament. Martin Brodeur was the starter, and we chased him in that game, so they went with Roberto Luongo. Luongo was better than Marty at that point in his career, and I think that's what won Canada the gold medal in the end. To this day,

I wonder what would have happened if we hadn't poured it on. What if we had scored only four goals? Would they have stuck with Brodeur?

After that win over Canada, I remember my son Patrick saying to me, "Your team seems a little arrogant."

"You know what? I had the same feeling," I told him. "They're smug. You have no right to be smug until you win something. Then it might be obnoxious to be smug—but you can be smug if you've got a ring or a gold medal." So I blasted our team the next day. Other than a couple of guys in our leadership group and our goalie, I told them we didn't have anything to brag about. We were relying too much on two or three guys and we weren't pulling hard enough on the rope.

To their credit, nobody pouted. They knew who I was yelling at. And they just started pulling harder.

The other thing I remember about that first Canada game was the experience of walking back to the hotel through the streets of Vancouver. The crowd that night was really hostile, really sour. I guess the US isn't supposed to beat Canada in men's hockey. People were yelling at me, "Fuck you, Burkie, you fucking American!"

I'm not good at taking abuse. I barked back at a couple of them. I was really worried I was going to get into a fight, and once you get into a fight in a mob you're dead. You can't fight five guys. Those Bruce Lee movies are full of shit. You get five people on you and you're going to get beaten badly and maybe killed.

There were cops everywhere, and they saw that I was getting worked up and said, "Mr. Burke, just keep walking." I had Jennifer walk 15 feet in front of me, and I told her, "If something happens, just go, get back to the hotel. Don't stop for me, don't stop for anything." In 2011, they had a riot in Vancouver after the Canucks lost the Stanley Cup final. I think we were one fist fight away from it happening in 2010.

The gold medal game was a heartbreaker for me.

We managed to tie it up on Zach Parise's goal in the last minute of the third period to send it into overtime, and at that point I really thought we had it.

The sequence of the winning goal—it's the "golden goal" for Canadians, but not for me—is something I'll never forget. Bill McCreary was the referee, and the puck bounced off his skate to Jarome Iginla (I always joke that maybe the Canadian referee *kicked* it to Iginla). Then Iginla made the pass to Sidney Crosby.

Brian Rafalski was right on Sid's ass, backchecking. Sid skated towards the net and it looked like he was going to move, and then he saw that Ryan Miller was going to try to poke-check him. Miller hadn't attempted a poke check the entire tournament. And if he hadn't done it there, if he had just waited and stood up, Sid would have tried to deke him, Raffy would have caught Sid and checked him, and the teams would've played on, maybe all the way to a shootout. Instead, the instant that Sid saw Miller tighten up his grip for the poke check, he snapped that shot.

It was a great shot, through the five-hole. There was no room to spare. It was almost as though the puck had to turn sideways to get through.

The only comfort I take in that loss is that there was only one guy on the ice who could make that shot. He deserved it. I have so much admiration for Sidney Crosby—the fucker.

The worst part of winning a silver medal is that you've got to watch the other team get the gold. It's really humiliating. While I watched, I remember thinking that it had been the worst month of my life—by a mile. We were so close. Phil Kessel grazed the crossbar in overtime, but nobody remembers that now.

Today, I can look back and understand that the silver medal was a great achievement. But you can't see that when you're sitting there after the game is lost.

And my son. I remember just sitting there thinking, "My life cannot get a whole lot worse than it is right now. It just can't."

I took my first trip to visit the troops in Afghanistan the summer after the 2010 Olympics. We had a family meeting about it, and my wife made me promise that I wouldn't go outside the wire. I stayed in Kandahar.

Most of the fighting is done out of the forward operating bases, and on a later visit, I'd get to one of those. But in Kandahar, you're still in an active war zone. You fly in on a Hercules transport wearing a flak vest and a helmet, and the plane makes a semi-tactical landing. Lights out the last half hour. You could have heard a pin drop on that plane. People were scared shitless—including me.

One of the guys told us it was going to be a rough landing. They hadn't secured the air space and the base was regularly being hit by rockets, so they were afraid we were going to get hit. It felt like we were going in vertically, then they made a hard bank and we were pinned up against the side of the plane. The plane hit the runway so fucking hard.

It was the middle of the night when we landed. We got off and walked to the end of the airstrip where we were met by a Canadian lieutenant-colonel. "Welcome to Kandahar," he said. "There are two rules you must know. First rule: if you hear a siren like this [he made the sound], it means there's a rocket attack. You hit the ground, you cover your face and head, and you pray the rocket goes somewhere else. Second rule: if you hear a siren like this [he made a different sound], it means the enemy have breached the perimeter and we are hunting them. You get inside and you stay inside."

We looked at each other. That part wasn't in the fucking brochure. You sign a waiver when you go over there, acknowledging that you could die, and that if you do, the government will pay your family $150,000. But suddenly, that sounded like a real possibility.

Visiting our troops in a war zone is a life-changing experience. It's so humbling. You think you have a tough, important job back home until you see guys who have just come out of the forward operating bases. They're exhausted. They've been marching in 50-degree heat in full packs and getting shot at. I picked up one of those packs—it weighed 80 pounds. I'm not sure I could have carried it, along with the ammo and the rifle, and I'm a big guy.

The soldiers were so grateful that we came over, but not as grateful as I was to them.

The following July, I returned to Afghanistan with our young defence-man Luke Schenn. He had started a program with the Leafs called "Luke's Troops," where at every game we acknowledged an active member of our military. I encouraged him to make the trip with me.

"If you're going to be a hero to these guys," I told him, "you need to get some sand in your shoes."

He was a little hesitant about going to a war zone.

"There is some risk," I acknowledged, "but we can trust the Canadian Forces to look after us. Their worst nightmare would be me or you getting shot."

The soldiers loved the fact that Luke was there. Here's an active NHL player working out in the gym with them, having breakfast with one unit one day, lunch with the snipers the next. One day, we were told that we were playing road hockey against the soldiers at 8 a.m. I asked, "Why so early?" The commanding officer told me that we needed to do it before it got too hot—it wound up being 46 degrees when we played.

The timing of that trip was always going to be a little bit tricky for me. The first of July is free-agent day in the NHL, and we had some irons in the fire that year—including plans to make an offer to the best player who would be available on the open market, Brad Richards. But the Forces like to have celebrities spend Canada Day with the soldiers on the base.

I talked things over with Dave Nonis, and we were confident that we had things covered in Toronto. We had prepared our offer to Richards on an iPad, which was cutting-edge technology then. It included a picture of a Leafs sweater with his name on the back, hanging in one of our dressing room stalls. It was pretty progressive stuff for 2011.

I told the CO that I would need an office I could use at midnight, which, with the time difference, would be the moment free agency opened. I also needed wi-fi and a good cell phone link, a live computer link and a working land line. They put everything in place. At around 11 o'clock, I talked to Dave and made sure we were ready to make our pitch to Richards, and also one to Ed Jovanovski.

When the hour arrived, it all went off like clockwork. We offered Jovanovski a three-year deal, and we weren't willing to go beyond that. He got four from Phoenix and signed there.

Our opening offer to Richards was six years at $6 million a year. I remember that, when his agent heard that, he asked if we were serious.

"You're not even close," he said.

"Well, then," I said, "we're not even close."

I think we added a seventh year at $6 million, but that's as far as I would go. We made a wise decision and walked away. I called Richard Peddie and told him what was going on and then went to bed in the barracks with the soldiers.

Richards wound up signing with the Rangers for $63 million over seven years. It turned out to be such a terrible deal for New York that they bought Richards out after three seasons.

I don't read the papers, but after the fact, someone sent me a copy of an article by Steve Simmons of the *Toronto Sun*, in which he implied that the reason we didn't get Richards was that I was in Afghanistan, as though it was a dereliction of duty on my part. Apparently, he said the same thing on television.

We were in a war zone. This is not some visit to an army base back home. The first time I was in Afghanistan, I witnessed a ramp ceremony for a 19-year-old kid who was killed in action. This shit is real. How twisted would you have to be to criticize someone for visiting soldiers in an active war theatre? I was putting my life at risk. The base got hit by rockets four straight days before we got there, and after we left, it got hit by rockets three days in a row. And meanwhile, this dirtbag was criticizing me for being there.

I was so outraged and offended. It was the lowest thing I've seen in journalism in my 30-plus years in the hockey business. It was a gratuitous cheap shot. And it backfired on Simmons badly. He got absolutely killed for writing that because he didn't think through the consequences.

Even if you don't like me personally, do you really think we should have given Richards $60 million? And were you really going to criticize me for being in Kandahar visiting soldiers?

Simmons never did get around to acknowledging that the Brad Richards deal was one of the worst in the history of the NHL.

As many of you may remember, I once referred to people in the media as "scumbags and maggots"—but I wasn't talking about everyone in the business. In fact, I've got a lot of respect for most of them. I don't think the average player or front-office person understands how hard they work. They are critically important to our business, and the vast majority are really good at what they do. They're well-intentioned and want to get the story right.

But there are a few out there who continue to spoil it for everybody. I thought Tony Gallagher in Vancouver was just mean. He took unnecessary shots at people, so I went after him. Larry Brooks in New York is a bad guy, and I sued him successfully. Al Strachan, who used to work for the *Globe and Mail* and the *Toronto Sun*, is also a bad guy.

Simmons is the worst of the bunch. Before the July 1 story, I barely spoke to him, and I never liked him. My theory is that he was bullied as a kid. He's got all the personality traits, the socially awkward part. Gallagher and Brooks are like that, too. Now they've turned into bullies themselves, and I really resent that. If you know the fear of being bullied, if you know the awful suspense, the feeling of being afraid to turn the corner, you have no right to bully other people.

Unlike them, the good people in the media try to learn and listen, and I have all kinds of time for them. When I was an agent, I realized very quickly that coverage played a role in what players got paid and how they were viewed by teams. So, I really encouraged my guys to have allies among the reporters. Give them the time they need and treat them respectfully.

A lot of people think I loved to pick fights, but that's not true. I don't. I never did. Almost all the fights I got into were on behalf of one of my players or a coach.

I learned at Pat Quinn's knee, and Pat taught me to work with reporters and to be honest with them. The one thing you can never do is lie to the media. And that's the one rule I have. If I can't answer a question, I say I can't answer it, or that the question's not appropriate. But I don't lie to them, and I trust them until they give me a reason not to.

When they do, though, I've got a memory like an elephant and I go right back at them. I have what I call "not today" days, when I decide that I'm not taking shit from anyone. At that point, I don't care about the carnage, and I don't care about my reputation.

———

One of the biggest changes I've witnessed during my working life is the rise of social media. When I started out, there was none of that, and now it's a huge part of our business—in some ways, as important as the mainstream media. When I was in Calgary, we held a seminar for our players before the beginning of the season to explain to them how social media works. They're all young guys, so of course they know how to use it, but we had to go through the dos and don'ts to help them stay out of trouble.

One of the downsides of the social media environment is that it allows people to operate anonymously. There are cowards out there who feel like they can say anything they want about you with impunity. And while you can sue the mainstream media for libel if they print or broadcast something defamatory, there's no real handbook for fighting back against someone using a fake name who tweets something about you that's untrue.

But when that happened to me, and to someone who I very much admire, I decided to try and fight back.

Hazel Mae at Sportsnet is a great journalist. I'm a big fan of hers, and of her husband, Kevin Barker. After I got fired by the Leafs, horrible stories started to circulate on Twitter, suggesting that I had had an affair with Hazel, and that that was the reason I was let go.

I have a Twitter account, but my daughter runs it for me. I don't follow anyone. The only reason I knew what was going on was because some friends called me and told me. Initially, I just let it go. And then, one morning, I woke up and decided I wasn't going to let it go. It was one of my "not today" days.

I called my lawyer in Vancouver, Peter Gall, and told him I wanted to file suit against the unnamed persons who had started the rumours on Twitter.

"Are you sure you want to do this?" he said. "You sure you're on really thick ice? There's no past? They're not going to find a picture of you and Hazel Mae somewhere?"

"We're professional friends. That's all," I told him. "I've never been alone in a room with Hazel Mae. I've met her probably five times, always in a business setting."

I called Hazel and asked her if she wanted to join me in the suit. In the end, she decided not to, but she issued a statement supporting me.

When the suit became public knowledge, I got overwhelming support, especially from people in pro sports and the entertainment industry. I admit that there were a few people close to me who wondered if it was a good idea—they felt that people who hadn't seen the original rumour were going to find out about it only because I was pursuing legal action.

But for me, it was a point of principle. This wasn't fair comment. It wasn't fair to Hazel Mae or her family, and it wasn't fair to me. I've never minded being on an island if I'm doing the right thing. If 99 people think it's wrong to do something and I'm convinced it's right, I'm going to go ahead and do it.

The best thing that came out of that lawsuit was that the judge ruled that we could force these people, living in their parents' basements and writing horrible things about Hazel and me, hiding behind their screen names, to be identified. They all had internet accounts, and to get one of those, you have to be a real person. The judge ordered internet service providers to produce the names. We got retractions and apologies from all the people involved. (Though they interviewed one of the guys who posted it, who was a student at Carleton University, and he tried to argue that he could post whatever he wanted because "[w]e have free speech in this country." The reporter who did the interview straightened him out on that.)

I think it was a very healthy process. It brought the level of attack on the internet down—at least for a little while. You're not immune on social media. People have to think twice now before they write something that is patently false.

I'm glad I did it.

I knew when I inherited Ron Wilson as head coach in Toronto that it probably wasn't going to work out over the long term. Even though we had been friends since college, our hockey philosophies were just too different.

In the summer of 2011, I went down to visit him at his place in Hilton Head, South Carolina, to try and get us on the same page. We were out on his boat when I told him, "We're at a critical point here. Something has to change. So, I can either fire you or I can fire your assistant coaches." He said that his assistants, Rob Zettler and Tim Hunter, were both good guys, and I agreed with him.

"But something has to change," I told him. "Don't fight me on this, or I'll have to fire you."

We brought in Scott Gordon and Greg Cronin to replace Zettler and Hunter, but in the end, it didn't help. Ronnie had already lost the media in Toronto, and he was starting to lose the room. And you have to have at least one of the two.

There are telltale signs that let a general manager know when a coach has lost a team. First, the agents start to call you and say, "My guy's had enough." The first time that happens, you tell the agent to fuck off. But when it happens two or three times, you have a problem.

Ron had become really aloof with his players. I like to be the first guy at the rink, and most days, I go down and have a coffee in the players' meal room. I watch them come in, make a bit of small talk, ask them about their wives and their kids.

When Ronnie arrived, he would come into the meal room, grab a bowl of oatmeal and head straight back to his office without saying a word to the players. I told him he had to start spending more time with the guys and talking to them. "You've got to get into this more," I told him. But he had isolated himself from the team at that point.

There was an interview with Phil Kessel around that time where the reporter made some reference to Ronnie and asked Phil, "What does your coach say about that?"

"I haven't talked to the coach in two weeks," Phil said.

When I heard about that, I tried to intervene. I went to Phil and told him we were going to go in and talk to Ron right now. Phil wasn't interested in doing that, but I marched him straight into the coach's office. Ron was sitting at his desk. He looked up and was surprised to see us.

"Phil says you haven't talked in two weeks," I said. "You two talk—now."

I got up, left the office and closed the door behind me.

Phil and Ron met for a good 20 minutes and they both told me it was really helpful. But talking to Ronnie privately, I made it clear that it wasn't my job to get him to communicate with his star players. I told him he had to be more interactive, but he just couldn't do it.

All of which raises the question of why I gave Ron a contract extension in December 2011, less than three months before I had to fire him.

The short answer is that it was the right thing to do. The team was playing well. We were 18–13–4 that Christmas after missing the play-offs the previous three seasons. I knew we had the makings of a playoff team, and I wanted to get Ronnie to that point.

I wanted to do the extension quietly. I knew what the reaction was going to be. But Ron decided to send out that tweet about Santa giving him a present. It was kind of smug, and people didn't like it. It fuelled the fire, and the Toronto media were happy to pour on more gasoline. They wanted him gone.

That was the winter when the 18-wheeler went off the cliff. We were 11–15–3 after Christmas, and 1–9–1 in that awful 11-game stretch that convinced me that Ronnie had to go. During the last game he coached in Toronto, 18,000 people were chanting in unison, "Fire Wilson!" I wasn't going to make him go through that again.

I already had a replacement in mind—Randy Carlyle, who had won the Cup for me in Anaheim, was available. I was scheduled to speak at an MIT conference in Boston, and I asked Randy to meet me there. I interviewed him, we spoke at length and I offered him the job. Then I booked a flight to Montreal, where we were playing our next game. I called Ronnie and told him I had to talk to him when he got there.

Ron knew what was coming. By the time we met, he had already packed up all his stuff and booked a flight back to Hilton Head. When I gave him the news, he thanked me. "I know it's time," he said. "Thank you for not making me go through that again." He hugged me and we said our goodbyes. Then I went out and introduced Randy Carlyle as the new coach of the Toronto Maple Leafs.

It was a really tough, sad day for me, having to fire my friend. It broke my heart. It still bothers me, but I know it was the right thing to do. And the truth is that staying loyal to Ron as long as I did was part of what ended up costing me my job.

Rumblings that the Maple Leafs' parent company might be sold began in December 2010. The story then was that Rogers, the big telecom company, was going to buy out the Teachers' Pension Plan, but that didn't happen, and then things quieted down. A year later—in December 2011—the sale was announced. The teachers were out, while Rogers and Bell were coming in as partners, each with 37½ percent. Larry Tanenbaum retained a minority stake—25 percent—but if the two telecom companies disagreed on something, he would have the deciding vote. The league and the Canadian Radio-television and Telecommunications Commission, which regulates the telecom business in Canada, both had to approve the sale, and by August 2012, it was finalized.

We had our first face-to-face meeting with the new ownership not long afterwards. George Cope was there to represent Bell, along with Nadir Muhammad from Rogers, Dale Lastman and of course Larry Tanenbaum. Richard Peddie, who would step down at the end of December, always carefully orchestrated those meetings. Each department would come in and present in turn—basketball, hockey, soccer. Dave Nonis was with me, while the next group waited in the hall.

I've always believed that when you work for a company you owe it to them to be prepared, so we were very thorough. We went through everything we were planning to do with the Leafs, but also talked about the farm teams and the guys we'd drafted who were still playing in junior, in Europe or in college.

Over the course of our presentation, I swore a couple times. I don't think I said "fuck," but I might have. I definitely said "goddamn" and "shit." Apparently, George Cope didn't like that.

I was told later that, after I left the meeting, George Cope leaned over to the person sitting next to him at the table and said, "Well, he's done here."

"He" being me. Apparently, Cope didn't like me. That was the beginning of the end.

It wasn't just that, though. I remember talking to Gary Bettman right after I got fired, and I asked him if he thought there was anything I could have done differently that would have saved my job. He said no—they were going to make a change when they got the team because they wanted to make a break from the past. That's especially Bell's modus operandi. When they take over a company, they immediately move to change the top management, and honestly, I have no problem with that. You buy a team, you get to bring in your own people. I've been let go twice when a team was sold—or about to be sold. It happens.

But that doesn't mean I saw my firing coming. In fact, three weeks before it happened, I had breakfast with Nadir Muhammad. He told me that if we missed the playoffs, "it's going to be hard for us to bring you back."

"Nadir," I told him, "if we miss the playoffs, you *should* fire me."

So forgive me for thinking I had the job for the rest of the season.

And by the way, we made the playoffs—or at least, the team I built, with my head coach, made the playoffs—for the first time in eight years. I was gone by then.

This is how it played out.

In the summer and fall of 2012, I was part of the NHL's labour negotiating team, trying to hammer out a new collective agreement with the players. Donald Fehr had taken over as the head of the players' association, and the league was determined to push the players' share of hockey-related revenue down to 50 percent from 57 percent. Everyone knew that there wouldn't be a deal without a fight, and probably not without another lockout.

I was there to negotiate hockey-related issues. As far as I was concerned, there were serious problems with the cap system that had come into effect after the 2004–05 lockout. I was fighting for a five-year maximum contract, a 10 percent cap on signing bonuses and the end of those "back-diving" contracts, where teams would agree to pay players over a ridiculously long term in order to circumvent the cap.

Around Labour Day, Carolina GM Jimmy Rutherford, who was working on the same stuff as I was, told Bill Daly he'd had enough. There were five or six major meetings over the course of that summer, and they could start to feel like Groundhog Day.

Bill suggested that maybe it was time for me to go home as well.

"I'm actually enjoying this," I told him. "I'm the first guy here and the last to leave. I love watching the lawyers work. I'd like to stick around to help make sure we wind up with a deal that makes sense."

Bill declined my offer. "We've got your list," he said, referring to the items the hockey people believed had to be part of the next contract.

The league locked out the players to start the season, and I suspected all along that in the end, they would sell us out in a heartbeat once they got the players down to 50 percent in order to get back to work.

Unfortunately, I was right. They gave the players eight-year maximum contracts. There was no cap on signing bonuses. But the part that hurt the most was that they let teams get away with those back-diving deals. The league had promised retribution—some kind of recapture, plus penalties. Gary told the general managers they would rue the day they cheated the salary cap.

I wouldn't sign those kinds of deals with the Leafs, even though we certainly had the financial resources to do it, and I must have talked 10 other GMs out of doing it. When the league challenged the Ilya Kovalchuk contract, I was their only witness during the arbitration process, the only one who had the guts to stand up and say it was a circumvention of the cap.

So, what did the league do in the CBA negotiations? They kicked me in the ass. Instead of penalizing the teams that cheated, they gave them two Get Out of Jail Free cards—compliance buyouts that didn't count against the cap.

The league sold out the guys who did the right thing. But the truth is, they were always going to sell us out to get the players back on the ice as soon as possible. They're like Abraham Lincoln, who viewed a promise as binding unless and until the greater good demanded that it not be binding. That's actually one of the things I admire about Gary Bettman. As I said earlier, he's always going to do what's best for the league. If that means a guy like me gets hurt, it's not the end of the world because it's for the greater good of the NHL.

Not that I was happy about it at the time. Not long before they reached a deal, Murray Edwards, a co-owner of the Flames, called me from Calgary and asked me if I'd be willing to come to New York and rejoin the negotiations.

"Let me get this straight," I said to him. "You want Brian Burke there so that when you give away all the stuff that the GMs thought was important, you can point to me as the Judas who gave it away? Murray, I'll never say no to the NHL. If you want me there, I'll be there. But I know that the only reason you want me there is to make your concessions look good. You guys have already fucked this up. All the stuff that was critical to me as a general manager, you've already given away."

I was downright rude to Murray (really, it's amazing in hindsight that the Flames hired me after the way I talked to him that day).

"I'd really appreciate it if you'd come," Murray said, and reluctantly, I agreed to go.

I flew down to New York and sat through the meeting. The league and the union were still squabbling. The league could have—and should have—held firm. There was no way players were going to stay out over an issue like eight-year contracts, since the vast majority of them would never have the chance to sign one.

In the end, the league gave the players what they wanted (and, as a result, maximum contract lengths and unlimited signing bonuses are still the two biggest issues in the current CBA). Once they got the players' revenue share down to 50 percent, they declared victory, and they weren't interested in fighting over the other details. Before I flew back to Toronto, I made it clear to Bill Daly that I didn't think they should agree to those terms. But the die was cast.

———

On January 9, 2013, three days after the lockout ended and five days before the beginning of what would be a truncated 48-game regular season, I was heading to the airport for a flight back to New York to ratify the deal. Mike Andlauer, one of the minority partners in the Montreal Canadiens, had kindly offered me a ride in his private plane.

I was halfway to Pearson Airport when my cell phone rang. It was Tom Anselmi from Maple Leaf Sports & Entertainment.

"You've got to come back to the office," he said.

"I'm on my way to New York," I said. "We are going to ratify the new CBA. I was on the fucking team that negotiated it. I've got to be there."

"No," Tom said. "You've got to come back right now."

I turned around and started driving back to the office, running through a checklist in my head of what could possibly be so urgent. I decided that they were probably going to fire Bryan Colangelo, who was running the Raptors, and wanted to give me a heads-up.

Tom, Dale Lastman and Larry Tanenbaum were waiting for me in Richard Peddie's old office—that was poetic: the office that used to be occupied by the guy who recruited me, whom I loved like a brother. The three of them wouldn't even make eye contact with me. They were looking at the floor as though they were searching for loose change.

That's when the penny dropped.

Oh fuck. It's me.

"We're making a change," Larry said.

I was in shock.

"You'll have to excuse me," I said. "I wasn't prepared for this meeting."

I walked down to my office and got a bottle of water, just to buy some time. My assistant, Catherine Grey, saw me walk by and said, "What's up, boss? You don't look so good."

"Just leave me be for a minute," I said.

Anselmi followed me into my office.

"Burkie," he said, "you can't talk to anyone."

"Relax, Tom," I said. "I'm just collecting my thoughts."

I picked up a bottle of water and then went back to Richard's old office, where the three of them were waiting.

I was fucking flabbergasted—which may make me the dumbest motherfucker in the world. When you get that call, you should figure it out. But after my talk with Nadir, I really believed I had the season. There had been no speculation in the media. No one was writing or saying that Brian Burke should be fired, because they could all see the positive direction we were headed in. We had the fastest team in the league and we had the toughest team in the league. If we got any kind of goaltending, we'd make the playoffs—and of course, we did. I just wasn't going to be around to enjoy it.

"Can I have some reasons?" I asked.

Larry said it was because I didn't use our financial might to make the team better.

That was a reference to an earlier fight I'd had with him and Dale Lastman about Roberto Luongo. I wasn't willing to offer the kind of long-term contract the Vancouver Canucks gave Luongo, because I believed it was a circumvention of the salary cap, and I figured that the league was going to come up with a way of penalizing teams who did that in the new collective agreement. The Canucks are paying dearly for that contract.

I remember a phone call with Larry. Dave Nonis was with me, but not on the phone. We were in the Newark airport after a CBA session. Dale was screaming at me over a speakerphone. It was really Dale's beef. Larry just repeated it.

"Everyone else is doing it" was essentially Dale's argument.

But I wasn't going to do it, on principle, and because I believed it would hurt our team.

"You didn't solve our goalie problem here," Larry continued.

Before they traded Luongo, the Canucks asked me for Jake Gardiner, Nazim Kadri and two first-round picks for him. You think I should have paid that price to get that goalie? Have you lost your minds?

"The day I take personnel advice from you lot would be a sad day indeed," I said. I still couldn't believe what was happening.

Next, they tried to cover their asses. They asked me if I would frame my departure as "a leave of absence." There was no way I was doing that. To the outside world, the minute you say "leave of absence," people assume you're having a nervous breakdown or are heading for the Betty Ford Clinic.

Then they asked me if I would stay around as a "senior advisor."

"Fuck no," I told them. "You guys are going to take the heat for this."

The point is, they knew they were going to take a hit with the public and press for firing me. There were a lot of people who thought I should have been given that season. There wasn't an angry mob outside the arena demanding that I be fired. The fans and the media saw the team progressing and thought we were finally getting there.

Then, Larry started giving me a pep talk.

"You know these things happen . . . ," he began.

I had been down that road before.

"Larry, is this a pep talk?" I asked him. "Do you really think I need a pep talk? I lost a kid on this job on your watch. I don't need a pep talk. Today's not a bad day for a guy who lost a kid. Today, I lost a job. That day, I lost a lot more."

To this day, I regret saying that to Larry, because Larry is a good person. When I said it, I could see that it hit him right in the nuts. And all he was doing was trying to be nice to me.

I still like Larry. Tom Anselmi and I remain good friends. Dale and I are . . . cordial.

And of course, the person who was most responsible for my firing wasn't in the room that day.

As I was driving home after the meeting, I started feeling really bad about the shot I took at Larry about my son. So I called Dale Lastman and told him that if it would help them, I would be willing to stay on as the senior advisor.

"Absolutely," he said. "We'd love that."

"Okay," I told him. "You can announce it, and then we'll figure out later on exactly what my role is going to be."

When I got to my place, I sat down at the kitchen table but left my coat on and kept my car keys in my hand. I had asked Dave Nonis to call me the minute that he knew the story was going to break, so that I could get my girls out of school and tell them the news myself. I didn't want them to hear it on the radio or from a classmate.

The phone rang, but it wasn't Dave on the other end. It was Cliff Fletcher, who had stayed with the organization as an advisor after my hiring.

"Hey Burkie," he said. "I'm really sorry to hear the news. I don't get it. Why wouldn't they let you finish out the season?"

I thanked Cliff for his kind thoughts, told him I'd call him back later and hung up the phone.

Now I had a problem. I love Cliff, but he and Gord Miller at TSN are very close. I knew that Gord was going to have the story in 60 seconds if he didn't have it already. Cliff might well have called him before calling me.

I called Dave Nonis and asked him why he'd told Cliff.

"I didn't tell anyone," Dave said. "Tom Anselmi called all the hockey ops guys together and told them. Everyone knows."

"Fuck you guys," I said. I was furious.

I hung up, jumped in the car and drove to the girls' school. I got Mairin and Gracie out of class, brought them to the library and told them I had just been fired by the Leafs.

"Do we have to move?" was the first thing they asked me. They loved living in Toronto.

"No," I said. "You're not moving anywhere. I may have to go somewhere to work, but I'll come back to see you just like I do with the older kids."

Then they went back to class, and I jumped in the car and pointed it north. I was a member of the Griffith Island Club, a private shooting club on an island in Georgian Bay, just off the Bruce Peninsula.

Normally, I would have been up for a traditional firing wake like the one after I got let go by the Canucks. But this time, I wasn't ready for it. I hadn't expected to be fired. And I didn't want to see anyone.

When I got north of the city, I called Ken, the manager of the club, and told him I'd be at the landing in two hours, and to send the boat to pick me up and take me to the island.

"Brian, I can't," he said. "The seas are too high. We can't make the trip across right now."

So, I turned around and drove back. By then, everyone was calling me to offer their condolences and plan the wake. We all got together at my condo—Jennifer came over, and Dave Nonis, Randy Carlyle, Claude Loiselle and all the rest. Everyone was great. But still, it wasn't the ending I had expected in Toronto.

The next day, I went back to work. I started packing up my office so that Dave Nonis could move in. Dave tried to talk me out of it, and said I could stay where I was, but I insisted. After all, he was the general manager now.

"So, what do you want me to do?" I asked him. "What's my role as 'senior advisor'?"

We had drafted a player named Andrew MacWilliam, who was playing for the University of North Dakota. They were playing in Minnesota that weekend. Dave knew that was my home state and that I'd enjoy going there.

That was more than fine by me.

"The sooner I get the fuck out of town, the better," I told him.

Ian Clarke, our CFO, told Dave that I had a travel budget of $50,000 for the rest of the year. The plan was that, after the Minnesota trip, I would go and take a look at all the kids we'd drafted, scout junior games, go to Europe. That plan lasted all of a few minutes—until Tom Anselmi came into my office as I was packing up. He closed the door.

"What are you doing?" he asked me.

"I'm getting ready to go to Minnesota."

"Burkie," he said, "you're not going anywhere. These guys want you out of here right now. They want me to take your computer and your phone."

"What was that bullshit about you announcing that I was staying on as a senior advisor?"

"That's not happening," Tom said. "They want you the fuck out of here. There is no job."

I'm still not totally sure what happened. The reason they offered me the advisory role in the first place had to be to reduce the public relations hit they were going to take for firing me. It made it look like I was still friendly with everyone and we were all in agreement.

Somewhere between that conversation with Dale Lastman and Tom coming into my office, somebody obviously changed their mind.

You can imagine how I felt about that.

"Well, I guess we're going to have fun at the press conference," I told him. "Because I'm going to tell the media that this was all bullshit."

"Let me get back to you," Tom said.

So now it was clear that we were negotiating. Under my contract, the Leafs' only obligation to me after I was fired was to pay my salary and cover my medical insurance. All my other perks and benefits instantly disappeared.

Tom came back to me with a proposal.

"What if we let you keep your season tickets for the rest of the season?" he asked.

I was provided with four tickets. And because of the lockout-shortened season, they were worth about $30,000.

"You think you can buy my silence for $30,000 worth of tickets?" I said. "Forget it. You can keep them."

Then he upped the ante.

"What if we make your pension contribution for this year and next year?"

That added up to something like $260,000. I phoned my lawyer and asked for his advice.

"So, you're saying that they are going to give you $260,000 to say at your press conference tomorrow that you're staying on as a consultant?"

"Yes."

"Am I missing something? Sign off on it before they change their mind."

So, that's what I did. The next day, I met with the media, and of course I was asked about the nature of my new role with the team.

"I don't know," I said, "but we'll work it out."

That, of course, was a bald-faced lie.

At least that final media conference gave me proof that there's a God. Steve Simmons had the temerity to stand up and ask me a question—something about where I stood with USA Hockey.

"You'll have to ask them," I told him. "The best part of today is that I'll never have to speak to you again in my life."

They packed up all the stuff from my office and shipped it to my house—there must have been 50 boxes in all. The following morning, I got up early, as always. But I had nothing to do. That's when it hits you. You get up and you're full of energy and you have your coffee and . . . now what?

I went to the movies. I had never gone to a movie on a weekday in my life, and I had never gone to a movie alone in my life. I went to the theatre and saw that *Jack Reacher* was playing, starring Tom Cruise. It was excellent.

And I thought, "So this is what it's like when people don't have to go to work."

So, what went wrong for me in Toronto?

At the press conference to announce my firing, I said that in an age where accountability was vanishing, I intended to be accountable, and I am. I got fired because the team didn't win enough games. It's as simple as that. The team was sold, and that may have sealed my fate, but if we had won enough games before that, they would have been forced to keep me.

Looking back, I'm not sure what I could have done differently. It took a while because of the no-trade clauses and all the overpaid Europeans, but we finally got the team I wanted, and that team made the playoffs the year I got fired.

The media was too negative in Toronto, and the stress of working there exacted a significant personal toll. Looking back, the strain of the job, and especially the strain of losing, contributed to the end of my second marriage. By the time I was fired, Jennifer and I had decided to split, and I was already living in my own place. It's amicable—we get along fine and we co-parent very well.

But despite the price paid, I wouldn't trade that opportunity for anything.

There are ghosts in the building in Toronto, even though none of those championship Maple Leaf teams ever played there. You look at the banners hanging from the rafters and you feel the power. I remember the day after my introductory press conference, I went to work out in the arena, and I grabbed a long-sleeved T-shirt the trainer had given me. I looked at the front of it and realized that I was about to put on that famous Leafs logo for the first time. I hesitated for a moment and just stared at it. Tim Hunter was changing, too. He looked at me, looked at the shirt and said, "It's a little different, isn't it?"

It is. It's not the Anaheim Ducks or the Vancouver Canucks. It's the Toronto Maple Leafs. When I finally put the shirt on, I felt so proud.

I will forever be grateful for the chance to run that team.

The Leafs are like the New York Yankees, the Boston Celtics, Manchester United. I remember telling my players that if they travelled to some remote location in South America and sat on a stone wall outside a village, the first person who walked up wearing a sports T-shirt or a hat would be wearing one with the logo of the Celtics, the Yankees, Man U, maybe the Dallas Cowboys . . . or the Toronto Maple Leafs.

That's no exaggeration. When I was in Anaheim, the year after we won the Cup, we started the season in London. Before the game, I stood outside the O2 Arena and watched the crowd file in. There must have been 4,000 NHL sweaters in the building that night. Half of them were Toronto Maple Leaf sweaters—and the Leafs weren't even playing.

When the league announced that it was going to hold the outdoor game at the Big House in Ann Arbor, with the Leafs playing the Detroit Red Wings, Gary Bettman called me and asked if we could sell 40,000 tickets. "I'll need 48 hours," I said.

He called back and asked me if we could sell 50,000. "Well, then I'll need 72 hours," I told him.

We had ticket requests from 32 countries, all from people who wanted to see the Toronto Maple Leafs play.

To be part of that was a great experience. The job brought me to Toronto, a city I love. I enjoyed the job. I had great support while Richard Peddie was still there. Larry Tanenbaum is a gem. The team got sold and they wanted a new direction and they were entitled to that.

But I'm not making excuses. You can win in Toronto, and someday, somebody will. I just didn't get the job done.

THE GREY HAIR IN THE ROOM

THREE OR FOUR DAYS after I was fired by the Leafs, Bob Murray called the team and asked for permission to hire me to do some pro scouting for the Ducks. I really like and respect Bob, and of course I had originally hired him in Vancouver. I was under contract with Toronto until the end of the season, but Bob said he would work something out with them so that I'd be free to take the job.

I was happy about it, mostly because I just had to get the fuck out of Toronto. I couldn't go anywhere without being recognized. Most people were nice to me, but the odd person would come up to me and say something like, "It was about fucking time they fired you, Burke." You get sick of being stopped on the street. Plus, the weather was awful at that time of year.

My first game back working for the Ducks, I actually wound up watching a game at the Air Canada Centre. I moved down to the front row of the press box, where the pro scouts sit. They were relentless!

"Hey," the guys said, "didn't you use to sit up there?" They were pointing to my old seats in the Leafs executive box.

After that, Anaheim sent me to take a look at their farm team in Norfolk, Virginia. The first player I met there was a young goalie from Denmark named Freddie Andersen. Freddie was battling a weight problem then, but it was obvious that he was such a good kid. He had been overweight at training camp, and by the time I saw him, he was still 20 pounds over. "Mr. Burke," Freddie told me, "I played 40 pounds overweight in the Swedish league and nobody ever told me to lose weight because I was the best goalie there. Nobody said a word to me. Now I will lose the weight."

We were sitting having breakfast at the rink. There was a whole spread laid out for the players, with bagels and everything else. But Freddie was eating a bowl of oat bran—the kind of healthy shit that I won't eat. I called Bob afterwards and told him the kid had it all figured out, that he'd be fine.

After that, Bob brought me out to Anaheim to watch the Ducks play. I stayed there for 10 days, saw three home games, and sat by the pool the other seven days and drank beer. It was just the tonic I needed.

Ken King and I were friends for many years. I was one of the first people who called him when he took over as president of the Calgary Flames 25 years ago. I'll never forget what I said to him then: "Congratulations, you dumb bastard." The Canadian dollar was at around 60 cents American, which made it nearly impossible to run an NHL team in Canada in the black—unless that team was the Toronto Maple Leafs.

When Ken called me about six months after the Leafs firing and asked if I was interested in becoming the Flames' president of hockey operations, my initial reaction was to say no. I wanted another chance to build a team from the ground up. "I think I still want to be a general manager," I told him, "and I think I will get that opportunity eventually."

Ken asked if I would at least meet with him so that he could explain the job properly and maybe change my thinking. Because I like Ken, I said I would, but I wasn't going to do it in Calgary. I told him about a trip I had taken out there with my daughter Molly, who moved to Calgary not long after the big flood. We got in at two o'clock in the morning, and when I left, I took a cab to the airport and went through security, where a woman took a picture of me. Almost immediately, I got a message from Bob McKenzie at TSN, asking me what I was doing in Calgary.

So, there was no way I could slip in and out of there without being noticed. I convinced Ken to meet me in Toronto instead. We got together at the King Edward Hotel, and Ken laid out the job, the responsibilities, the pay.

I was intrigued by it.

A president of hockey operations is really the grey hair in the room. For a team that has a proven, experienced winner in that role, it expands the pool of general managers it can hire, because the team can bring in a young guy and take a chance on him without worrying about the young GM making mistakes the way John Ferguson Jr. did in Toronto. John didn't have that kind of support with the Leafs. He would have been a great success if he had. The president of hockey ops can take care of all the speaking engagements—the charity lunches and Rotary Club meetings that are important for the team and for the community. In a place like Calgary, there are probably 75 to 100 of those a year. The same goes for league meetings. There are four every year. The president attends those while the GM focuses on the hockey team. A president of hockey ops can also keep an eye on the farm teams, so that the GM is free to concentrate on the 23 guys on his NHL roster and work on ways to improve it.

Those two people need to communicate well and have a good working relationship. The president has to be clear and honest when he thinks something is a bad idea. When we were talking about the job, Ken compared it to being business partners. You would never walk in on your GM and say, "I just traded this guy," just as you would never walk in on your business partner without warning and say, "I'm taking the next two weeks off." You'd discuss it and have things worked out three weeks in advance.

Ken told me I would have the final say—including the ability to veto any deal. But the idea was to never let it get to that point. Instead, we'd talk organically about trades as they evolved to make sure we were on the same page.

I really enjoyed Ken. He was a good guy and he was really smart. He could be erratic as a boss—he had his bad days—but in general, he was a terrific person to work for. The more I heard from him, the more excited I became about the job.

The next step was a meeting with some of Ken's bosses, the people who own the Flames. I did have to fly to Calgary for that one—I was actually in the middle of an RV trip with my daughters, and came in from Salt Lake City—but I managed to slip quietly into town, and we met behind closed doors in the private dining room of a downtown restaurant (La Chaumière). Murray Edwards was there, and so was part-owner Clay Riddell.

I thought the meeting went really well. I did warn them that if they hired me, there would be times when they'd roll their eyes over my methods. I told them it was inevitable that I'd get into a fight with the local media at some point. But they said they were fine with that.

They asked me for my opinion on their general manager, Jay Feaster. "Tell us if we've got the right guy or not."

I was honest with them. I didn't think Jay had the right vision for building a winning team. He won a Cup in Tampa, but I think that was really Rick Dudley's team. He just didn't work at the job the way I think you have to work at the job. But I said that I was willing to give Jay a chance—that's always my policy when I step into a new job.

After the meeting, I flew back to Salt Lake City to resume our RV trip. By the time we rolled into Las Vegas, the Flames had faxed me a formal job offer. My hiring was announced in September 2013.

Accepting the job did mean that I'd be spending time away from my kids. But Calgary was an hour closer than Anaheim or Vancouver, and that hour felt like a fucking week. I kept my house in Toronto, and I would pick up the girls after school on Thursday, then take them to school on Monday morning every other week.

I loved my time there. Of all the places I've lived, Calgary is my favourite.

Vancouver was really cool because our teams got better both times I was there, and we started filling the building. It was like riding a surfboard on a big wave, with everyone thinking you were a genius and buying you dinner. And in the summer, Vancouver is one of the most beautiful cities in the world. But the weather in the winter gets you down, and I was a long way away from my kids.

Anaheim was great because we won a Stanley Cup and the owners were great. You drink out of the Cup and your life is never the same.

Toronto was cool because it's the centre of the hockey universe. It's the Vatican. All those clichés are true.

But Calgary is really special. This might sound obvious, but it begins with the physical beauty of the place and the way they have preserved open space around the city. In the summertime, at 11 o'clock at night, the sun is just setting over the Rockies, and it looks like a postcard.

What I loved most were the people there. They could not have been nicer. I was treated beautifully there, even though we went through some tough seasons. And it seemed like every person you'd meet was involved in at least one philanthropic activity. I have never worked in a city where it seemed like everyone gave back to the community. It's just expected in Calgary. Everyone has a cause, and it's not just writing a cheque—they commit their time. When you ask for volunteers, they show up. I've never seen a city that was more anxious to help people who needed help.

The Flames' fans are great. It's a different dynamic than in Toronto. I remember that when Richard Peddie was running the Leafs, they did some research into their season-ticket base and found out that the average ticket holder attended six games a year. They sold or shared the rest of the package because of the high cost. Richard didn't think that number could possibly be right, so they narrowed their survey to an especially loyal group of individual season-ticket holders—in other words, not the corporate crowd. Those people attended an average of eight games a year.

The number in Calgary is closer to 30 games. The tickets are priced more moderately, so you have more individual ownership, which means you have more passionate fans in the building every night. They love their team and they really hate the Oilers and Canucks. It creates a fantastic atmosphere.

———

I've been lucky enough to have some great captains on my teams. I had
Chris Pronger, Scott Niedermayer, Mark Messier. I had Pat Verbeek in
Hartford, who was a really underrated player, a great leader and tough
as nails. But when I look back on players that I really admire, Mark
Giordano, whom I inherited when I was hired by the Flames, would
be right near the top. He's small, he was never drafted, and logically,
he should not have been a dominant NHL player. But he is because of
three things. First, he's got a great hockey mind. He reads plays and
anticipates. He's not the biggest guy or the fastest guy, but he knows
where the puck is going to go and he gets there first. And second, he
has a huge engine. His effort level is unmatched. And third, he's really
tough and really physical for a little guy. His puck skills are average, but
he gets so much out of them, he ends up better than average. His shot
is average, but he scores lots of goals. He does everything better than
he should be able to, because of his hockey mind and his willpower.

And away from the rink, Mark does more charity work than any
other player I've had, including the Sedins. It's amazing how much he
and his wife, Lauren, do in Calgary. Together, they are a dynamic duo.

Mark Giordano is one of my all-time favourites.

Our team got off to a terrible start in 2013, and by December all my
suspicions about Jay Feaster had been confirmed. We let him go, and
I stepped in as interim general manager for the rest of the season. The
next spring, we introduced Brad Treliving as the new general manager of the Calgary Flames. Brad was one of the bright young minds
in the game, and he had been working as an assistant GM under Don
Maloney in Arizona.

I first met Brad when he was in training camp with us in Vancouver,
when I was the assistant general manager.

In fact, I was the guy who cut him.

Brad was a defenceman who played junior hockey in the Western
Hockey League and then kicked around the minors for four or five
seasons. He was a studious player. He wasn't the most talented guy,
but he did things the smart way. You could tell he was always thinking

the game. And he had guts. He was the one guy in our camp that year who was willing to fight Gino Odjick. He didn't do well in the fight, but to his everlasting credit, he was willing.

When I pulled him aside to tell him we were letting him go, Brad said to me, "You're making a mistake. I'm going to play in this building someday."

"Son," I told him, "the only way you're going to see a game in this building is if you buy a ticket."

He comes from wealth. His dad is Jim Treliving, who founded Boston Pizza and is one of the dragons on *Dragons' Den*. Brad owns a couple of Boston Pizza outlets himself, and he stands to inherit millions and millions of dollars someday. But still, he's got a tremendous work ethic. When I was an assistant GM, I was known for always being on the road, turning up in one rink after another to scout players. But Brad may have outdone me. You'd see him at a college rink one day, then the next day you'd walk into an AHL rink, and he'd already be there. He worked like a dog.

When the league was running the Phoenix Coyotes and Brad was part of the front office, Bill Daly used to rave about him, talking about how much he had his shit together.

So, Brad was a great hire for us, not just in terms of his hockey IQ, but his values as well. He's a good family guy. He's fair with players and employees. He has a really big heart to go with a really big brain. He's a joy to work with—we still text or talk to each other nearly every other day.

We also have a similar vision of what winning hockey looks like. Brad doesn't like it quite as crude as I like it, and he thinks the style of game I like is outdated—and to be fair, there's some truth to that. But he's a terrific person, and in Calgary we formed a very strong partnership.

The highlight of my time in Calgary was the 2015 win over Vancouver in the first round of the Stanley Cup playoffs. It was our first post-season appearance since 2009, and the first time a Flames team had won a series since they made the run to the Stanley Cup Finals in 2004.

We were kind of a surprise team that year. No one expected us to do anything—only one member of the hockey media picked us to make the playoffs. It was Johnny Gaudreau's rookie season, and he was sensational playing on the first line with Sean Monahan and Jiri Hudler. We were especially dominant at home in the Saddledome. We went 23–13–5 at home.

The Canucks finished only four points ahead of us in the regular season, but pretty much all of the experts predicted that they would beat us in the playoffs. Then we stole Game 1 in Vancouver 2–1, after being down 1–0 entering the third period. Kris Russell got the winner with thirty seconds left in the game.

The Canucks handled us pretty easily in Game 2, winning 4–1, but there was a line brawl at the end of that game that was a defining moment for our team. Deryk Engelland grabbed a couple of guys, and ended up taking three game misconducts. We sent a message that our team was not going to take a back seat physically to the Canucks. Guys like Engelland and Micheal Ferland let Vancouver know that we could play the game any way they wanted to play.

Twenty years from now, what people will remember about that series was the battle between Ferland and Kevin Bieksa.

I drafted Kevin when I was in Vancouver. He's a smart player, an elite defender who makes good outlet passes. He's also really hard-nosed, and he used to terrorize the Flames. The liberties he took with players were just astonishing. Until that series, we didn't have an answer for the kind of bite that he delivered.

And then Ferland provided the answer. He said, "Not today. . . ."—a man after my own heart.

Micheal is a great kid. He's a really good hockey player with a great shot and he can skate like the wind. At his best, he's belligerent and hostile, but he doesn't play that way all the time. That's the puzzling thing about him—he goes quiet sometimes. But not in that series. Our coach Bob Hartley did a really good job of convincing him that he could be a difference maker. He told him to go out there and hit Bieksa, and he did, every chance he got. When Micheal Ferland hits you, you feel it. He drove Kevin nuts. Kevin was beside himself wondering what to do. He insulted Ferland in the press, called him names. Micheal really got in his head.

And if you ask me, that was the difference in the series.

We won the next two games in Calgary to go up 3–1. The Canucks staved off elimination at home, and then we finished them off in Calgary in Game 6. They went up 3–0 early, but we roared back. Matt Stajan scored the winning goal and Ferland added an empty netter.

That crowd went nuts. The fans in Calgary hate Vancouver almost as much as they hate Edmonton. When I worked for the league, I was in the building when the Stanley Cup was awarded all five years. So I've been in a lot of loud arenas. But that night, I couldn't talk to the people standing right next to me. I had to yell to be heard by a person a foot away. It was crazy. After the game the fans spilled outside and headed for the Red Mile, a stretch of a downtown street where people went to celebrate. It was just like the old days—when they won in '89, and when they made the run to the Finals in 2004.

It was the highlight of my time in Calgary, for sure.

After that, we went out with a whimper. Anaheim, who we drew in the second round, had our number, especially in their building, where we hadn't won in something like 10 years.

One of the things I remember about that series is that the night before Game 1 in Anaheim was the same night as the Floyd Mayweather–Manny Pacquiao fight. Mark Giordano told me that the guys wanted to watch it, so I talked to the hotel and we set up a private screening. The only problem was that they charged us by the viewer—$100 a head. So it cost us close to $7,000 to show the fight to the players, plus the team staff, family and friends. Add in the catering and drinks, and the night cost us about 10 grand, but I thought it was worth it to provide a diversion heading into a rink that had been so daunting for us.

And then the fight was awful.

I remember Gio came up to me afterwards and said, Thanks for putting the fight on, but what a dog. He was sour. So it didn't really accomplish what I thought it would in terms of team morale.

We won only one game in that series—Mikael Backlund scored the overtime winner in Game 3 back in Calgary, but that was it.

Looking back, I think we overachieved a bit that season, but I also think we were legitimately coming on. We drew some confidence from winning that series against Vancouver, which I thought would turn into momentum heading into the 2015–2016 season.

But instead, we slipped back . . .

In January 2016, there was an incident during a game between us and the Nashville Predators. One of our defencemen, Dennis Wideman, was clearing the puck out of our zone when he took a pretty good hit from Miikka Salomaki. Wideman got up slowly and skated along the boards to our bench. Just before he got to the door, he ran into linesman Don Henderson. Henderson went down to the ice face-first. Wideman kept going and took his seat on the bench.

I want to mention a couple of things before I get into what happened behind the scenes.

Dennis Wideman is a really good guy. He's very smart, and also very hockey-smart. Of all the guys we had in Calgary, Mark Giordano was probably the best if you wanted to talk hockey, but Wideman was right there behind him. He was a terrible skater, so a big part of the reason he had a long career was that he was a student of the game. He's really bright, and I enjoyed having him on our team.

Donnie Henderson is also a really good guy, but the truth is that by then, he was pretty long in the tooth as a linesman. He was having trouble getting out of the way of the play, and the league had already told him that it was going to be his last year.

If you watch the tape, Dennis is skating with his head down, and then he does a hard right pivot when he looks up and sees Henderson— clearly, in an effort to avoid him. At the end, he reflexively brings up his stick and knocks him down. It looked bad in the moment, but Dennis did not intentionally run into Henderson, and he certainly didn't intentionally cross-check him.

After the game, Brad Treliving went down to talk to Dennis, who had no clue what the fuss was about.

"What's up?" he asked Brad.

"The league is going to look at this," Brad said.

"Look at what?"

"You kind of cross-checked Donnie Henderson."

Dennis honestly had no idea.

The league suspended Wideman indefinitely, pending an in-person hearing. Sometime between the incident and the hearing, somebody got to Wideman. I suspect it was one of his teammates, or maybe somebody from the players association. They must have convinced him that it was a bigger deal than he thought it was, and that he could be facing a serious suspension.

Wideman did get hit pretty good on the play, and he banged his head. He told us at the time that he had a slight headache. But that was it. No light sensitivity. He went through the concussion protocol, but as I recall, his concussion score was very low—I think out of the maximum 163 points you can get on a concussion test, he might have scored 7.

Before the hearing started, Brad and I went over to the reps from the players association and asked them how they planned to defend him, just so that we were on the same page. They told us they were going to take the position that Dennis shouldn't be facing any supplementary discipline at all because he was concussed before he ran into Henderson.

We knew we had a big problem, because that wasn't our defence. We were going to argue that Wideman was simply trying to get out of the way, and that the collision was an accident. We didn't think that a theoretical concussion was a factor at all.

Henderson was in the room for the hearing, along with Dan O'Halloran, who was the head of the officials union. Colin Campbell and Kris King were there to represent the league.

Brad spoke first. He showed the tape, went through the play, and argued that you could clearly see Wideman's attempt to avoid Henderson—he pivots 90 degrees on his skates at the last second to try and get out of the way.

Next, it was my turn.

"Colie, I used to do your job," I said. "And I used to stay awake at night, praying that a guy would come in for a hearing that I really wanted to fuck, that I really wanted to throw the book at. But this is not that guy." Dennis had played 600 NHL games, and the only major penalties he had ever picked up were from a handful of fights, where the other guy got one as well. He wasn't a dirty player at all.

"I know you've got to give him something, but this is not the kind of guy you want to come down hard on."

At that point I thought we were probably looking at a 10-game suspension.

But then the union started talking. They argued that Wideman shouldn't get any kind of suspension at all, because he was concussed on the play.

While they were talking, I could see Colie put his pencil down and stop taking notes. I knew exactly what he was thinking: "I don't believe they're doing this."

The league gave Wideman a 20-game suspension, and Gary Bettman upheld it on appeal. (The NHLPA later appealed to an independent arbitrator, who eventually knocked the suspension down to 10 games. But by then, Wideman had already sat out 19 games—and in the end, he never played another game in the NHL.)

I was appalled by the way the union had decided to argue its case. But what upset me even more was what happened afterwards.

Before the Wideman incident, the Flames were the least penalized team in the NHL. Afterwards, for the next 30 games, we were the most penalized team in the league.

Obviously, the officials had decided it was time for some payback, professionalism be damned.

We asked for a meeting. Colie and Steve Walkom, the NHL's head of officiating, came to Calgary and sat down with us, and we went through the stats. It was crystal clear that this was retaliatory, and we told them that if it didn't stop, we were going to go public with the whole thing. People in the media were already starting to figure it out, but it would be a whole other thing if a team came out and said that the officiating in the league wasn't fair, and had the stats to prove it.

Happily, we didn't have to go that far. After that meeting, it stopped. The calls against us went back to normal. To his credit, Walkom put an end to it. I lost a lot of respect for Dan O'Halloran.

———

At the end of the season, we made the decision to fire Bob Hartley. That year, Bob started being really hard on players—too hard in our view. He was picking on individual guys. It got bad enough that when guys got on the charter after a loss, they'd walk by Bob and he would give them a hard time right on the plane. The atmosphere just got to be too negative.

There is a cycle to coaching. Every coach has a shelf life, and if you're a tough, demanding coach, your shelf life is shorter than average. Bob was like that, and he had hit that wall with our guys.

We replaced him with Glen Gulutzan. He had a different, lighter style. He's a great guy and really good head coach, and I think we made some progress with him behind the bench. But what happened to him, and what eventually led to his firing after two seasons, was that our senior player group influenced him too much.

That's common with a young coach, and it's not a particular fault of Gully's. It happens on a lot of teams.

A young coach will call on their senior player group and ask them what they think he should do, who they think should be in the line up, that sort of thing. That particular group in Calgary kind of banded together. They didn't exactly bully Gully—he's stronger than that—but they definitely influenced him. Veteran players always look out for the interests of other veteran players, and sometimes that can hurt a team.

The most obvious example is what happened with Brian Elliott in the playoff series against Anaheim in 2017. He was awful in Game 4, when the Ducks took a 3–1 lead. Brian—his nickname is Moose—is a great guy and he was usually a really solid player for us, but he was obviously struggling in the playoffs. I remember asking Gully why he was putting him back in for Game 5. "You're the head coach," I told him, "and you get to pick the starting goaltender, but please explain the logic to me."

"The senior players think he deserves another chance," Glen said, "and I have a hunch . . ."

"Well, you'd better put him on a Chihuahua leash then," I said. "The first bad goal, you have to yank him."

Brian let in a terrible goal on one of the first shots of the game, and we had to make the goalie change. But by then it was already too late.

Glen was fired at the end of the following season, after we missed the playoffs. We felt the team should have taken a step forward, and we didn't. We concluded we needed to make a change. But there's no question that Glen is an excellent leader. He'll get another chance to be head coach in the league some day—and he won't make that same mistake again.

If you're going to talk about my legacy in Calgary, I guess the most important part of it was the 2016 draft.

Brad Treliving decided to send me to represent the team at the lottery—Irish good luck charm that I am—and, predictably, we dropped from fifth to sixth.

The draft was held in Buffalo that year. Toronto and Winnipeg had the first two picks, where they took Auston Matthews and Patrik Laine, respectively.

After that, there were a bunch of guys in play for picks three through six: Pierre-Luc Dubois, Jesse Puljujarvi, Olli Juolevi, and Matthew Tkachuk. We liked all of those guys. But we really liked Tkachuk. When Columbus took Dubois with the third pick, I remember we were doing fist bumps under the table, because we were pretty sure where Edmonton and Vancouver were going to go with the next two picks, and that we'd have the chance to take Tkachuk at six.

That was a turning point for the franchise.

Matthew was so mature for his age, as a person and as a hockey player. When he came to his first camp as an 18-year-old, we had planned on sending him back to junior. I almost always send 18-year-olds back. But after the last two pre-season games we knew Matthew was ready for the NHL and that our team needed him right away. We went to Ken King and told him that we had to keep him. We had already told ownership that Matthew was going back to junior for another year, so Ken had to go back to them and sell the idea of keeping him up with us—which he did really well.

I don't think I've ever encountered a player that young who understood the game so well. He would bring up the same things that I noticed as a general manager who has spent most of his adult life in the sport. He'd talk about a pressure point in the third period where we hit the post instead of scoring and how that changed the outcome. I thought, "Man, this kid sees the whole game."

He can score goals, he can make plays, but he also drags his teammates into the battle. He knows the game so well that he can tell when it needs some life. Then he throws a big hit, even though he's not that big a guy. Or he gets in a fight, even though he's not a good fighter—but he's a willing fighter. When he senses that a game needs a boost, he provides it.

Matthew also makes great decisions on the ice. If the puck comes around the wall to him in our own zone, he always gets it out safely. He makes a perfect outlet pass to his centre or he goes back across the grain and throws the puck to the off-side D. That's very rare, especially with young players. A lot of times, the defenceman rims the puck because he's under pressure, and that just puts the forward under pressure and he makes a mistake. In those situations, Matthew Tkachuk always gets the puck out of the zone. If he doesn't have a play, he chips it out, and if he does have a pass, he makes it and you're out of the zone with speed.

He's not a particularly good skater but he works like a dog, catches up to the play, and in front of the net, he's one of the best puck tippers I've ever seen. The only guy I can compare him to from my teams is Tony Tanti. There's no secret as to why he's good at it. Matthew stays out after practice every day and stands in front of the goalie while a defencemen shoot pucks at him—at least 30 pucks a day. He works on the tip over and over again. That's why his ability to score goals in close is so unbelievable.

I'd be shocked if Matthew Tkachuk isn't the next captain of the Calgary Flames, when Gio is done.

———

When I took the job in Calgary, the deal I made with Ken King was that we would take things year by year. At the end of every season, we would go over what was working and wasn't working, and then decide whether or not I would stay on.

At the end of the 2017–18 season, Ken told me he thought it was time to make a change. The whole thing was handled very professionally, and I have no hard feelings towards the organization. They thought Brad was ready to fly solo, and they had brought in Don Maloney as an assistant GM, so he could be the grey hair in the room if Brad still needed it.

I would have been happy to stay, but it was time to move on.

The year after I left, the Flames had a 107-point regular season. So, we obviously did something right. Of course, they went out in five games in the first round of the playoffs—but that was Brad's fault. I only want to take credit for the 107 points!

After Calgary let me go, I immediately set up a meeting in New York with Gary Bettman and Bill Daly. I was hoping that they might be interested in adding me to the NHL office in Toronto, but there wasn't anything there.

My next calls were to the two all-sports television networks in Canada, TSN and Sportsnet. Both of them were interested.

Mark Milliere, my old boss at TSN, was willing to offer me a job. But Sportsnet had the national rights to the NHL, and he said that he really thought I ought to be on the national show.

I met with Sportsnet's Scott Moore and Rob Corte at my place in Toronto. The first question they asked was whether I was just passing through—was a TV job just a place to park while I waited for another job running a team?

"No, I'm getting out," I told them. "I'm done."

They said they'd never stand in my way if I got a big job, but I finally convinced them that was unnecessary. This was as much a lifestyle change as it was a career change.

I had decided right after I left Calgary that I was sick of moving, sick of travelling, and that I wasn't going to do it anymore. Since I've been with Sportsnet, I have been approached by two teams with offers of significant high-level jobs, and I turned them both down.

I'm getting more time with my daughters now. I can go to their basketball games and concerts—the kind of stuff that I missed for 30 years. I'm sleeping in my own bed. I like the people I work with and I like talking about hockey. I hope—and think—I'm making a contribution. I intend to do it for as long as people think I'm doing a good job. I'm working very hard at it. I think I'm getting better. I can get better still. But the main thing is, I'm enjoying it.

To me, retirement is something that happens when there's no one left who wants you to work for them and wants to pay you for it. And even if that happens to me someday, I'll probably just shift over to charity work full time. Sitting on a beach or hanging around a golf course—I just can't see that for me.

But I'm working four-day weeks during the hockey season, and that's nice. It means I can hunt a little bit more. I can fish a little bit more—especially during my annual trip to Langara Island Lodge in B.C. I've missed only two years there in the last 26, and I've brought along a bunch of hockey people. It's an amazing place—whales, sea lions, bald eagles, and some of the best salmon fishing in the world.

CONCLUSION

ALMOST EVERY TIME I give a speech, someone comes up to me afterwards and says something to the effect of "I never liked you. I thought you were a real jerk. But after listening to you, I guess that maybe you're a good guy after all."

It happens with astonishing frequency. And my ex-wife would say that it's an opportunity to make a friend. I guess the polite response when someone says that to you is a simple "Thank you."

But that's not me.

When someone tells me that they thought I was an asshole, and then decided after meeting me that they were wrong for all those years, I find it extremely insulting and condescending. I didn't care what they thought about me yesterday, and I don't care what they think about me now. I make that crystal clear. I should make a friend that day, but I don't. That's just the way I am.

I really only truly care about the opinions of a couple of handfuls of people. There are very few people who can call me and tell me I'm wrong that I would listen to—and those people who come up to me after the speeches are never on that list.

To be honest, the same thing goes for this book. I don't care if it changes your view of me. I'm not running for office. I'm not out there kissing babies. If I were, I'd probably be a much nicer person—but I'm not, and I don't intend to be.

What I do hope is that you found the book interesting, that you couldn't put it down, that you thought, "This guy has had an interesting life and an interesting career," and that maybe you decided to do some things differently based on the way I've done things. Maybe acceptance of gay people. Maybe doing more charity work. Maybe doing more to support the military.

If it doesn't change your view of me, I don't care. But there are things that I do care about, things that I hope I stand for, and ideals that I hope I live up to. I am honest. I am ethical. I care deeply about the communities where I have lived. I am a devoted dad. Education is critical. Community work is critical. Self-improvement. Honest self-evaluation—you have to admit when you make mistakes. Having a moral compass. Doing the right thing. All of that matters to me.

And you can stop right there. Notice that I didn't mention anything about hockey? At my funeral, I hope that hockey never comes up, and that when people remember me, they remember me for those other things.

But if you do run into a former player of mine, I think he'd tell you, "Brian Burke never lied to us, he always had our back and he was quick with praise. If we had any kind of personal problem, he was right there for us." So you might not like me, but my players sure seem to.

If you go to Vancouver, I think they'd tell you that in addition to playing entertaining hockey, we put that team to work in the community and I put myself to work in the community—and I hope I made a difference. If you asked in Anaheim or Calgary, I hope they'd say the same thing.

In Toronto, I get stopped on the street all the time by people who thank me for settling here, for making my home here, which I think is the ultimate compliment.

The other day, a guy came up to me out of the blue.

"Our city is better with you in it," he said.

I told him he had just made my week.

ACKNOWLEDGMENTS

I need to thank a ton of people. This starts with my amazing parents and siblings, particularly my three brothers. But I also had wonderful aunts, uncles and cousins: Burkes, Reynolds, Sammons and Mirantes. Some incredible talent that pushed us all.

I had the great fortune in 1970 to fall in with remarkable guys, all athletes, and fairly serious students. We remain best friends to this day. They have been constants in my life for close to fifty years now. They are (in alphabetical order): Mark Heigl, Rob Johnson, Doug Olson, Ron Olsonoski and Geoff Raile. We lost Rob a couple years ago, and I miss him every day. The rest were and are simply astounding. And later we added John McMorrow to our group, a high school and college teammate and roommate.

Providence College next. The Dominican Order are extraordinary men and women. The History Department was special. Lou Lamoriello and Bob Bellemore. Doc Baynes and Bo Riendeau. Players: every single one. Special teammates: Ron Wilson, Jim Tibbetts and especially Rick Moffitt. Also Dave Kelly, Peter Valenti, Rick Cabalka and Dan Kennedy. Students Jim Parks, John Schiffner, Nancy Davidian, Roseann Thomas, Marlene Macauda, Lou Buffalino, Nick Fucillo, Barry Sullivan, Ted Patrikas, Bob Cayer and Mike Cuddy. Thanks too to the Friars' Club and St. Joseph Hall.

Maine Mariners: Ed Anderson and Bob McCammon. Mike "Doc" Emrick. Captain Dennis Patterson, Blake Dunlop, Terry Murray, Drew Callander, John Paddock, Frank Bathe, Mike Busniuk, Pete Peeters but most of all, TJ Gorence, one of the best guys ever.

Harvard Law School: Gary Toman, Steve Eckley, Norm Bartczak, Todd Cronin, Dave Boyer, Maureen Manning and especially Mike Moran.

Lawyers: Ron Garmey, Walter St. Onge.

Clients: Franke Bathe, Mike Busniuk, Pete Peeters, Joel Otto, Gord and Kevin Dineen, Brett Hull, Ray Staszak, Peter Taglianetti, and Scott and Kurt Kleinendorst.

Vancouver Canucks (first tour of duty): The legendary, unforgettable Jack McIlhargey and his wonderful wife Karyne. Frank and Emily Griffiths. Arthur Griffiths. The late and great Pat Quinn, and his lovely wife Sandra. Mike and Yvonne Murphy, Stan and Jennifer Smyl. Steve and Denise Tambellini, Darcy and Kathy Rota, Dave and Susan Nonis. Bob McCammon, Glen Ringdal, Ron Delorme, Jack McCartan, Curt Fraser, Ron and Maureen Wilson. Larry Ashley, Jim Robson, Tommy Larscheid and Dan Russell.

Hartford Whalers: Richard and Dee Gordon, for my first GM job, I will always be grateful. Paul and Doreen Holmgren. Kevin and Rhonda McCarthy. Pierre McGuire. Tommy Rowe. Joel Quenneville, Pat and Diane Verbeek, Geoff Sanderson. Chuck Kaiton, Rick Peckham, John Forslund and Skip Cunningham.

National Hockey League: Gary Bettman—cannot thank you enough. Jeff Pash—a quiet genius. Steve Solomon, Arthur Pincus, Bernadette Mansur, Glenn Adamo, David Zimmerman, Bill Daly. The legendary Jim Gregory. And Bryan Lewis.

Vancouver Canucks (second tour of duty): John and Gwen McCaw—thank you. Steve Bellringer. Marc Crawford, Mike Penny. John Shorthouse. Pat O'Neill and Mike Burnstein. Mark Chipman and Zinger. Dave Cobb, Victor de Bonis and Harvey Jones.

HNIC, World Cup, 2004: Ron MacLean, Kathy Fielder, Glenn Healey, Harry Neale and Kelly Hrudey.

TSN: Mark Milliere—thank you. Bob McKenzie, James Duthie, Steve Dryden and Anju King.

Anaheim: Henry and Susan Samueli, the best owners in professional sports. Thank you. Mike and Sherry Schulman. 2007 Cup Team. Randy and Corey Carlyle. Bob and Betsy Murray, David and Kari

McNab, Dave and Roxanne Farrish, Newell and Lori Brown, Francois Allaire. Joe Trotta. Tim Clark, Mark O'Neil, Kevin and Annie Dineen. John Allaire and Brian Hayward. Steve Carroll and Dan Wood.

Toronto: Larry and Judy Tanenbaum. Fantastic owners and even better people. Richard and Colleen Peddie, Dave and Laurie Hopkinson, Tom and Sharon Anselmi. Rob and Shannon Zettler, Tim and Marilyn Hunter. Greg Cronin and Scott Gordon. Brian Papineau, Bobby Hastings, Tim Blatchford. Paul Ayotte. Robin Brudner. Dallas and Gretchen Eakins. Joe Bowen, Jim Ralph, Pat Park and Noah Foreman.

Calgary: Murray and Lysanne Edwards, Clay Riddell, Alan Markin, Alvin Libin, Jeff McCaig. Wonderful owners—thank you for everything. The prodigious Ken King—the reason I went there. Thank you, Big Man. John and Rhonda Bean and Jay Feaster. Brad and Julie Treliving, Brad Pascall and Cassie Campbell-Pascall. Craig and Jessie Conroy. Chris and Kelsie Snow, Don Maloney, Mike Burke, Brenda Koyich, Anita Cranston, Brian McGrattan, Ron Sutter, Derek McKinnon, Sean O'Brien, Ryan Huska, Ray Edwards, Marty Gelinas, Jamie Pringle, Tod Button, Fred Parker, Rob Sumner, Steve Pleau, Jim Cummins, Terry Doran. Ian Auld. Mark and Kelly De Pasquale. Kent Kobelka. Ryan van Asten, Jordan Sigalet. Glen Gulutzan. Bob Hartley. Clint Malarchuk.

Sportsnet: Scott and Becky Moore. Rob Corte, Ed Hall, Brian Spear, Matt Marstrom, Ron MacLean, Jeff Marek, Elliotte Freidman, Chris Johnstone, David Amber, Anthony Stewart, Greg Millen, and Gord Stellick. Justin Bourne, Christine Simpson, Doug MacLean, Nick Kypreos and Don Cherry.

USA Hockey: The luminary Jim Johansson; Lou Vairo, Bob O'Connor, Dave Ogrean, Bob Johnson, Dave Peterson, Herb Brooks, Ray Shero, David Poile. Pat Kelleher, Stan Bowman, Dale Tallon and Don Waddell.

Life friends: Bill Polian, Ned Colletti, George McPhee, Trevor Whiffen, Will Meany, Jim Treliving, Mike Milbury, Glen Sather, Harry Sinden, Peter Gall, John Tortorella, Dean Lombardi, Joe Weiler and Bruce Allen.

And my two wives, Kerry Burke and Jennifer Burke, both exceptional mothers and people. And all six of my outstanding kids, who are truly the absolute highlight of my life.

I spent a lot of time putting this list together. Some omissions have undoubtedly occurred. Most were unintentional, and for these I apologize. Many were not. And for those I do not apologize.

Finally, with regard to this book, many thanks to my publisher, Nick Garrison and Penguin, for giving me this opportunity. And to Stephen Brunt, who added polish to my laboured prose. And to my agent, Rick Broadhead, who always provides sound advice.

INDEX

Brian Burke is an American-Canadian NHL executive and analyst, who in 2021 was named president of hockey operations for the Pittsburgh Penguins. He has served as the president of the Calgary Flames, the president and general manager of the Toronto Maple Leafs, and the general manager of the Anaheim Ducks (winning the Stanley Cup with the team in 2007), the Vancouver Canucks, and the Hartford Whalers. Burke was the general manager of the United States national men's ice hockey team for the 2010 Winter Olympics in Vancouver, and has served on Rugby Canada's board of directors.

Stephen Brunt is an award-winning writer and broadcaster for Sportsnet and the co-host of The FAN 590's *Writers Bloc* with Jeff Blair and Richard Deitsch. He is the author of the #1 national bestselling *Searching for Bobby Orr* and *All the Way*, with Jordin Tootoo. He lives in Hamilton, Ontario, and in Winterhouse Brook, Newfoundland.